MW00996571

Dialogues with
Creative Legends

Aha Moments in a
Designer's Career

For Kathleen —
A creative legend in
your own right!

7·29·2013

Dialogues with Creative Legends

Aha Moments in a Designer's Career

DAVID CALVIN LAUFER

FOREWORD BY

RICHARD SAUL WURMAN

New
Riders

VOICES THAT MATTER™

Dialogues with Creative Legends:
Aha Moments in a Designer's Career

David Calvin Laufer

New Riders
www.newriders.com

New Riders is an imprint of Peachpit, a
division of Pearson Education.

To report errors, please send a note to
errata@peachpit.com

Copyright © 2013 by David Laufer

Project Editor: Michael J. Nolan
Development Editor: Margaret Anderson/
　Stellarvisions
Production Editor: David Van Ness
Copyeditor: Gretchen Dykstra
Indexer: Valerie Haynes Perry
Proofreader: Jennifer Needham
Design: Brandbook LLC, Atlanta

ISBN-13: 978-0-321-88564-7
ISBN-10: 　 0-321-88564-3

9 8 7 6 5 4 3 2 1

Printed and bound in
the United States of America

In Loving Memory of
Craig Brian Eric Dieter
Scott Calvin Dieter

Acknowledgements

Dialogues with Creative Legends pays tribute to many generous people with very influential ideas. There are many more who, though their names do not appear in the narrative, made important contributions that helped bring this book to fruition.

Special thanks are due to five friends who read the manuscript during development and provided great comments and insights: Prof. Geoffry Fried of the Art Institute of Boston at Leslie University, Elizabeth and Kurt Seidel, Scott Walters, and Michael D. Spring. James P. Cramer of the Design Futures Council also read the manuscript and provided insight and encouragement.

Many people assisted by providing contacts in my search for visuals and permissions. Richard Anwyl of the Center for Design Studies, and Eileen Millard were very helpful. Generous support and assistance also came from Jenn Shore in Richard Saul Wurman's office, Kelsey Osgood of Overlook Press, Doreen Minuto, Steven Heller of School of Visual Arts (SVA), Francis Di Tommas, also of SVA, Doug Sery of MIT Press, Eric Fowler of the Society of Illustrators, Steve Curtis of the Society of Typographic Arts, Chicago, and Carol Wahler of the Type Directors Club, New York. Simón Cherpitel also assisted with photography, a treasure trove of *U&lc* originals, and background information. Hearty thanks also go to Don and Tina Trousdell.

Thanks also to Francis Di Tommaso of the School of Visual Arts and Dr. Bob Hieronimus of 21st Century Radio for their assistance with the work of Heinz Edelmann. Valentine Edelmann made valuable contributions. Special thanks to Lawrence L. Gellerstedt III and Heather Burdette of Cousins Properties, and also to Pam Tipton and Lisa Kaminski of Emory University. I am grateful to Doris Wells Papanek and Bryleigh Morsink, Archivist at the Victor J. Papanek Foundation at the University of Applied Arts, Vienna.

Genevieve Fong and Eames Dimetrios at the Eames Office assisted with expert research and visuals.

The AIGA staff were also generous with their time, permission, and information, especially Ric Grefé, Mike Joosse, Heather Strelecki, and Amy Chapman.

I owe a debt of gratitude to Nathan Shedroff for introducing me to New Riders Press. At New Riders Press, my special thanks to Nancy Davis and Michael Nolan for supporting this publication. Margaret Anderson deftly and patiently helped me shape the concept of the book to its present form. Also in my all star line-up at Peachpit, Glenn Bisignani, Gretchen Dykstra, Mimi Heft, Jennifer Needham, Valerie Haynes Perry, and David Van Ness, all made important contributions to devlop and promote the book.

My online friends and contributors to the Design Leadership Project on Facebook are a continuing source of encouragement.

Special thanks to Richard Saul Wurman for his support of the project, his perceptive reading, and foreword.

I would thank my extended family for their support: Bette L. Laufer, Nancy Collander, Beth Dieter, and Steve Gregory. My deep gratitude goes to Laurence E. Laufer and Vincent A. Laufer for their insights and friendship. I am grateful beyond measure for my wife Geraldine Adamich Laufer who—to pick just a few superlatives from a very long list—is a fine author, an insightful editor, and an extraordinary life companion.

Contents

Richard Saul Wurman
FOREWORD: DESIGNING YOUR LIFE

Richard Saul Wurman, FAIA, (1935–   ) is an architect, graphic designer, and polymath with a prodigious and influential career. Born in Philadelphia and educated at the University of Pennsylvania, he coined the term "Information Architecture," and is its leading practitioner. Mr. Wurman is the founder of the TED conferences, and has written 83 books (and counting). Among his best-known publications are the Access Press travel guides, the groundbreaking *Information Anxiety (1988, revised 2000)*, *Understanding Healthcare* (2004), and his semi-autobiographical work *33: Understanding Change & the Change in Understanding* (2009). Wurman is a fellow of the American Institute of Architects (1976), an Art Directors Club Hall of Fame honoree (2003), and an AIGA medalist (2004). He is a senior fellow of the Design Futures Council and is the 2012 recipient of the Lifetime Achievement Award from the Cooper-Hewitt Museum of Design. Mr. Wurman has been awarded three honorary doctorates, two Graham Fellowships, and many National Endowment for the Arts grants.

If I throw 140,000 words on the floor and connect those words with a sentence or two, we wouldn't call that a dictionary. A dictionary or an encyclopedia—many of the collections of data in our world—are based on being able to find something. The ability to find something goes hand-in-hand with how well it's organized.

The thoughtful structuring of information is an essential skill for the graphic designer, information architect, or information designer.

The Information Age has been in existence for more than two decades now and yet, does it inform?

It's not the age that has been addressed by designers. Because of their access to computers, like everybody else, designers do make prettier pie-charts, now in millions of colors, now in three dimensions, now exploding apart in wedges, floating in space, with shadows on some strange ethereal background. Each of these decisions has made the information less understandable. But apparently they are applauded by other graphic designers and by clients who don't seem to care about understanding, or are convinced that jazz and beauty and design as they know it—making things prettier—is the wave of the future.

We continue to flatter the makers of these things and invite them to speak at our major design invocations. They are followed by students around the country whose main claim to fame is to make type unintelligible, to break it up in abominations of understanding. Do the different as opposed to doing the good.

And yet, through this field of black volcanic ash has come a group of people, small in number, deep in passion, called information architects, who ply their trade, make themselves visible, and develop a body of work on paper, in electronic interfaces, in some extraordinary exhibitions. These people are now and they are the future.[1]

Recently I gave the keynote address at an *Economist* conference on big data in San Francisco. As I drove into the city, I saw not one, but three different signs that included the word "innovation." One was for the city itself, calling it the Innovation City. The word, I realized, had achieved the ignoble status that frequently used words sometimes do: it had lost its meaning.

Twenty-plus years ago I was intimidated by the prospect of figuring out how many ways one could organize information. After boiling down the unique options I could think of, I came up with only five. Now I've taken it upon myself to think of the ways one can innovate and to bring meaning back to a word that's become meaningless through overuse, abuse, flagrant generalization, and use as a marketing ploy. Once again, I've come up with five: addition, need, opposites, subtraction, and epiphany. That is, A NOSE. (I find this humorous, as I scratch my nose when I'm trying to think of an idea.)

Since I've only been asked to write an introduction, I won't go into an explanation of each of these things. I'm sure readers of this book will quickly find examples in each category. One of the five is subtraction. The Bauhaus movement in design and architecture was heavily focused on subtraction, on minimalism, on clarity of communication, as exemplified by Paul Klee's design courses and his books, *The Thinking Eye* and *The Nature of Nature*.

When I created the TED Conference in the early 1980s, I approached it with the idea of subtracting. I subtracted the panels of men in suits talking about a single subject, I subtracted the lectern, I subtracted saved seats, I subtracted selling from the stage, I subtracted long speeches, I subtracted a focus on a golf tournament. I took away all the things that didn't interest me, and I arrived at the convergence of technology, entertainment, and design in the form of a dinner party that I'd like to be at.

Recently, I invented the WWW Conference, and subtracted the last two things that I could: time and presentations. I introduced one of these conferences as a great leap backwards, and went on to explain that this gathering could have taken place 2,500 years ago in Athens, in a small amphitheater with no amplification or electricity. It was Aristotle, Socrates, or Plato or whoever was on speaking terms with one another having a chat in front of an audience. It was a conversation.

Likewise, this book by David Laufer is a pleasant leap backwards, a collection of conversations with graphic designers working over the last forty years. Some are well known, some are obscure, some are charming, some are acerbic, and some are a combination of charm and abrasiveness. But they all have opinions, they all have stories, and they are all in conversation about their passion for design.

I think it's interesting that he starts with Victor Papanek, someone I met when I was 25 at my first teaching job at North Carolina State College. I knew him for only a brief period of time, as he was soon fired for being one of those acerbic chaps, but he will be forever appreciated by those who observe the fork in the road that presents itself to all designers. To the left there's a sign that says "Looking good," with another sign below it that says "This way to rewards and awards." To the right there's a sign that says "Being good," with a sign below it that says "Do good work." The seduction of the left fork is with the graphic designer, the industrial designer, the architect—all of us—every day. It is our nemesis.

The central idea of this book is the importance of mentors and mentoring—the big brother or big sister who leads by example; the idea of reading, listening, and being in the presence of those who've pulled themselves out of the slime, who've become worthy and therefore can help us choose our path. My life has been hugely influenced by people vastly more intelligent than me—people who could make the complex clear; who by their example, by their writings, by their work, gave me permission to expand my curiosity and my interests. In fact, giving permission, either actual or implied, is a cornerstone of learning—not copying a style, not being lectured to, not emulating someone else's work, not duplicating an example, but merely being in the presence of good work was really quite enough.

I recently started my 84th book, *Threads 322*. It's about the thread of permissions, about giving oneself permission to make constructive/ objective criticism at the deepest and most uncomfortable level; to connect with individuals and mentors of all ages, even deeply flawed people; to understand the word "quest" in the word "question" and the word "inform" in the word "information"; and to admit the difficulty in aspiring to design one's life. I think the individuals David has chosen to include in *Dialogues* define that idea of mentorship, and I hope you'll take advantage of their insights.

The big design problem is not designing a house for Mom or Dad or designing a toaster or designing a book. It's designing your life. By the design of your life you create the blackboard to bounce all your thoughts against. What is it you like to do every day? Time is the only commodity. What other do we have?

I really measure my life by what I want to do every day and that's a design problem, if you want to call it that, that we have an effect upon. We can decide what to do, what our trade-offs are.

Mies van der Rohe was a notable German-American architect who lived in Chicago and was considered one of the pioneers of modern architecture.

One day, late in his life, he was sitting in a big chair, a little chubby like me, a cigar in his mouth and his students were interviewing him. They wanted him to say his secret. He didn't say anything. They asked again. He didn't say anything.

Finally, he said, "Do good work." And I thought that was so profound, so clear. The ultimate is to do good work and that's all we try to do. Good work, and then we die. You're not around, you won't read your own obituary, you just do some good work, have some fun and indulge yourself, and make yourself clear to other human beings. That's all we are, human beings, and have some good conversations, and hopefully do some good work.[2]

—Richard Saul Wurman

1, 2 Richard Saul Wurman, *33: Understanding Change and the Change in Understanding* (Greenway Communications, 2009)

Introduction

It is a brutal fact of the free market system that there are always more new, talented, and enthusiastic creative people entering the marketplace than there are situations where their talent can be utilized to its fullest potential. I see dozens of young design professionals each year, and I am always glad when I hear that one has landed a job. Sadly, too many highly talented people do not find a place to flourish; some give up and take other career paths, some take positions where they cannot be mentored or developed. For a society—and a world economy—that depends on innovative thinkers, this seems like a double loss.

While no book could hope to right this wrong, I undertook writing this one to accelerate the arrival of some crucial aha moments for creative professionals—the realizations that guide and expand career opportunities. It is my hope that *Dialogues with Creative Legends* will help reestablish the importance of mentoring as a fundamental design activity—on both sides of the interview table. The process of selecting, vetting, and promoting new creative talent is opaque. There are no road maps. There are, however, some attitudes that help; some ways to remain enthusiastic and persistent in the search until opportunity opens a door.

My own search began while I was a student at Carnegie Mellon University in 1968. At the time, CMU ran several programs to bring leading design practitioners to lecture, and there were usually either Q&A sessions or workshops where students could interact with the design luminaries. My first few contacts with highly accomplished creative professionals were transformational; the idea of design— which in a classroom setting can seem abstract—became alive and vital. As a result, it became my obstinate idea that if I could meet and question other great practitioners in design, and learn how they had steered their careers to such heights, then I might discern a pattern and follow that pattern myself. This necessitated tracking them down and getting them to agree to give me an interview. The process of obtaining the appointments was frequently as educational as the interviews themselves. I have included interviews in which special mentoring or coaching took place, as well as those with designers whose work was highly acclaimed. These interviews form the first two sections of the book and are presented chronologically. Later in my career I was privileged to be hired by some dynamic business leaders, and to learn from their personal style and observe their leadership. A few of these interviews with business leaders form the last section of the book.

MOTIVATIONS & CHOICES Everyone with creative impulses confronts a certain set of questions as they mature:

> *What is the nature of my talent? Does my talent measure up?*
> *How do I find and contact the people who need my abilities?*
> *How do I get noticed, get experience, and get connected?*
> *Can my talent change the world for the better?*
> *How do I support myself while trying to figure all this out?*

Even against a background of revolutionary change in technology and society, many of these questions for creative individuals are constant. They must be posed and wrestled to the ground by each new creative soul. The questions and answers vary because each talent is unique, yet there is much to be learned from the conclusions of the seekers who have gone before.

> *What is there to be learned from the great practitioners of design, and their counterparts in business, from this recent and amazing period of graphic invention? What constants connect the rising generation of visual designers to the grand masters who preceded them?*

It is these questions about creativity, mentoring, self-discovery, and interdependence that drove the interviews in this book. I set about asking questions—frequently the wrong questions—without much foreknowledge. Some of the interviewees are legends in design and business; others are less well known but nevertheless read me deeply and taught me extraordinary things. There were dozens of interviews I chose to leave out, to concentrate on those that, regardless of their professional standing or name recognition, enhanced my understanding in ways I could never have discovered on my own.

SETTING The latter half of the twentieth century was a time of intense social change, upheaval, and creativity. Nuclear weapons ended World War II, but began a cold war built on "mutually assured destruction." Advances in birth control brought about far-reaching changes in family, vocation, marriage, and gender equality. An explosion in music and visual culture paralleled rapid evolution in business, education, and technology. The Civil Rights movement exposed inequality and hypocrisy that had clogged America's morality since the founding of the republic.

This period was also a coming of age for graphic design. The larger family of design professions was just beginning to see female practitioners join its topmost ranks. It was striking that, while my graphic design class at CMU was half women, the university's lecture series for famous designers was still called Men with Ideas. Rapid improvement in communications media gave designers a host of new tools. Between 1950 and 2000, several generations of phenomenal creative talents put those tools to astonishing use, responding to their stormy surroundings with an outpouring of daring, dazzling, and iconic imagery. As the millennium drew to a close, the digital revolution transformed every area of human endeavor, including the design profession.

TECHNICAL AND HISTORICAL BACKGROUND Much has changed about the practice of graphic design since the period of these interviews. I have purposely avoided as much as possible writing about history or technique, since it is the more timeless psychological and social issues that are important to career development. Yet, a quick review of the technical and historical context will make the interviews comprehensible. Let me do that here, to minimize the necessity for historical asides in the main narrative.

In the late 1960s, most graphic design was created with artists' media: pastels, gouache, cut paper, and analog photography. Designers relied heavily on the use of photographic prints, from film negatives; if you were in a hurry, direct to paper "photostats" were used in great profusion for design decision making. Felt-tipped markers flourished for a decade or two as an essential sketch medium. Also widely used was collage, a technique requiring great skill and a large library of old magazines. Artwork was prepared on boards to be photographed for printing or filmed for broadcast. Much of what is now transacted via the Internet was then delivered in person or by professional couriers. Photocopiers, which were then coming into common use, changed many of the techniques of design and illustration. Color copying was in its infancy, though it was embraced as quickly as it became reliable.

The graphic designer's portfolio was—then as now—the defining component of an early creative career. A professional portfolio had printed samples and tear sheets from magazines, stills from TV, photographs of installations. Until then, an early-stage portfolio was filled with drawings, studies, and mostly handmade approximations of design ideas. Most students and young professionals recorded their portfolios on 35mm slides, primarily as a backup. Portfolios had to be viewed firsthand.

Because of the manual nature of design, the portfolio of a young professional emphasized manual skills. Drawing, lettering, skilled use of wet media, and the ability to indicate the space and gesture of typography using only a pencil were the designer's stock in trade. One of my professors, Ed Fisher, Jr., repeated his mantra to four decades of student designers: "Quick expression is the designer's salvation." Another professor, Herbert Olds, said, "I draw because it's the fastest way to see what I'm thinking." I believe both will always be true, no matter how much the tools and methods change.

Beginning in the 1960s, typography underwent a series of technical revolutions. The typositor appeared briefly, a bizarre contraption that was half workstation and half darkroom, facilitating variations in headline type unimaginable with metal type. This began an emancipation of typography that gave graphic design a blast of freedom. The typositor also reduced the cost of introducing new fonts, from tens of thousands of dollars for a foundry font, to a few thousand for a typositor font. A wild outpouring of typographic innovations—and plagiarism—ensued. Herb Lubalin's font Avant Garde, with its many ligatures and tight kerning, is an early example of how alert designers began exploiting their newfound freedom. A succession of electromechanical, photographic, optical, and digital methods for typesetting caused waves of wrenching change that eventually abolished the typographic unions and put typesetting in the hands of everyone with access to a computer.

When I began the interviews in this book, fax and automated teller machines were two decades in the future. Telephones were hardwired—no mobile—though in most cities telephone booths were abundant. There was no Global Positioning System—one either asked for directions or carried a paper map. In the early 1970s, mechanical answering machines began to replace answering services staffed by live operators. Prospecting for work by telephone was slowed by the necessity of collecting recorded calls from a machine or a remote human operator. I purchased my first answering machine in 1977; it cost several weeks' pay and weighed 15 pounds!

The tsunami of change brought about by the Internet has made it considerably easier to make the work of new talent easily visible. Yet interactive and social media have also made *more difficult* the essential task of obtaining face-to-face interviews with top talent. Employers can anonymously view and eliminate all but a very few portfolios for interviews. For that reason, it is my hope that this book will convince rising designers to apply their creativity to making personal contact with their creative idols and to soliciting mentorship. I certainly hope it will remind gatekeepers everywhere of the crucial mentoring activity that goes on in face-to-face interviews, and of the necessity of hiring, in the words of Ruedi Rüegg, "people, not portfolios."

ABOUT THE INTERVIEWS This book spans approximately 40 years. I did not begin with the intent to write a book, so many of the dialogues were recorded in note form and transcribed later. While I have presented the interviews here in present tense using a dialogue format, I cannot represent them as verbatim. Some, such as those with employers, teachers, and clients, are summarized from conversations that took place over the course of weeks or even months. Others, such as the lectures in Pittsburgh and job interviews with famous designers, were from notes made soon after the fact. The Lubalin interview is an example.

I have been privileged to meet and serve many creative and business leaders of the first rank who are not included in this book. This is not because their advice was not excellent, not because their creativity or leadership is not great. Rather, I felt compelled for the reader's sake to make the most concise and revealing collection of dialogues, not the most comprehensive.

It has been my intention throughout to be true to what was being communicated, and to give the reader the immediacy of firsthand experience in a narrative edited to give context and continuity. First and foremost, *Dialogues with Creative Legends* is meant to convey the cumulative effects and connections—the aha moments—brought about by the insights of these mentors. Where possible I have sent my remarks to the interviewees to obtain their agreement. There are many references to people in the narrative who were not interviewees but who played roles necessary to the development of a point. For a few individuals playing supporting roles whom I have not been able to track down for comment, or whose real names I have forgotten, I have elected to give fictitious names. These are: Dan Small, Jonathan Green, Walter Papillion, John Wright, Squire, and Jimmy Saronsen.

PATHS AND GOALS The fundamental goal of graphic design is still to communicate with precision, power, and finesse. The goals of showing a portfolio are remarkably constant as well. For the interviewer the goal is to assess the creative skill, experience, and personality of the young talent. For the interviewee, the goal is to make an impression, ask and learn, and ideally find an employment opportunity. In the larger sense, the interviewer's role is to gain insight into the ecosystem of young talent, and to help it thrive.

For new talents confronting the necessity of making a living by their art, and especially to those whose zeal is missionary in its intensity, I offer this narrative not as a template to be followed, but rather as encouragement. Showing one's creative work can seem terrifying and insurmountably difficult. Youthful interview experiences often include mistakes, tongue-tied moments, and embarrassing faux pas. Each new talent has to indulge a few interviewers who are rude, insensitive, dishonest, manipulative, or misinformed. I hope the ideas in this book will help interviewees maintain their poise, stay alert to serendipity, and shrug off the few inevitable bad experiences. If *Dialogues* imparts nothing else, let the reader understand that the majority of creative interviewers have been through the same trials, and want to be helpful even if they can't offer employment.

Each time a portfolio is shown, the creative community is strengthened in some small way. The process deepens the interviewer's knowledge of the talent pool and strengthens the interviewee's creative work through commentary and experience in the spotlight. It also helps prepare the interviewee for a seat on the other side of the interview table. Many interviewees later find that the interviewer's job is often just as challenging! And I hope that *Dialogues with Creative Legends* will help impart a sense of the long tradition in the creative community of helping everyone who asks: stranger, friend, competitor, and collaborator alike. It is a wonderful tradition. One rarely regrets generosity; I greatly regret the times I was unable to extend it.

I received many invaluable comments, a few well-deserved insults, and much encouragement from the designers whose time I begged away from their clients, their families, their much-needed nourishment or rest. Those are debts that cannot be repaid; at best they can be paid forward. I am thankful for the opportunity to pass along insights from some truly extraordinary creative and business leaders.

—David Calvin Laufer,
Atlanta, November, 2012

Dialogues with Creative Legends

Aha Moments in a
Designer's Career

TEACHERS

In my childhood hometown of Cleveland, Ohio, lives Mr. A. Reynolds Morse, a successful entrepreneur and one of Salvador Dalí's most devoted patrons. His home and factory are crowded with his growing collection of Dalí paintings, which Morse opens to the public. My mother is lukewarm about Dalí, but nevertheless feeds my interest in art with occasional visits to study the artist's oeuvre. (Morse's collection will later be donated to form the Dalí Museum in St. Petersburg, Florida.) I ask for paints so I can emulate Dalí's work and life.

At age 17, I see an advertisement for the first issue of *Avant Garde* magazine. The inclusion of an interview with Dalí is enough to convince me to part with a couple weeks' earnings from my newspaper route for a subscription.

When my first issue of *Avant Garde* arrives, the interview with Dalí proves to be moderately interesting, but the page layouts are spectacular! Although I don't realize it, I am looking at the work of Herb Lubalin; one day, my zeal to meet the man will lead me on an odyssey. At this moment, all I know is that I am seeing a new category of creative work—graphic design—that is creatively exciting and accessible in a way that fine art is not.

The arrival of *Avant Garde* sets up an unexpected contrast between the work of a famous artist and that of a famous graphic designer, and begins for me a lifelong interest in the relationship between

these two types of creative work. Dalí's imagery comes purely from his own imagination; it is stimulating to see. It offers ideas without words or explanation. Or rather, it gives the viewer a starting point for new ideas, leaving him or her to make a new journey from there. The magazine takes ideas from a wide range of art and culture and makes them exciting, comprehensible, and chic. And someone gets paid to create it!

I begin experimenting with definitions. Artists can make whatever they like (sometimes) and may get paid a lot or nothing at all; designers get a salary (sometimes), but they have to work with subject matter provided by others (sometimes). Art stimulates imagination (for some, or revulsion for others); design popularizes and explains, and then is (usually) discarded with yesterday's papers.

Creative work involves a tension between freedom and security, though I struggle to express it. It is a dialogue that is to last for many years, and the resolution will come from mentoring and soul searching. This book is, in part, a chronicle of that dialogue.

Victor Papanek
PORTFOLIO AND CAREER

When Victor Papanek (1923–1998) lectured at Carnegie Mellon University (CMU) in 1969, his landmark book *Design for the Real World: Human Ecology and Social Change* was just beginning to have an impact. Papanek interned with Frank Lloyd Wright in 1949, graduated from Cooper Union with a degree in architecture in 1950, and completed his master's degree in design at the Massachusetts Institute of Technology in 1955. By the age of 44, Papanek had worked in residence with Navajo and Balinese societies, and done some far-reaching designs for populations whose needs had never before been considered by industrial designers.

Papanek taught for most of his career, beginning at the Ontario College of Art, then moving on to the Rhode Island School of Design and Purdue

University before becoming dean of the California Institute of the Arts. He headed the design department at the Kansas City Art Institute. He lectured widely, and also worked, taught, and consulted throughout the world. Papanek was the Constant Professor of Architecture and Design at the University of Kansas from 1982 to1998. Papanek challenged his students to take on difficult problems, and they did, designing low-cost agricultural equipment, furniture, communications devices, and healthcare products. This growing body of work was highly unusual for its time, and led to consulting offers from the United Nations Educational, Scientific and Cultural Organization and the World Health Organization. Swedish automaker Volvo contracted him to design a taxi for the disabled.

Among many honors, Papanek was awarded a Distinguished Designer fellowship from the National Endowment for the Arts in 1988, and the IKEA Foundation International Award in 1989. He wrote six books.

FALL 1969 I'm on my way to my dorm at CMU when Mark Perrott, an industrial design major, says, "Hey, aren't you going to the Victor Papanek lecture?"

"Who?" I ask. University life has resulted in sensory overload. I start to make my excuses, but Perrott insists I grab my design portfolio and accompany him. "He's a really socially conscious designer. This is more important than whatever assignment you are doing."

Papanek is a fit, confident man with a broad smile, amplified by an even broader mustache. It is evident from the moment he enters the room that he loves this type of session. He does not go behind the podium, but walks around the room. He has a stage presence, yet we're all on the stage with him. He opens with visuals of some of his signature projects and talks about his upbringing and his time spent living in nonindustrialized societies.

"I make no secret of the fact that the design work I am the most proud of is that done by my students. I seem to be a good designer, but I'm better as a framer of design questions. I frame problems that industry sees no profit in tackling, and my students, who don't know what is impossible, dive right in." He is grinning.

"So that is why I encouraged you to bring projects tonight—not so I can tell you what is good, but so I can see what brilliance is brewing here at CMU." Nobody wants to be first to open his or her portfolio, so Papanek suggests we lay them all open. It is not a critique of

> **❝ I make no secret of it: the design work I am the most proud of is that done by my students. I'm a good designer, but I'm better as a framer of design questions. ❞**

individual work. As it happens, we have three generations of CMU industrial design professors there: the highly ethereal artist-as-social-theorist Robert Lepper, the devoted technician of heavy industry Richard Felver, and the agile interdisciplinarian Joseph Ballay, who balances the demands of user, manufacturer, and investor. Papanek looks at a senior industrial design student's portfolio and says, "Tell me about this work."

"I'm making this portfolio because I want to get a job as a designer. The portfolio is a means to an end. I have to demonstrate to somebody that I can do what they need."

The four professors pause and exchange glances. Papanek decides to see where the other students are. "Anybody else? Does that sum up the function of the design portfolio?"

Another volunteers, "My dad wanted me to be an engineer like him, and wouldn't pay for me to go to art school. We decided we could both live with industrial design. I'm not sure whether anyone will hire me, but my portfolio is sort of a record of trying out my wildest ideas." Everyone nods a certain sort of satisfaction with this position.

I decide that I have nothing to lose since I'm the lone graphic designer in the bunch, and say, "I'm energized by the projects we are given in class, and sometimes I am proud of the results, sometimes not. Even if I pick my best work, my portfolio seems like a jumble. I'm not sure what a professional portfolio is supposed to be like."

Lepper, whose humor adds depth to the most serious subjects, replies, "Designers are always worrying about their portfolios. The only designers who aren't fretting are retired!"

Felver offers, "Industrial design in my lifetime has moved from engineering to planning. We used to have to demonstrate that something was mechanically possible. Then it became intertwined with the financial side: we have to demonstrate that a product can be manufactured and distributed at a set unit price and break even after so many thousand units. Then it moved into styling, making your client's product look more 'current' and sell better than the competitor's product."

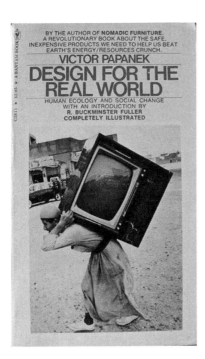

With equal parts social theory, bombast, anthropology, and delicious ingenuity, *Design for the Real World* is a wake-up call for designers everywhere to seize the initiative and set an agenda for socially responsible innovation. Papanek eschewed style and preference; his work was always about making life better for underserved populations.

Papanek's emphasis on carefully studying user populations influenced the teaching and practice of two generations of designers who followed. Above, a hydrotherapy device for movement-impared children.

The famous ten-cent radio (above), developed by Papanek with George Seeger, was made from a tin can, an ear piece, and wires, and powered by burning paraffin, or dung. These radios became the first mass-communication devices for millions in isolated populations in the developing world. Appreciative users decorated their radios using local materials and cultural tradition. Papanek and his students also designed irrigation pumps, vehicles, and even an $8 hand-cranked refrigerator created for UNESCO. *Nomadic Furniture,* cowritten with James Hennessey, suggested ways to live simply and relocate easily, including designs for collapsible furnishings made from cardboard.

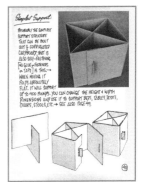

66 *Nobody chooses the body they get! Let's design products that benefit people who don't fit the norms, as well as those that do.* 99

The group opens up a bit and there is a feeling of mutuality.

Papanek now offers some foundational material. "Okay, this is not atypical of the kind of conversations that go on in design schools everywhere. We sharpen our talents to take orders. We concentrate on product making. We get absorbed in details like maximizing the revenue that can be gotten out of a certain investment in tooling. We take as gospel the programming we get from industry. Westinghouse hires us to help them overtake GE in such and such market area. What I want to challenge you to do is look at the whole thing through the other end of the telescope."

Ballay, who is responsible for booking the speakers for the Design Issues series, smiles. He probably knows that what is coming will make his colleagues uncomfortable and says, "Go on, Victor."

"Industry makes things to sell," Papanek continues. "It's so easy to get wrapped up in the selling end that we sometimes forget about who has to own and use the stuff. You look at how you would design a chair or a car or a toy for your own family, and it looks different than what you design for other people to manufacture for a profit.

"Understand, I'm not saying profit is bad—we must make money to stay in business. But," Papanek looks each student in the eye in turn, "you have an important decision to make right now in your career. Are you going to be an order taker or a product innovator? Industries are great at making lots of a product and shaving the unit cost of it to make it profitable. They are great at finding what will sell to the largest number of people. But there are always many people who fall outside that largest number market.

"Henry Dreyfus was commissioned by the US Army to do an exhaustive study of ergonomics, which was published as *The Measure of Man*. It details that most human adults fall within a certain set of dimensions. Le Corbusier's Modulor made similar assumptions as a starting point for proportioning buildings. Both of those examples were tremendously important, but both of them marginalize the people who fall outside those norms. Why can't we make a world that works for everybody? Nobody chooses the body they get! Let's make a world that fits people who don't fit the norms, as well as those who do.

"Industrial designers create tractors that increase the number of acres a single farmer can till, but the vast majority of farmers in the world will never own a tractor. Can't we design something at a profit that improves the productivity of all those farmers?"

Papanek is doing something that great designers everywhere do all the time: he is reframing questions. He changes tack.

"Any of you coming out of a professional design program will have a very good-looking portfolio." The Papanek grin and moustache flash my way with a good-natured glance. "You don't really need to worry about whether your portfolio is flashy enough. What will make your work irresistible to industry is if you demonstrate that you can identify populations that are underserved and design something that helps them live more fully." He is walking while talking, and he stops for emphasis.

I'm not an industrial designer, but a question pops out, without much forethought. "I really love beautiful cars. Stylish design commands a premium in the marketplace. Isn't that important, too?"

"Now let me say that my attitudes about industrial design have gotten me kicked out of a few universities, and uninvited to an industrial design convention. I was supposed to be a speaker, but after my book came out, somebody on the board told me, 'There was the feeling that we didn't need Papanek to chastise us for catering to affluent markets.' So I take it as a compliment that my book pricked some consciences.

"If you decide to be an order taker and work with what industry thinks it needs, OK, that's a viable career choice. But I'm saying, think of design not merely as a profession, but also as a calling, a mission. Design can be about making life nicer for the people who can afford to have nice lives. That's where the profession started. But why can't it be about making a better life affordable for everyone?" I decide to ask for clarification, because he seems to

> **66** *Don't worry about whether your portfolio is flashy. To make your work irresistible to industry, demonstrate that you can identify underserved populations and help them to live more fully.* **99**

> **" A good portfolio demonstrates that you're a problem solver. The assignment is the problem; your design is the solution. An exceptional portfolio shows that you have the empathy to identify and solve a problem on your own. "**

be missing the point that students need to get hired in order to eat: "Professor Papanek, I love the idea of design being a force for a better world. But where do I go to get hired for that?"

Papanek is not taken aback. "Not just a good question, it is the question. A good portfolio demonstrates that you're a problem solver. The assignment is the problem; your design is the solution. An exceptional portfolio shows that you can identify a problem on your own, empathize with a population of users, and transform the problem into an opportunity. I want you to understand why I'm so energized by student portfolios. A professional portfolio has projects that have been brought to fruition. They demonstrate that you know what is possible and what can deliver. They are about credentials and they create trust. Student portfolios are about learning what is possible, but also about suspending disbelief and proposing radical solutions. They can be unfettered by the technical details. Or put another way, great design—whether professional or academic—makes an imaginative leap to a desired goal: making life better for people. If the solution is compelling enough, the technical details can often be filled in retroactively.

"And by the way, striving for pure utility is a sure path to lasting beauty. Have you ever seen industrial design as beautiful as the lunar lander we put on the moon? President Kennedy gave the aerospace community an inspiring, visionary assignment: 'Put a man on the moon within the next decade.' He didn't know how it would be done, but he believed in his people. So, the scientific community rallied to the cause with many innovations to fill in. Without that vision, the design community would not have made the innovations of microcircuitry, metallurgy, and satellite communications that were necessary. On a smaller scale, that's the skill that a student portfolio needs to demonstrate. To imagine a solution outside technical boundaries, then work to achieve it."

Papanek concludes, "So, back to your question, how do you get hired to make the world better? For every generation it's a bit different, but I think it's by demonstrating that there is hope for ambitious goals, by being unafraid to think beyond narrowly defined technical or styling problems. Part of it is design skill. Part of it is your enthusiasm. You can make up for a lot of shortcomings and technical inexperience with heartfelt enthusiasm. In making the transition from student to professional designer, that enthusiasm is your trump card. Make sure your portfolio plays it convincingly!"

I experiment with a new way of stating the difference between art and design: Great design makes the world better by lifting people's standard of living. Great art makes the world better by lifting people's spirits. It still doesn't draw together all the ends, but there is something stirring in this attempt.

Buckminster Fuller
WORLD GAME

Richard Buckminster "Bucky" Fuller (1895–1983) studied at Harvard University and at the US Naval Academy. Among his early inventions were a winch for rescuing aircraft downed at sea and a new method for building with reinforced concrete. He wrote a book—at a young age—about the far-reaching consequences of Einstein's Theory of Relativity; publishers shunned the project until Einstein himself endorsed it, lending great credibility to Fuller's early career. Teacher, theorist, architect, cartographer, industrial designer, educator, and outspoken futurist, Fuller wrote seven books, including *Nine Chains to the Moon, Operating Manual for Spaceship Earth,* and *I Seem to be a Verb*. As a college professor, he taught his students to practice "comprehensive design science," and he expanded the design vocabulary with "tensegrity" (for structures that combined elements set in tension with one another) and "dymaxion" (for dynamic maximum, a philosophy of doing more with less). Fuller crystallized his design process as "synergetics," which he used

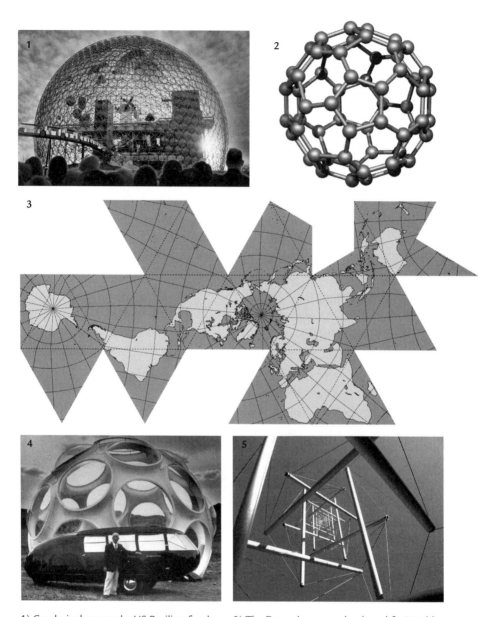

1) Geodesic dome at the US Pavilion for the 1967 World's Fair, in Montreal
2) Molecules of carbon with geodesic structure, discovered two years after Fuller's death, were named Fullerenes (known to his fans as "Buckyballs") in his honor. Fullerenes in many configurations are now a foundation of nanotechnology.
3) The Dymaxion map, developed for World Game, allows the continents to be viewed together with minimal size distortion.
4) Fuller with his Dymaxion Car and a modular geodesic structure.
5) Fuller demonstrated new, highly efficient structures made possible by "tensegrity," the use of tension and compression together.

in his projects and taught his students. His writing is by turns densely theoretical, then profoundly simple and beautiful; Fuller held an honorary chair in poetry at Harvard. Among his best-known creations are the Dymaxion House, the Dymaxion car, and the Dymaxion map. Although the design for what Fuller dubbed the "geodesic" dome was invented by someone else, Fuller patented some technical advances that made geodesic domes more practical to build.

As a teacher at Southern Illinois University Carbondale, he instituted World Game, in which he challenged teams of student designers to view all the world's resources and the needs of all life forms as a single system, and to improve the quality of life for all inhabitants of "Spaceship Earth." His ideas laid the groundwork for the modern environmental movement. Fuller's breadth of knowledge, intellect, and passion made him one of the most visionary—and controversial—figures in modern design.

DECEMBER 1969 The announcement that R. Buckminster Fuller has been added to the "Men with Ideas" lecture series at CMU causes considerable buzz. Fuller is famous but his work is controversial—one of the school's architecture professors calls him a "charlatan." A clueless kid from Ohio, I know almost nothing about him. The Carnegie Mellon bookstore is sold out of all of his titles except *I Seem to Be a Verb,* which I purchase and browse the day of the lecture. It's like a comic book of political and cultural paradox, and a lot of fun, but it doesn't give me much to go on.

So I attend the lecture with relatively little foreknowledge. Fuller is in the big auditorium at the Carnegie Museum, and the event is standing room only. He is introduced with some fanfare as a modern Leonardo da Vinci. At 75 years old, he is rather slight in build and wears very thick glasses with circular lenses that make him look a bit bug-eyed. He is, however, a veteran of many presentations, and he takes the stage like a conquering gnome. His sentences are long, his large vocabulary is further expanded with words of his own invention, and he dives right in. For the audience, it is sink or swim, and within a few minutes the intensity of his voice has us all swimming.

"We will be talking tonight about World Game—a way of applying a comprehensive design science to achieve the most far-reaching consequences. Everyone here can participate and I hope you will. There's certainly nothing as important you can apply yourselves to at the present time."

Several things become clear. First, Fuller hops between many subjects, so taking notes is very difficult. Second, Fuller is not interested in teaching us how to design. He is interested in galvanizing youth to boldly envision a practical Utopia. He talks method only to explain that it is possible to create a better quality of life with less waste. He touches on many of the same social themes that Victor Papanek had in an earlier lecture. But where Papanek is willing to do detailed work for very specific populations—such as toys for children with muscular dystrophy—Fuller wants to design on the largest possible scale. He is impatient with the politics of entrenched interests. He peppers his description of corporations with descriptors such as "legally piggly." He wants Earth's resources to be used for the benefit of all Earth's inhabitants. Fuller has wit and passion, and an ability to make bold changes seem not only possible, but within one's grasp. Clearly, Fuller has read everything worth reading, and either rejected it or integrated it into his thinking. He is a visionary.

"We set out to look for ways to make the earth's resources more equitably available. How many of you know about Malthus?" Some hands go up. "Malthus, you know, tried to convince us that we had exceeded the capacity of our planet nearly two centuries ago, so shortages of food, health care, and shelter are inescapable. While these are facts of life for far too many, World Game asserts that there is now no reason that all of Earth's inhabitants cannot have food, shelter, and livelihood, if we make that our goal.

"We think we have reached our limits of efficiency, yet our whole history is one of making accidental discoveries that improve efficiency. Our Earth is a beautiful spaceship, but it came without an operating manual. Where are the resources? Where are the best places to live? So my students and I set about to study these questions, and we soon discovered that there was no map of Spaceship Earth suitable for large-scale planning. All the available projections distorted the size of the continents and made them look like separate land masses. So we set about making a new map." He shows a slide of the world as a globe, then one with the land masses mapped on a sort of soccer ball made of triangles. "We were able to project the world onto an icosahedron,

> **The bigger your ideas are, the greater the inertia—resistance to change—you must expect to face.**

which has triangular sides—which minimizes distortion to the size of the continents—then open it up to a view that is much more useful for big-picture planning.

"So, if you find you don't have the right information to make informed, long-range choices, start by making the informa-

66 If you don't have the right information to make informed, long-range choices, start by making the information you do have easier to understand—more visual. 99

tion that you do have easier to understand, easier to present. This Dymaxion projection is the first new world map to be patented in a century and a half. Why? Because until now, we have had abundant resources and a tacit acceptance of waste, poverty, and inequality. Nobody needed a radically new map because nobody was thinking about planning on a global scale. World Game required a new map— it is a precondition for a new way of planning."

His pace is picking up, and he changes visuals.

"So we see that when the Western Hemisphere is working, its demand for electricity can outstrip its supply, but at the same time, the side of the earth that is asleep has excess electrical capacity. What if we could transmit the idle capacity from Russia to the United States, then twelve hours later, reverse the flow? We would reduce the resources we have to tie up in generating capacity, and make our nations interdependent. There would be a few technical challenges to moving electricity across the Arctic," he pauses for the audience, which he knows is filled with engineers and architects, to have a short laugh. "But the technical hurdles can be solved if we can get governments to stop posturing and do the right thing."

Fuller moves from one demonstration to the next. (I later learn that Fuller has glossed over some important map advances, including the 1909 Butterfly Projection by B.J.S. Cahill from which his Dymaxion projection has clearly benefited. One sees where the controversy comes from!)

Fuller suggests that a central dilemma faced by all designers is inertia—resistance to change. The bigger your ideas are, the more visionary, the greater the inertia you will face. Change creates opportunities for improvement, but change also interferes with established norms, and, more to the point, established spending habits.

> **❝ All the information in the world is available right here in this room. It's just a matter of presentation. ❞**

The "power seeking and profit seeking" who stand to lose revenue can find a thousand reasons why the change you propose won't work, or is too expensive, dangerous, unconstitutional, or whatever. A crucial part of good design is explaining why the design is good. Change, innovation, new ideas all must be made palatable. Very few ideas are so revolutionary that they are wholly without precedent. When you present innovative ideas, you must demonstrate how they are connected to past experience. The more innovative your concept, the more important it is that it appears to the world as merely a new twist on a safe, tried-and-true idea that has been tested and proven a hundred times.

"We had a hard time getting geodesic structures approved for construction until we began demonstrating their kinship with insect nests, atomic structures—things that had been working in the natural world for millennia."

Fuller speaks uninterrupted for two and a half hours, and he's just gotten up a full head of steam. Professor Goldman comes on stage to remind Fuller to make time for questions.

At first there are no questions—Fuller seems to have covered almost every subject in the world—so Professor Goldman asks whether there is ever enough information available to a team to allow planning on such a large scale as World Game.

Fuller responds, "All the information in the world is available right here in this room. It's just a matter of presentation to make sense out of it." I realize we are hearing all of this futurism from a man who spent his formative years without a telephone! Fuller seems to be saying that the availability of information through modern media has finally caught up with the designer's need for information. This gives him confidence that planning on a global scale is at last within reach of humans, precisely because of more accessible information. A student asks how to get a job with World Game.

"World Game is a way of thinking, a set of mental tools," Fuller explains. "You learn it as a student, when you have time to experiment. Once you graduate, you take your World Game tools with you wherever you go."

Many hands now go up, and Fuller is favoring students. He fields a statement about wanting to do designs that are worthy of the Museum of Modern Art, and "isn't that equally important and valid as making maps and domes?"

Fuller responds, "You can't do everything. You have to make tough choices about where you will spend your career time. I have work in museums, but that's a byproduct, not a goal. I never set out to design beautiful things, but when I am done designing, if the result is not beautiful, I know I have done something wrong."

A professor stands to speak: "Isn't World Game really a giant international welfare scheme—a form of Communism?"

The place goes quiet. Communism is a hot and dirty word. But Fuller has heard all manner of criticism, and steps up the pace of his delivery. He suggests that capitalists can be just as socially conscious as Socialists—he avoids the "C" word. It is important to differentiate, he suggests, and World Game players must be "confident that good design ideas will be adopted by governments of all types. In fact, that is one of the criteria we factor in to World Game. Governments and corporations act first in their own self-interest."

The professor is not letting Fuller off easily. He asks a long question, suggesting that the World Game is the type of centralized planning that has led to so many failures in Communist "command economies." Fuller is patient. He suggests that politics are never really the problem or the solution. He also acknowledges that planning does not guarantee success. Usually large-scale failures are either due to bad planning—planning that is too narrow in focus—or no planning at all. Hence his stress on a "comprehensive" design science, one that considers the connectedness of large-scale and small-scale problems. He suggests that World Game projects are a training exercise for a new generation of planners who can succeed by surrounding the problem. Planning on a larger scale than the problem yields a better solution. He suggests that World Game solutions have to serve the interests of capital, labor, and government. Fuller does not buy arguments that require either/or choices. He wants his Dymaxion solution that delivers optimum performance for all criteria.

> **❝ I never set out to design beautiful things, but when I am done designing, if the result is not beautiful, I know I have done something wrong. ❞**

> **❝ If we give in to Malthus and assume that no amount of planning can end suffering, then we fail in the very endeavor that makes human beings unique. ❞**

He concludes, "Of course, sometimes governments have to change when their citizens have already instituted change on their own!" Fuller seems confident that his ideas cannot be ignored, and that when they get broad enough exposure, the politics and economics will sort themselves out. What is so striking about Fuller is that he's so *certain* he's right!

A student asks, "Isn't such an emphasis on planning unnatural? Isn't nature efficient because it relies on competition, not cooperation?" Fuller is delighted with this question and his theoretical side takes over, producing a lengthy answer.

He refers again to the social philosopher Malthus. "If we give in to Malthus and assume that no amount of planning can end suffering, we fail in the very endeavor that makes humans unique." At the end of a few minutes, he realizes he has not answered succinctly, and says, "Look at how natural competition between species results in efficient life forms—plants that thrive in hostile environments. Look at the beauty of a hummingbird that can fly a thousand miles. Nature is both competition and symbiosis interacting over thousands of years. So, don't think in terms of natural competition vs. design. Think in terms of a design science that can learn from natural forms and accelerate the discovery process."

The crowd begins to thin out after three hours, but Fuller is still taking questions. I put on my biggest voice and ask, "What is the relationship between Design and Art?"

Fuller finds no dilemma, or even a need to differentiate between design and art. His poetry and his drawing, his teaching and and his many designs are "a passionate search for doing more with less." He does not ornament or decorate, but he does find beauty through utility. The gallery experience is all a part of displaying, sharing ideas, and kindling enthusiasm for change. "Start with the search for learning, usefulness, efficiency. The resulting discovery will tell you how it wants to be expressed, and where it should be shared. And also, how you will be paid for your efforts."

Charles and Ray Eames
THE CONNECTIONS

Charles Eames (1907–1978) and Ray Eames (née Kaiser, 1912–1988) were among the most influential designers of the modern era. Ray, an abstract painter and graphic artist, was in the Avant Garde in New York in the 1920s. Charles studied architecture at Washington University, but was dismissed for his espousal of the work of modernists like Frank Lloyd Wright and Eliel Saarinen. Charles and Ray met at Cranbrook Academy. Among their earliest collaborations was a furniture exhibition with Eero Saarinen. The breadth of their creative output was exceptional, encompassing furniture, graphic design, exhibition design, film, product design, and teaching. Their house in Pacific Palisades, made entirely from off-the-shelf industrial components, became a touchstone for modern residential design and brought them considerable publicity. The Eameses displayed an exceptional talent for picking projects that brought modernism into the mainstream. They experimented with bent plywood, then a new manufacturing technique, to produce a generation of stylish, comfortable, and affordable furniture, and made good design more affordable for a large market. Their films and displays for IBM made mathematics and computing much more exciting for the post–World War II generation of students. The Eameses' clients included IBM, Herman Miller, and the Smithsonian Institution.

FEBRUARY 1970 The auditorium is packed for Charles and Ray Eames. They have brought in special 70mm projection equipment to show some of their experimental films, including the just-released *Powers of Ten*. Their theme for the evening is "Connections." This word is a mantra for them, useful for describing the process of design, the relationships between designer and client, and the layering of generations of designers, each one upon the preceding. They

1) Mathematical display for IBM
2) Promotional coasters for the Eames design office
3) Chair designs for Herman Miller in wire and cast aluminum
4) Furnishings, with lamp and modern decorative birds
5) Galaxy frame from the Eames film *Powers of Ten*
6) Herman Miller chair and ottoman
7) Entrance to the Eames residence in Santa Monica, California

show their work and bring the lights up for remarks and questions. To my astonishment, about half of the audience gets up to leave when the films are done. We move closer to the front.

As a husband-and-wife team, the Eameses are at ease with each other as creative peers. They express many of their ideas contrapuntally. They are too coherent to be improvised, yet their enthusiastic repartee feels too spontaneous to be rehearsed!

Ray says, "When we talk about connections, it's important to understand the science of heuristics. It is an enthusiastic intellectual wandering, a search for patterns of meaning. We as designers must constantly look to make connections between successes and innovations—sometimes between seemingly unrelated disciplines to see what might be useful to our current project.

"We made *Powers of Ten* because our clients at IBM were concerned that mathematics are not well taught in school nor well understood by the populace. We wanted to take math out of the textbook and put it into visual terms to make it easily accessible."

A student asks a rambling question, which Charles deftly interprets for the audience as "Why do we choose such difficult media for our projects, like bent plywood and motion pictures?" The question strikes Charles and Ray as humorous, and the audience picks up on their mirth.

Charles answers, and demonstrates his talent for making connections and analogies, explaining, "Film is actually a very easy medium—you just load the camera and shoot. But the camera lets you do all sorts of meaningless imagery with barely any effort at all! Doing something meaningful and entertaining—that is more difficult. Now bending plywood, I grant you, is difficult. You might go off and start shooting film without an idea just to see where it takes you. You probably would not start bending plywood without some fairly specific ideas about what you wanted to do. There is a relationship between

66 The science of heuristics: it's an enthusiastic intellectual wandering, a search for patterns of meaning. We as designers constantly seek connections—sometimes between seemingly unrelated disciplines— to see what might be useful to our current project. 99

❝ There is a relationship between the difficulty of medium and the amount of forethought you put in. An easy medium lets you do something bad with little effort and no forethought. ❞

the difficulty of the medium and the amount of forethought you put in. In an easy medium you can do something bad with little or no effort. A difficult medium fights you; it restricts your ability to play with it, so if you're going to use it, you're more likely to plan and treat the medium with respect. Our plywood chairs required a healthy respect for the limits of the curves that could be made, and some experiments into what curves were sittable. It was not easy to do something good, but it was also hard to do something bad. The reward with difficult media is usually that they are very durable, permanent. But easy or difficult, it's the connections that hold the key. You have an idea of something you want to say."

Ray takes advantage of the pause. "Or that your client wants to express in some positive way."

Charles says as an aside, "Right, first you have to sort out—simplify—what they really want to say, then you have to figure out how to say it in a way that will hold the audience's attention!" Then he picks up his media thread. "The message drives the choice of media. We talked about making *Powers of Ten* an exhibit, moving from one order of magnitude to the next, but it only took a few minutes of discussion to realize that it wanted to be a film. The exhibit format had some interesting possibilites in terms of scale, but the film medium gave us the ability to control the timing of the experience so much more closely than an exhibit."

Another student asks a long question, which Charles fields as, "How do you get playful results with 'difficult' media? Is that right?"

Ray suggests, "I think she's asking how you sketch your ideas for the difficult media to keep the playfulness of ideas."

The questioner nods vigorously. This pair has a great talent for reframing questions to be more insightful than their originals.

"Right, great question. Would you agree that is largely a personal question?" Charles asks, raising his brows to Ray.

Ray begins. "Charles and I work with different sketch media. You want something to play with that lets you work fast. Pencil on tracing paper is inescapable. For 3-D I like clay—actually we use Plasteline. Film is much harder. We end up taping all sorts of stuff to the wall so it can be rapidly reordered."

Charles picks up as if on cue. "I should say that it takes a few tries to get a good ensemble of media before you really get one that gives you great results. Penciling out each scene may give way to making paper or clay models and taking still photos. The key to maintaining that playfulness you asked about," Charles gestures to his questioner, "is working as fast and loose as possible until you can convince yourself—and your client team—the whole concept is working. Then you go into the finish mode, where the medium is more rigid, more unforgiving."

Ray adds, "And more expensive. You want to make your experiments, your mistakes, your false starts, your near misses, early and cheap; preserve as much of your budget as possible for getting good imagery and sound in a finished take."

Charles carries on. "We actually want to redo *Powers of Ten* in more detail. It is going in the right direction, but it is really a sketch for a film, as the title says. Looping back to what Ray said a minute ago, there's another inverse relationship in media. A spontaneous little sketch in an 'easy medium' like pencil is not all that remarkable. Seeing sculpture in very durable medium like marble or steel that still appears spontaneous—lifelike—is truly extraordinary."

Ray finishes the evolution of this answer. "The ability to retain something transitory—an emotion, a personality, a fleeting moment—in a very permanent form, that ability is highly prized. It is one of the ways we judge the mastery of a designer or artist."

As the presentation winds down, there's a charge in the audience

> **Make your experiments, your mistakes, and your near misses early, fast, and cheap; preserve as much of your budget as possible for getting good image and sound in the final production.**

> **The ability to retain something transitory—an emotion, a personality, a fleeting moment—in a very permanent form, is one of the ways we judge the mastery of a designer or artist.**

that seems electric, a feeling of unity of mind more akin to the experience of a rock concert than an academic lecture. There is vigorous discussion of the topics in class and over coffee for the next few weeks. It hits me. The Eameses took questions during their presentation as a way to be more directly connected with their audience. It was disruptive, but it gave the audience a way to shape the direction of the discussion. That is where the buzz came from, and that was, in a profound way, the subject of their presentation. Connecting for the Eameses is not an abstract design principle; it is essence of a creative life.

Saul Bass
NOTES ON CHANGE

Saul Bass (1920–1996) leaves a lasting imprint on two important areas in design: motion picture titles and branding systems. Bass was—like Paul Rand, Herb Lubalin, Lou Dorfsman, and a number of other influential designers of his era—a child of eastern European Jews who immigrated to New York. Like Rand, Bass got his early training by studying at night at the Art Students League. He also studied under design theorist György Kepes, then at Brooklyn College. Bass moved to Hollywood in 1941, where he designed movie posters. His big break came when he created a poster for Otto Preminger's 1954 film *Carmen Jones*. Bass's work so impressed Preminger that the director invited the young Bass to design the titles for the film as well. This led to a Hollywood career that included titles for more than fifty major films. Bass was among the first to treat titles as an integral part of the film, setting the mood for the action to follow. Bass also possessed a natural aptitude for business, and parlayed his visibility in film into branding for corporations. He helped establish many of the design management techniques needed to administer consistent branding to large companies with global operations.

JANUARY 1971 Saul Bass is an energetic man with a push-broom moustache and a personable grin that radiates all the way to the last row of the lecture hall at the Carnegie Museum. He is seated with a bundle of notes under his arm as Francis Esteban, Pittsburgh's ranking expert on branding, introduces him with smart brevity as "the man who, whether he is designing the identity of a corporation, a film, or a charity, makes work that has a timeless quality, something that never stops looking new and exciting."

Bass suggests that he'd like to screen a few of his titles and his film *Why Man Creates* (1968), then he will make some remarks and take questions at the end. The film rolls. I realize that I've already seen the movie in a theater and thoroughly enjoyed it. It is not a story, but a series of short observations about human creativity. There are quite a few laughs in it, and when the lights come up the audience applauds warmly. Despite Bass's suggestion that we hold questions until the end, a number of students begin peppering him with questions. The auditorium is a bit too big for this style of discussion, and Bass knows it, but he good-naturedly goes with the flow.

"OK, let's do a few questions about the film you just saw. I want to save the larger filmmaking questions for after—I have a surprise for you." He points to a student near the front row who can barely contain himself.

"Mr. Bass, there is a part in the film where you have a ball that appears to hop up and down—how do you do that?"

"If I tell you, you won't believe me," he says, pausing as though he might not say any more before continuing. "We bounced the ball," pausing again while the audience chuckles, "then we ran the footage backward and forward as needed to make it look like hopping."

He adds a few sentences to satisfy the film students about technique, then summarizes Occam's razor: Given two ways of doing things, the simpler one is usually better. He notes that this applies to all forms of design, but doubly so to filmmaking.

Bass points to another student, who is too starstruck to be coherent, but Bass listens and graciously finds a question worth sharing.

"The question is about editing, how you determine the pace to get the humor to work. Yes? Yes, it is probably the hardest part about film for me. You write your script and record it, for timing, when you start to plan your shots. You end up looking at the same

> **With experience comes the ability to view your design many times and still see it 'for the first time' as the audience will do.**

sequence fifty, maybe a hundred times. You get so familiar with it that it seems to slow down, like there is too much space between laughs, so you cut it tighter and tighter as you go on. Then you discover that one laugh is obscuring the next joke because you've cut it too tight. What comes with experience is the ability to view your design numerous times, modify it and still see it 'for the first time' as the audience will do."

He invites one last question, and a very petite woman in the back row stands up to project her voice."I just graduated and started doing freelance design. I'm having a lot of trouble getting paid enough. How do you explain what you do so that people are willing to pay a decent fee?"

Bass smiles knowingly, restates the question and says, "I know what you mean, you can't afford to turn it down, and you can't afford to take it on! Well, part of the trick is to be able to explain what you do in terms that your mother can understand. No jargon." He pauses as the audience laughs. "You know how I learned this? I explained graphic design to my mother."

He pantomimes conversing with his mother, beginning with a comical doting mother voice: "So, you printed this nice brochure?"

Son: "No, Mom, we hired a printer."

Mother: "So ... you made these photographs?"

Son: "Well, no we hired a photographer and models and directed the photographs."

Mother, increasingly baffled: "So, you ... wrote the words?"

"No, we hired a writer."

"You ... set the type?"

"No, Mom, we *designed* it. We coordinated things to make it nice."

Mother, feigning comprehension: "Oh! I see." Then, incredulous, "You get paid for that?" Bass begins talking again before the laughter subsides—he wants to save time for his script, but he wants to help his questioner. "Seriously, though, there probably is not a straight answer. Some people want a low price and don't care if the work is bad. Forget them. Some want good work, and they are just trying to see

> **Design? You get paid for that?**

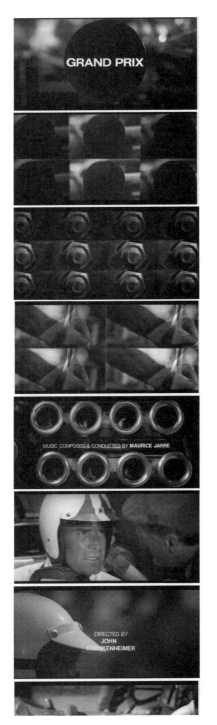

Whether branding telephony, household goods, or entertainment, Saul Bass achieved simplicity, power, and just the right emotional undercurrent.

> **The only power you have in a professional relationship is the power to withhold your talent—to say 'No!'**

how low you'll go. The only power you have in a professional relationship is the power to withhold your talent—to say 'No!' They'll let you turn down the job and hang up or walk away, but if they are convinced that you are in demand, and you seem enthusiastic about their project, maybe they'll call you back the next day. You have to decide in your mind how much—or how little—the job is worth, and stick to it. If you let them know you really need the work, you are done for. If you convince them you do great work and are confident about your prices, you are more likely to get a fair value. Every creative person, if they are blessed, finds a few clients who believe in them so fully that they give their designer extraordinary freedom. You have to earn that trust." Bass moves on. He sits at a black folding table to one side of the screen and starts describing a new project.

"I've never tried this before, but I'm going to walk you through the script for a film called Notes on Change. It's sort of a sequel to *Why Man Creates*, but also totally different. *Notes on Change* is all about the dilemma of our species—we must adapt to survive, but we also resist change. We like our comforts and our familiar surroundings." For nearly an hour, he paints word pictures. The film is to open with a super slo-mo scene of a wrecking ball breaking through a brick wall. It's an aged brick wall, with letters that look like they were painted there many years ago saying "Notes on Change." A voice-over begins as the wall starts to deform and crack, ever so slowly, from the impact of the wrecking ball. Being a title designer, Bass naturally starts with the most spectacular titles he can dream up. I realize I am seeing a master storyteller at work. Before he can do the design, he has to tell his story to many people: clients, collaborators, employees, and investors. Finding a compelling way to get from words to visuals is a crucial skill for a successful designer.

Bass finishes his reading and the house lights come back up. The audience has been quiet and spellbound.

"I guess we have time for a few more questions."

An aspiring director asks a succinct question. "Mr. Bass, when I make a film, I have a hard time getting my team to follow my directions. We seem to waste a lot of time disagreeing over details. What remedies can you suggest for this?"

Bass is already nodding before he responds, "I know exactly what you mean. You can slide on through your preproduction meetings and everyone seems perfectly in accord. Then you get to the morning when you're going to shoot scene one, and there, standing on the set with the meter running, things start to unravel." Bass starts another pantomime, this time playing several characters standing in a circle.

> **The creative director needs to know when to be democratic, when to negotiate, and when to be, well, downright dictatorial.**

Scoffing voice: "No, that will not work!"

Passive-aggressive voice: "We will need different equipment."

Detached voice: "Just do what we agreed on; we're wasting time."

Whiny voice: "Just tell me where you want the lights."

Exasperated ingenue throwing up her hands: "What what what?"

Bass breaks in again in his own voice, "What was working great as a democracy has become a food fight. Group input is great early on in the creative process. When you start to narrow your options and explain your vision to key people, you barter and cajole. But when the camera rolls, you have to be prepared to become a despot. The creative director needs to know when to be democratic, when to negotiate, and when to be, well, downright dictatorial!"

He pauses to reflect. "You just saw the titles we did for *Grand Prix*. That was the most complex shoot I had ever been on. I had a couple dozen race cars, drivers, more than a hundred people on set, and a thousand people in the stands. It could easily have been chaos. I could see immediately that we would never get anything done if I gave the slightest hint of uncertainty. I strode onto the set and started barking orders, almost at random: 'I want the 400mm lens there. I want the cars to take a flying lap and start rolling the camera as they appear around turn 3. I want the stands bustling with fans along the straightaway.'"

Bass enacts the scene, pointing this way and that with Napoleonic command. "All the while I'm saying to myself, 'Why am I doing this?' Then I realized, it will take them an hour and a half to set this up, so I commandeered a Jeep and took the assistant director and drove off. We went and scouted, and found a few shots we

> **❝ My bedrock philosophy that underpins all my film work is that we—humanity—will probably continue to screw everything up, but we'll somehow manage to stay one step ahead of utter doom. ❞**

really wanted. We came back to find everything waiting. I looked through the lens—it was a terrible shot—so I shouted 'Roll em!' Zoom zoom, the roar of the cars rattled everyone's bones. I shouted 'Cut! Print! Next shot!' and started barking orders for the second shot—which was really the first shot. Everyone said to each other, 'This guy really runs a tight ship!'" The young filmmaker who asked the question is laughing with the rest of us. Bass addresses him directly: "I guess what I'm saying is that you must at all costs look like you know exactly what you're doing, and if you don't, fake it until you can figure it out." I conclude that it really helps to be an actor—both to command and to entertain.

There are a dozen questions. Bass continues to demonstrate a remarkable ability to tell stories and become many characters. A serious-looking fellow with round glasses stands and attempts a complex intellectual question about solving problems through design. Bass, for the first time this evening, does not attempt to repeat the question. Widening his winning grin, he intones with warmth and sincerity, "I guess my basic, bedrock philosophy that underpins all my work is that we—humanity—will probably continue to screw everything up, but we will somehow manage to stay one step ahead of utter doom."

I compare and contrast Bass with Fuller. Both are invigorating and inspiring, but where Fuller relies on intellect and big ideas to engage his audience, Bass exudes warmth, humor, and emotional understanding. Design, it seems, is not a fixed product or method.

> **Aha:** *Design, it seems, is not a fixed product or method. Both the process and the outcome are deeply influenced by the personality of the designer.*

It is a process, and the outcome is deeply influenced by the personality of the designer. It appears that Bass's philosphy shares a fundamental optimism with Fuller, but their ways of expressing optimism could not be more different!

DESIGN IN THE REAL WORLD

MAY 1972 I graduate. My portfolio is a neatly presented jumble of student projects, a few freelance jobs, and half a dozen scruffy sketchbooks. I start making calls to potential employers.

Monday: "This is a student portfolio, not a professional presentation. Get serious."

Tuesday a.m.: "Your portfolio has some interesting pieces, but I'm not convinced I can make any money by hiring you."

Tuesday p.m.: "This is all you have to show for four years of college?

Wednesday a.m.: "Hey, John, come and see what your alma mater is turning out now."

Thursday a.m.: "We are looking for a designer but we don't have time to train you, we need a couple years experience minimum."

My first dozen interviews are a dose of harsh reality. After each, I reorganize, take out every piece that has drawn criticism, and obsess over order and what to say about each piece.

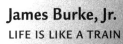

James Burke, Jr.
LIFE IS LIKE A TRAIN

James Burke, Jr. (born 1941) was raised in Wilmington, Delaware. He received a BFA from Penn State and an MFA in design from Rochester Institute of Technology. He began his design career at Pittsburgh Ad Art, becoming a partner when the company was reborn in 1972 as Graphic Center. In 1976 he cofounded, with Ernie Witalis, the agency Witalis and Burke, which rebranded in 1998 as Quest Fore. Burke's design activities were characterized by exceptionally long-lasting client relationships. Over the course of his 60-plus-year career, Burke's design thinking benefited the communications of most of the major industries in Pittsburgh. For two decades he served on the board of the Early Learning Institute, serving children with special needs. His lifelong passions are railroad and automotive design. Since retiring he has focused on documenting vintage cars and trains in illustrations, exhibits, and books.

JUNE 1972 After two long weeks of phone calls and punishing interviews in the Pittsburgh community, I have an appointment with Jim Burke. He is a partner in a twenty-person design studio called Pittsburgh Ad Art.

Sitting in the firm's conference room, I try to convince myself that the many bruises from my previous interviews are visible only to me. Burke is different from the other interviews. I'm still nervous, but he is relaxed and tells me up front that they are looking for someone, and what they're looking for. I fumble with my stack of work, trying to pick out a few pieces that I think will be most interesting based on his criteria, but I flip by a piece I have made of a locomotive. It was an animation experiment, drawn with a ruling pen. I'm about to learn a fundamental of creative interviewing.

Burke stops to admire the locomotive. "I have an O gauge model of this engine," he says, his gaze deepening. "This is mechanically accurate." Ed Fisher, Jr., one of my design professors at Carnegie Mellon University, always insisted that we know our subject matter. His epigram on the subject was something like, "Even if you're going to exaggerate, you must know your subject if your work is to be credible."

We talk about collecting—how you learn so much about people from what they collect and how collecting gives you a point of view in the world. The interview is going well. I, too, am now relaxed, so I tell him, "I collect photographs of street furniture, especially manhole covers." Up until this point, I've never thought of my photographs of manhole covers as a collection, but Burke makes me see that it is in fact similar to his trains, though not as extensive.

Burke says, "Weird idea—your photos have no intrinsic value, but they still constitute a collection."

After working for him for a few months, I realize that Pittsburgh Ad Art had several dozen applicants for the job; some were probably better designers, but the train was the bit of luck that made my work memorable. Trains are Burke's passion, and the fact that I drew his favorite train with considerable detail probably did the trick. It was practically an accident that I found a good, detailed picture to draw from, and certainly an accident that I picked Burke's all-time favorite. My interviewer saw some of me in my portfolio, but also he saw something of himself. It was luck, not skill, but I like having a job. The idea strikes me that, if I can learn more about the people with whom I am going to interview, I can use that knowledge to improve my appeal. It's the first in a long line of aha moments about interviewing for creative work, and certainly one of the most far-reaching.

> ***Aha:*** *My interviewer saw something of me in my portfolio, but also he saw something of himself.*

"Enjoying your work is important, but nobody's going to go out of their way to make your job fun. You have to do that yourself." I begin to see the reason for Burke's preoccupation with model trains. Most of his best friends are train collectors. They pass work around, and they see each other on weekends. He publishes a book about model trains, lavishing extraordinary care on the photography and design. He gives out copies to promote his business. His boss, the majority owner, never complains about the time spent on trains.

"To be successful in design, you have to have a personal passion, and you have to do your work with that passion as your energy source." Burke's living room has relatively little furniture; it is mostly glass display cases filled with model trains. I guess his family congregates in other rooms!

"It's especially important when work is slow, or uninteresting, to have a passion to propel you forward. Every creative person has periods of intense output, and other periods that are fallow. Having a creative center, an inner fire, helps you maintain your momentum."

"Why model trains?" I ask him at one point.

Burke reflects and offers, "I don't know, exactly. I played with them as a boy, but lots of other boyhood hobbies that seemed as important then have lost their interest. It's almost as though the fascination with them is too big and too mysterious to be explained. There are more types and more variations than any one collector could ever own or know about. In fact, I think that's one of the characteristics of any passion, any collection, any profession. If you can

> **Everyone has periods of intense output, and other periods that are fallow. Having a creative center, a specific passion to collect or make or travel or act out, helps you maintain your momentum.**

master it, and know everything about it, it ceases to satisfy. For some people, it's golf. For others, it's stamps, antiques, or music. If it appears a vast and rich source of wonder, you will meet other people who are also jazzed about it, and you'll engage with them on some deep level. For me, it's trains. They are art and design!"

I get quite a few routine assignments: fixing someone else's work, making client corrections. Having hired many student designers in his day, Burke knows that I'm antsy to add to my portfolio. Now and again, he says, "Here's a portfolio builder!" It's his way of keeping my interest level high, and it works. The first time this happens, though, it has an unintended effect: I lavish a lot of work and creativity on the first design ideas, only to have them all rejected. Burke comes to my desk to explain how it went.

"This is really my fault," he says obligingly. "I should have given you a better sense of the customer expectations."

This isn't true; he gave me a pretty detailed design brief.

"Let's review what the customer requested," he says before going over the design brief point by point. "Here's one way to think about this. The customer ordered a quart of milk. You'd really like to serve a milkshake with whipped cream and a cherry and nuts on top. It's OK to let the customer taste the milkshake, but you absolutely must deliver the quart of milk as a starting point." This is a lesson I am destined to learn and relearn many times, and also to play back to young designers who work for me. It's probably a conversation as old as prehistoric cave paintings!

> **The customer ordered a quart of milk. You'd really like to serve a milkshake with whipped cream and a cherry. It's OK to let the customer taste the milkshake, but you absolutely must deliver the quart of milk as a starting point.**

At lunch one day, I bring up my continuing interest in trying to find a succinct way to compare and contrast art and design.

Burke takes a stab. "An expression that begins with a desire to share a highly personal interpretation of the world is art. An expression that begins with a desire to solve a problem, or serve some need for living, is design."

"But," I point out, "you think of locomotives as works of high art, and that definition puts them squarely in the realm of design." Burke's brow furrows momentarily, and we discuss the narrow definition of art as something that goes in galleries or museums.

> *Sometimes art is utilitarian. Sometimes design can be aesthetically pleasing—may even make museum collections. Classifications don't always work. There will be overlap.*

Then he observes, "Sometimes art is utilitarian. Sometimes design can be aesthetically pleasing and be exhibited in museums. You can't assume that your definitions will always correctly classify something as only art or only design. There will be overlap."

I leave Burke's employment after two years to travel Europe and seek enlightenment. We both are sorry to part company.

"You asked me once, why model trains?" Burke recalls. "I didn't have a good answer then, but maybe I do now. Life is like a train: you're traveling along, changing cars here and there. Some are your choice, some are imposed by others. As the engineer, you have to stay on the tracks, but from time to time you get a choice. Between choices, you have to content yourself with enjoying the scenery and making the passengers comfortable. And the vehicle itself is a marvel! Silly analogy, maybe, but it's as close as I can get in words."

Walter Herdeg and Jack Kuntz
A VISIT TO MT. OLYMPUS

Walter Herdeg (1908–1995) was born in Zurich, Switzerland. He came of age in a family of modest means and was able to attend the Kunstgewerbeschule thanks to a professor, Ernst Keller, who offered him a full scholarship. After studying at the Hochschule für bildende Künste in Berlin, he worked doing package design and trademarks. During the dark days of World War II, Herdeg made plans to launch *Graphis* magazine, and when the war ended, he seized the moment. *Graphis* became the gold standard for designers, design-conscious clients, and design educators and students throughout the world. *Graphis* ran for 355 issues; Graphis Inc. continues today as a publisher of high-quality graphic design compendia. Herdeg retired in 1986 and was named an AIGA Medalist that same year.

APRIL 1974 Until my first visit to Switzerland, much of my conception of that marvelous country was based on *Graphis* magazine. The open expanses of slick, white pages seemed to correspond to snow-covered mountain ranges, undisturbed and brilliant. The orderly presentation of words and images, together with the columns of text that were always in perfect balance, gave me a mental picture of a country like a Bauhaus dream, governed by an invisible grid.

Switzerland is a revelation to the first-time visitor. The dramatic natural scenery and the orderly, well-proportioned architecture seem to have a common source. The scale of everything is harmonious, the architecture has soul, the streets are breathtakingly clean, and the public transit runs with precision. The cool, clear simplicity of Swiss graphic design, balancing poetry and precision, seems such a logical extension of their society.

I call the *Graphis* office. The phone is answered in German, but I begin in English, explaining that I'm a subscriber and two years out of school.

The receptionist doesn't miss a beat, saying, "Mr. Herdeg is very busy. When will you be in Zurich?" She has no doubt heard this lead-in from a thousand aspiring subjects. I give her a range of dates, and wait a Swiss minute. A Swiss minute is shorter than a New York minute, but passes more slowly because the surroundings are so orderly and serene.

"I'm putting you through to Jack Kuntz," she rejoins, "Mr. Herdeg's editorial designer."

"Helllloha." This is not a Swiss national. Indiana? Illinois? Somewhere Midwestern.

Despite the reassurance of a familiar greeting, a bit of nervousness creeps into my voice, the trepidation of a mortal foolish enough to approach Mount Olympus. Kuntz, too, must be used to this type of call, and his voice has the calming temperament of a person who has found the perfect vocation.

"Yes, certainly I can see you. Call me when you arrive in Zurich and we'll set a time."

When I arrive at the magazine's offices, I'm greeted by the *Graphis* sign—small, reserved, impeccable. The lobby is very simple, but for large backlit displays of *Graphis* covers. I'm shown down a corridor to Kuntz's office.

He is relaxed, even slightly cordial. We establish that we grew up in neighboring states, and I ask how he came to be in Switzerland. He served there in World War II, learned German, and came back after the war. He looks at his watch.

"We're going to try to introduce you to Walter," he says, stretching out his hand to receive the slide sheets I'm holding, "if the timing works. He has to see so many advertisers."

Kuntz pulls out an instrument of Swiss make that resembles a medical microscope, and peers at my slides. He has a large viewing area in his office with a light table and color-balanced lights.

"This is a great setup," I think aloud, taking in the purposefulness of the room.

"Uh-huh, uh-huh, uh-yes." Kuntz lets out little affirmations as he moves from slide to slide, taking in the type of experience and the experiments performed in each piece. His office is quite large; it could be a workroom for four. There are several workspaces for performing particular tasks: marking up proof sheets, specifying and proofreading type, and writing. A classic Olivetti typewriter sits squarely on an L-shaped table, flanked by an Eames chair standing at attention.

Kuntz asks, "Who makes your slides?"

I explain that I was the audiovisual assistant in Pittsburgh, so our photographer shot them, and I mounted and labeled them.

"You have good small motor," he says. "I see a surprising number of talented people whose presentation of their work ranges from casual to sloppy—as though manual skill didn't matter!"

I have the sense that he's placing me somewhere in a spectrum of many young designers whose work he has seen—in form as well as content. Kuntz asks about the purpose of my trip.

I answer, "The major art museums, the main botanical gardens, and—I guess it's OK to admit it—to visit as many as possible of the great designers whose work I see in *Graphis*."

Kuntz nods. "Whom do you wish to meet?"

"Herdeg first, of course," I tell him, "then Günther Kaiser, Jean-Michel Folon, Hermann Zapf, Josef Müller-Brockmann, and Heinz Edelmann. If I have enough money left to get to London, then Pentagram." I trail off after ten, feeling my request might be excessive.

Kuntz, who had been nodding almost imperceptibly as I said each name, takes out a mechanical pencil and writes a dozen lines. He opens his address file, scrolls past a few cards, and finishes writing.

"Here are some phone numbers that will help you." I realize that he's written down the numbers for nearly everyone on my list from memory, having to consult his file for only a few. The handwriting is a sixteenth of an inch tall, and looks like the Swiss font Akzidenz Grotesk Light.

Kuntz says, "Names and introductions matter everywhere, especially where quality standards are high. Use my name when you call Heinz, he works by himself and is very hard to see. He often doesn't answer the phone for a week because he has so many demands on him. A brilliant man, and so completely without pretense. Edelmann is neither self-important nor self-effacing. He is, at all times and with all people, just himself."

> **❝ I see a surprising number of talented people whose portfolio presentations range from casual to sloppy, as though manual skill didn't matter! ❞**

"You'll need to have a name when you call these designers or they won't see you. They know," he pauses, searching for a way to say it that Herdeg would approve, "how important they are. Their

> **Names and introductions matter everywhere, especially where the quality standards are highest.**

time commands a price. Use my name until you get a better one."

I'm about to say something about how there couldn't possibly be a better name, and he smiles a knowing Midwestern smile.

"If you get to see Müller-Brockmann, ask him for introductions to these same names. He is the grand master. All doors open to him."

We move on. I tell him I started subscribing to *Graphis* in college, when a subscription cost more than a month's groceries. Kuntz is very candid. "Herdeg knows he is a kingmaker, and he is very careful with this power."

"He clearly likes Push Pin," I observe.

"Until Push Pin, America was not a major focus of our coverage. Oh, we published Paul Rand, and Saul Bass, and Don Trousdell. In retrospect, it may have been snobbery, but back then, the bulk of American design looked too brash, too ignorant of aesthetics. Herdeg could have boosted circulation in America with more coverage of Americans, but he knew he would lose his European base, and he refused to do an American edition. He didn't feel he could live with a double standard." Kuntz pauses to look at me directly. "Then along came your Push Pin. Always innovating, always one jump ahead of the imitators. They were American, they were brash, but they were sophisticated in ways that Europeans were not. It was impossible to ignore them. They really broke design wide open. Herdeg realized it was a sea change, and decided it was his signal to become much more international."

His eyes dart over my shoulder. "Herr Walter!" he calls out.

I turn to face an intense man of angular features. His head barely reaches my shoulder, but he towers over me. Kuntz says a few sentences in German, and Herdeg grasps my hand firmly.

"We are delighted to have subscribers from the States. You have made a good investment in your future! Do keep us apprised of your career."

Before he can move on, I blurt out, "Mr. Herdeg, I must ask you

Graphis magazine's special recipe combined part art gallery, part creative resource, part arbiter of quality and taste. Its covers have always been thought provoking, and featured work by the foremost graphic artists in the world—frequently with their signature. There was never any sell copy, no price, it was pure creativity; even the magazine name itself was fair game for the designer's interpretation. Inside, the pages were always immaculately produced, with a perfect balance of white space and imagery.

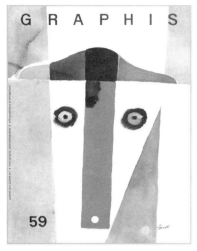

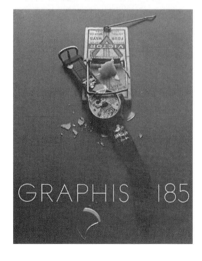

to clarify something for me." Herdeg nods, polishing his glasses, as though to inspect this impudent American more closely.

"What is the relationship of design and art?"

He replies without hesitation. "My career is devoted to proving that design and fine art are, if not one and the same, at least on equal footing." Herdeg puts his glasses back on. "There has long been a difference in the way people look at designers and artists, but as design has gotten more sophisticated and art has gotten more commercial, really, the only difference is in how one is paid." He asks about my itinerary in Europe, then he is off again.

I am left with Kuntz who says, "Now normally, I'm not to take up his time with subscribers. If you had been one of his published designers, or important advertisers, you would go to him first, then me. But I told him you were from my town—a slight exaggeration, but—so there you have your Herdeg introduction. He will never forget your name, so be sure to send your best work. You won't hear from us until we publish you a few times, but"—another direct look from Kuntz—"he remembers everything."

I'm close to overstaying my visit, but I'm really interested in how *Graphis* chooses articles. Herdeg is like a window into a world I had formerly only known on the printed page. There are many American illustrators who command good fees and are widely published, but never appear in *Graphis*. I suggest some of their names.

"I see what you mean. We have published some of those names— individual works here and there. To appreciate the editorial process at *Graphis*, you have to understand that Herdeg—and all good editors, regardless of their medium—have definite opinions about the people they put on their pages. Walter sees mountains of excellent professional work, but what excites him are the relatively few that have originality. I've seen him in our editorial meeting, flipping through a stack of work, saying—" Kuntz reflects a moment, and a German cadence creeps into his voice—"'Too glib. Too slick. If you have so many styles, you never have your own point of view.'"

> 66 *My career is devoted to proving that design and fine art are, if not one and the same, at least on equal footing.* 99

Kuntz pauses to summarize what I've been trying to grasp. "Day in, day out, editors have to decide whom to cover. They are opinionated just like everyone, only more so! They like to be the discoverer, the first one to say, 'Look! Here is someone who sees the world differently!' And in a larger sense they have to identify—or shall we say intuit—when a sea change is at hand. Good designers get seen, and published. Great designers change the way we see and comprehend. They cause their peers, editors, industries—sometimes even whole cultures—to subtly change course."

> **❝ Good designers get seen, and get published. Great designers change the way we see, and comprehend. They cause editors, industries—even whole cultures —to subtly change course. ❞**

I have to admire Herdeg's audacity. I'm here struggling to articulate the relationship between design and art; Herdeg just decides they are equal, and goes about bending world opinion to his point of view! I am also struck by the fact that Herdeg has found a way to be at the vortex of great design. He publishes a beautiful magazine, which he also designs. But for the most part, he keeps his own creativity on a tight leash, and lets others have the creative spotlight. For that matter, Jack Kuntz is doing the same thing, putting his creativity in the service of Herdeg's vision. Do all designers have to make such compromises in their careers?

Josef Müller-Brockmann and Ruedi Rüegg
PEOPLE, NOT PORTFOLIOS

Ruedi Rüegg (1936–2011) was born in Zurich and studied at the Kunstgewerbeschule. Josef Müller-Brockmann, one of Rüegg's professors, recognized his talent immediately. Rüegg interned for Müller-Brockmann and, upon graduation, worked for him for two years. Traveling to the US in 1963, he worked as an assistant to Paul Rand until 1964. He returned to Müller-Brockmann & Co. in 1965 and continued there until 1976. In 1977 he cofounded Baltis and Rüegg Studios, which later merged into Designalltag. Rüegg taught in Zurich and at Kent State University in Ohio. He was president of the graphic design association AGI Switzerland from 1976 to 1981. He collaborated with Carnegie Mellon University to curate one of the most complete collections of Swiss poster design in the world. Rüegg's book *Basic Typography*, published in Switzerland in 1979 and in English in 1989, remains one of the best books on the subject.

APRIL 1974 I have Jack Kuntz's name ready to drop when I telephone, but the receptionist at the Müller-Brockmann agency recognizes my name. She confirms that they received my letter (sent before leaving the US) and sets an appointment with friendly Swiss efficiency. We arrive at the train station in Zurich, but we have lost our map of Zurich. As we are looking about for a taxi to the Müller-Brockmann agency, I ask a passerby in my broken French for directions. She guesses correctly that we are not French, and asks in impeccable English how she might assist us. I show her the address.

"Yes, I have heard of this man. He makes our opera posters." She begins to give us directions, looks at her watch, then says, "Look, walk with me, it's only a block out of my way and this way you will not be lost." The Swiss set a very high standard for hospitality!

She is small of stature but sets a brisk pace. The air is bracing, and clouds of frosty breath stream out behind us, like a visible trail of her enthusiastic voice. She is interested to hear our itinerary, and is pleased by what we tell her.

"Good. You are not just sightseers. Europe unveils its secret treasures only to those who seek." Is this is why Herdeg and Kuntz were also interested in my itinerary? Perhaps it is human nature to want visitors to see the true beauty of one's hometown, not just the facade. American cities have icons that define them, but the differentiation between European cities seems both more subtle and vastly greater. We talk about Müller-Brockmann's opera posters.

"Oh, yes, every child likes stories about herself. We Swiss love anything that reminds us that we are cultured, noble, and intelligent." She is having a bit of sly fun at her own expense, but what she is saying is also universal. "Many people who can afford opera only seldom still can discuss what is playing because they enjoy the posters. Myself included!"

Our volunteer guide has added a valuable picture to my internal gallery about the art/design dichotomy: Art is an aesthetic experience that not everyone can afford; design can extend that aesthetic conversation to those who cannot experience high art firsthand. Design and art are perhaps two ends of the same continuum, between beauty and utility; between hidden beauty and overt appearance. It's not a definition so much as an observation, but I add it to the stew.

We find ourselves at our destination. We ask how we might repay her kindness and stay in touch. She waves us off cordially. "Enjoy your visit to Switzerland."

The Müller-Brockmann agency might have doubled as a museum of Swiss posters. Large sheets in spare, unornamented frames line the staircase, the lobby, and the hallways.

Rüegg is seated and working when I am shown in. He does not rise, but motions me to a seat. He does not spend much time in the portfolio, leafing through it once.

"We interview people, not portfolios," he remarks, perhaps as an explanation. He squares to me so he can take me in.

"If you're going to work here, your work will look like Müller-Brockmann's house style. That is why clients come to us, and we are all delighted with it."

He is at ease talking about design, history, and commerce. I remember from my research that he has worked for Paul Rand, so I ask him about working for Rand and Müller-Brockmann.

"Oh, they are like polar opposites!" Rüegg says jovially. "Rand likes to use lots of fonts. Garamond, Caslon Old Style, Baskerville, Railroad Gothic, even his own handwriting! Müller-Brockmann discovered early on that with one good font you could say everything you need. Helvetica provides us with a unity—a voice—that allows us to experiment with the other graphic elements and still have a style that everyone recognizes. Of course, the fact that Helvetica is of Swiss origin helps. But in a way, Helvetica became ubiquitous because a few designers like Hoffmann and Müller-Brockmann

> **We hire people, not portfolios. If you're going to work here, your work will look like our house style. That's why clients come to us, and we are all delighted with it.**

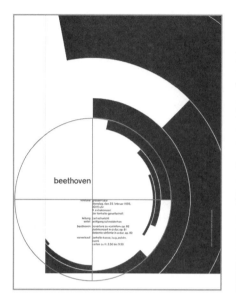

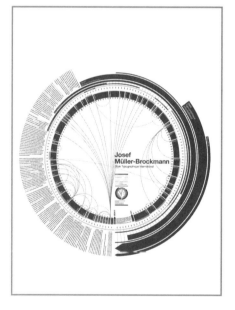

Four posters by the Müller-Brockmann Agency. Swiss posters are first and foremost about balance. Compared with other visual communications, they appear formal, perhaps even sometimes rigid. Yet the best balance structure with freedom, serious subjects with whimsical tone. Rüegg's designs (opposite page) display a willingness to explore and invent without sacrificing an abiding sense of order.

demonstrated how much could be done with it. They created a new vocabulary. Tschichold wrote *Die neue Typographie*, but he couldn't really make it happen. The evolution of the Grotesk alphabet was not quite far enough along, and the printing processes were still too tethered to the mindset of metal type. It took the Second World War and the beginning of the atomic age before there could be a truly liberated visual language."

I say, "I read a lot about design, but I have never heard that connection made so explicitly!"

Rüegg responds, "Well, I can't prove it, but I think having the world at war all around us and only our mountains and our neutrality to protect us made us feel that from our summit, we could observe the madness and make some sense of it." Here is a man capable of beautifully detailed design, and at the same time large-scale vision. I find myself wishing I could take Rüegg's class.

"I'm going to write a book about all this, if I can get time away from my client works," he says. He returns to the Rand comparison. "Now, Rand and Müller-Brockmann do have some things in common. They are both doctrinaire—one might risk saying opinionated. Each one—how could you say it fairly? Each feels he has scrubbed away the inessential and gotten down to the real, true source of design excellence, and they both seem to defend against intrusions, or additions that get in the way. They are both very direct. They both believe that graphic design can help people think more clearly and businesses run more efficiently. As different as the two masters are, they are both exceptionally disciplined in the way they work. The real value in working for a Rand or Müller-Brockmann is not learning to do work that looks like theirs, but in the discipline they bring to their work. What you find is that only when you have complete discipline do you finally have complete creative freedom." He pauses for a clandestine smile. "They both make you want to be like them. And surprisingly, I find that working with Josef and for him, I can learn the kinds of choices he makes, but ultimately I have to break away and do my own work, for different clients, for different reasons. Working for a giant in the industry

> **" Only when you have complete discipline do you finally have complete creative freedom. "**

is sort of like a barter. They have the visibility and the clients who will give you some measure of freedom. You have to do what those clients expect, but ultimately you cannot help but be yourself. Once you have learned the way your mentor thinks, then you can begin to enlarge upon that voice, that style."

"We would very much like to have a bright American designer. The work rules here make it difficult. If you were to come here to study, and become one of Josef's students, it might be possible to get a work permit." This makes a graceful way to end, so I agree to look into the application process, and we part cordially.

Heinz Edelmann
EVERY TEN YEARS, BURN YOUR PORTFOLIO

From the very beginning of his career, Heinz Edelmann (1934–2009) had a knack for finding clients and venues that gave his imagination free rein. Born in Ústí nad Labem, Czechoslovakia, he studied printmaking at the Düsseldorf Arts Academy, and worked in England, the Netherlands, and Germany. His illustrations for the innovative German fashion magazine *Twen* (1959–1970) made him a rising star in Europe. When the animated film *Yellow Submarine* opened in the US in 1968, Edelmann's fame went global. The effect of this film on the emerging creative community of the day was beyond description; it was unlike any animated film before it. A subsequent attempt to produce an animated version of J.R.R. Tolkien's *Lord of the Rings* foundered, but Edelmann went on putting his imaginative stamp on world's fair mascots, posters, magazines, and book jackets. He taught illustration and continued to publish illustrated books until shortly before his death at age 75.

MAY 1974 The way the phone rings in The Hague is unfamiliar, so I'm unsure whether I'm getting a busy signal or a ring. On the third try, Heinz Edelmann answers. I tell him I am in town for three days. I admire his work. It is noisy and I'm not sure he speaks English.

After listening for a sentence or two he says, "I am busy. I have a dozen book jackets going, but why don't you come by for 10 or 15 minutes and I will have a quick look."

Edelmann's house is modest but very stylish, bright white, very nicely kept, very Dutch. He greets me wearing white pants, a white shirt, and bare feet. His manner is at once sincere, impish, and intense, so the immediate effect is extremely likeable.

"Yes, welcome, sit down, so glad you called." He hands me a Coca-Cola. You are American, perhaps you could help me finish these off?" He *really is* working on a dozen book jackets, and most of them are multiple-language editions. He tells me casually they all are due at the printer the next day.

"How do you do it? How do you get approvals so fast?" I ask.

"Oh, well, approval, that is something you work on." He speaks in a measured cadence, often pausing between sentences to reflect. "You find a client and you build up a good understanding of what they like, and after a while you find yourself thinking just as they do. It takes, oh, sometimes a few days, sometimes a year. Sometimes it's instantaneous! If you haven't got it in a couple years, forget them, you need a different challenge."

Edelmann is a quintessential designer-illustrator, achieving an excellent integration between visual and verbal. Curiosity about how he achieves this is largely what drove me to contact him, and I'm about to get a short course.

> **❝I make a little sketch, the size of a postage stamp. I may make three or a dozen, no more than a few seconds each, to convince myself I have the idea. The sketch is intelligible only to me, but I know when I have it.❞**

"So, how I work. Well, for book jackets, the pay is not so much, so I have to finish each one in an hour. I make a little sketch, the size of a postage stamp. I may make three or a dozen, no more than a few seconds each, to convince myself I have it. The sketch is intelligible only to me, but I know when I have it. From that, I set the type.

I put German, the language that takes the most space, on the first layer, French on the next, English above that, then Dutch on the top layer, sometimes Italian and Spanish, too. I do all this to keep

> **❝ I get an idea of the subject, and I ask, what would make someone curious enough to spend money? ❞**

as much time as I can for the illustration." I can't imagine having anything left of an hour after preparing press-ready artwork in multiple languages! "Next, I take my colors and work directly on the illustration board, where I can refer to the type overlay and see picture and words in relationship." As he says this, he is creating a multicolor puddle of gouache. Keeping several brushes charged with color, he makes a few swooping motions, and a scruffy little animal appears on one of the illustration boards. It looks like a fuzzy dog, with a crooked smile and a funny tongue, that makes you want to present your cheek to be licked. The illustration appears in less than five minutes. The astonishing part is, he keeps talking.

"I like to read the book before starting, but usually I can't, so I read the short write-up they send. I used to call the author and ask what their book really means. Some publishers get upset with that. So I get an idea of the subject, and I just ask, what would make someone curious enough to spend some money? You get them thinking, you know? They buy because something gets under their skin, and they are curious, so they say 'All right,' and pay."

I am enthralled with the fearlessness of his approach, and ask, "How do you get the drawing the right size, in the right place?"

He replies, "So, yes, that takes a bit of practice. But I usually see the picture there on the white board, like a ghost. If I don't see the picture yet, I have to go to the next book and come back.

"I have to listen to music while I work, to keep up my speed," he continues. His phonograph is serving up an album of African chants, even though he is working on fiction, a poetry anthology, a biography, and a reference book. "Always something different, something new to think about."

A tumbler drops into place. I glimpse the origins of his style, mercurial and constant. I can't help but exclaim, "I know of no other designer whose clients allow him the latitude to create illustrations without submitting a sketch!"

He cruises around his drawing board, setting things in certain places, and talking as he goes. "Early on, I took work from an agency art director in Frankfurt. His assistant used to call me and say, 'Fritz is going to need three illustrations: the first, 145mm x 192mm; the next 188mm ...' and so on. He had no idea what he was going to put in the boxes. We had to go through half a dozen sketches before he figured out what he was trying to say. He had a hard time because he didn't draw well."

He pauses. "I get in a period every few years where there is too much interference and I just fire them all, and go out and see some new people. The meddlers don't call you back, but the good ones, they call you back and say, 'OK, Heinz, we'll do it your way, when can I get it? You have made me late.' Sometimes you even get a raise!

"How did you know my name—in America? I don't think you can get work papers here, so I can't help you get a job."

Note to self on good interview etiquette: If you can't help your interviewee, say that up front. I try to explain how I know his name without sounding obsequious. "Well, I read *Graphis*, and of course, I saw *Submarine*. The whole country was upside down with it."

"Oh, that whole project, such a nightmare," he says, obviously pleased with my comment about the movie.

"A nightmare?" I ask, surprised. "Not exactly what I expected to hear about one of the most groundbreaking pieces of graphic design in history."

"It was very difficult," he says. "They gave me this script, it had a long scene about Davy Jones's locker; nothing at all interesting about it. But they were paying me to do storyboards, so I said to myself, why not just draw something I like? So, I ignored their script and made storyboards while listening to Beatles songs. The characters came spontaneously. All this I do working in a tiny rented flat in London, freezing cold. I worked to exhaustion and fell asleep hunched over a little portable heater. I got burns on my arms. The whole thing was very difficult. The Beatles, you know,

> **❝ When you get too much interference, you have to fire your customers and go see new people. The meddlers won't call you back, but the good ones will call and say, 'OK, we do it your way.' ❞**

Heinz Edelmann's spontaneous excecution brought vitality to a wide range of subjects. His fast-evolving style meant that clients had to "expect the unexpected."

Aha: Adversity is not an excuse for bad work. Difficult circumstances are as routine a part of design as picking fonts and colors. What matters is the finished work. That is all the public sees.

they're so popular, we could get no access, barely a handshake." Edelmann talks a bit more about the development of the movie, the struggle for creative control, and confrontations with executives and even lawyers. Edelmann's vision for the film eventually prevails.

I think of the many pieces in my portfolio that fell short of my expectations because of uncontrollable circumstances. Edelmann's example seems to be this: Never let circumstances, or a bad script, or even physical pain become an excuse for doing less than your absolute best. The suffering, the impossible circumstances, the politics are, apparently, as routine a part of design as picking fonts and colors. The finished work is all the public sees. He is clearly pleased with the result, but hearing about the process behind a masterwork prepares me for the future. Chaos and conflict are part of the atmosphere in which creative talent thrives.

Edelmann trails off looking at my work. He does not criticze any individual works, but suggests, "You need clients who are more flexible. Theaters—they always need posters and they don't have money, which means it is harder for them to reject—so you can usually do something ..." He waves one hand with a circular motion, which I read as the conclusion to the sentence meaning "exciting."

He is seated on the edge of his chair, looking at my work, hands folded, looking intently, getting up, changing the music, looking at his illustration, moving from one idea to the next. I take this as a sign that it's time for me to go. I pack up.

"Mr. Edelmann, you have been very generous with your time. Thank you so much."

"Not at all," he says, his mercurial accent colored by his work in London. "Sit down, we'll still talk a bit." Perhaps he has more to tell me. I know I should leave, but he is such an entrancing teacher!

He continues amiably, "When you are starting out, you look for freedom. You get some awards; you are still negotiating for flexibility. You build a portfolio, then after a while your portfolio is exciting to others, and they want you to do something like your portfolio, but you are past that place. You want to do something different. Then they are disappointed that it doesn't look like your past work. So you see, you are always negotiating for more flexible relationships."

Aha: **As a business proposition, a recognizable style is salable. But as an innovator, that style can inhibit growth and invention.**

I say, "One of the reasons I admire your work is that you seem to have figured out how to be original and continually evolving. I just visited Jack Kuntz at *Graphis* magazine. He agrees you are a real maverick."

Edelmann cocks his head; the word "maverick" is apparently unfamiliar. "Cowboy? Herdeg is a real king maker, and he knows it. You get on his pages and you raise your prices the same week." His attention shifts again, like a chess master playing multiple games simultaneously.

It strikes me suddenly that this is in marked contrast to Jack Kuntz's comments of just a few weeks earlier. Editors like to see a style they can recognize. And Edelmann is saying that clients sometimes feel they are paying for a style. As a business proposition, a style is salable. But as an innovator, the style can inhibit growth and invention.

I'm curious how he resoves this problem. "So, what do you do when your portfolio becomes a barrier..."

"Yeah, every ten years," he says. He stops to mix paint, an activity that takes all his concentration. "After *Submarine*, a few years, I got very depressed. My work was very similar, so many people want Pepperland and Meanies. The money was very good, but I stopped growing. So I threw it all away. I made a batch of new work—different style, looser, so I could work faster—and I stopped making sketches for approval."

"You threw away your work? Literally?"

"Well, I burned it, actually. If you put it away in a closet, you are not free of it. If you pitch it, then you have to experiment. You force yourself to take big risks. Can I really do something better? If you get comfortable, you get lazy." Edelmann is silent for 15 seconds, staring at a piece of cardboard, a brush charged with gouache hovering. He attacks the surface with his brush, painting. Something like a puppet or harlequin appears in bright hues.

"Every ten years, burn your portfolio. Then you have to experiment, take big risks. Can I really do something better? If you get comfortable, you get lazy."

"So you see the image there, and the place where the words reach out to meet, and you paint into it." Anyone who has studied calligraphy has learned to visualize the letter and to move the eye to where the pen or brush must go to complete it, so that the hand follows the eye. Here Edelmann is doing the same thing. In the middle of painting, he opens another Coca-Cola and hands it to me—what made him think of that? The thick American finally figures out that it's time to go. I offer my profuse thanks as he protests that I should stay a bit more.

So I ask without any preamble, "What is the difference between design and art?"

Edelmann looks at me quizically. "You know, I studied printmaking, not design. Part of me is always wanting to be free of supervision. I have a theory about this question. So, designers admit that they are answerable to their clients, even though we fight it. Artists aren't answerable to anyone, or if they are, they don't like to admit it. Because of the complex relationship with creating for a client, being a designer is more complex than being an artist. The client may give you certain expectations: 'This audience isn't very sophisticated, you have to beat them over the head.' It's what designers think of as bad—ugly. But if that particular audience likes it and that particular client makes money, they come running back to you. You are in the mentally unstable position of having done a 'good' bad design. So design is more complex: there is 'good' good design, 'bad' good design, 'good' bad design, and 'bad' bad design. Art is just art."

I thank him again and step out into The Hague's sharp, late-afternoon sunlight. He has given me more than two hours and some outstanding insights. He scarcely missed a beat in his work! I had hoped he would differentiate art and design in a simple way, but I find his answer troubling; it is more complex. Surely there is both good art and bad art? Perhaps

"Design is more complex than art. There is good good design, bad good design, good bad design, and bad bad design. Art is just art."

what he means is that, if the artist is happy with a work, and considers it complete and ready to exhibit, then it is by definition a work of art. What the world does with it is irrelevant to the creative process. I put this theory to the test. Does it help define which is which? Diego Rivera had a mural torn out of a bank lobby because his client didn't like his anticapitalist imagery. He was beholden to his client. By Edelmann's definition, that must have been a work of design. But Rivera was an artist—an artist doing commissioned work. Jim Burke was right: the definitions are going to overlap.

Charles and Ray Eames find their freedom in making heuristic connections. Edelmann fights for freedom; Herdeg gets it by surrendering it! Rüegg finds freedom by learning disciplined work habits from his masters.

I return to the US with more answers, more questions, and a deep thirst for more dialogues with creative legends.

TITANS

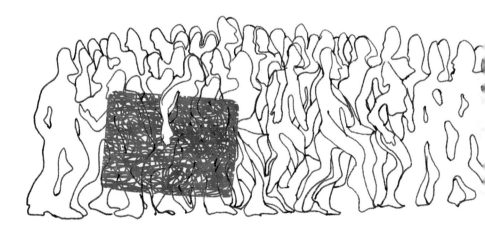

THE GREAT MIDWEST MOUNTED VALISE

JULY 1974 I arrive in New York's Penn Station. It's a steamy morning. I am filled with the energy from my European experience and armed with examples of design unlike anything New York has ever seen. I carry them in a large sample case made of black bonded leather, quite possibly the largest sample case that can be carried by a single human; nothing less could hold the voluminous ideas I have to offer. My friend Otter Hallstein finds it comic, and dubs it "The Great Midwest Mounted Valise." Something about the name fits: a dominant aesthetic that rides east and arrests the attention of New York. Absurd, impractical, and hi-yo, Silver!

To begin my assault on New York, I have three telephone numbers on an index card. The first is for Dan Small, a fellow creative squid from Cleveland, who, according to his mother, has a great job in the fashion industry and can undoubtedly get me some gigs. The second is that of Walter Papillion, a creative director in advertising whom I met at a university lecture and who will surely get me some interviews at top agencies. The third is for Ed Gottschall, the executive director of the American Institute of Graphic Arts (AIGA).

Penn Station becomes my office, my toehold in New York City. There is a telephone center: thirty telephone booths in two banks flanking a desk where one can obtain change and assistance with overseas calls. The booths have small, upholstered seats, and each booth has a bifold door with glass panels. Closing the door from the inside activates a light and a ventilation fan. The crucial amenity for a job seeker is a steel shelf, just big enough for taking notes.

In Pittsburgh finding my first job after graduation took two weeks, so with two years of professional experience under my belt, New York should be ... no big deal.

I enter Booth 6 confident that one of my three contacts will quickly lead to a great job with a slick office. Over the course of the next three minutes, I leave three messages. Not to worry, several things to do. First, find newspaper, review want ads. Next, examine the other phone booths. The portfolio that New York is breathlessly awaiting does not fit in Booth 6, and I wonder if perhaps one of the other booths might somehow accommodate it. I also need to explore Penn Station for food, a shoeshine stand, a street map, and some three-by-five cards.

PENN STATION BOOTH 6

Booth 6, selected impulsively, is in fact about the best of the lot. Its upholstery is nearly new, the fan is quiet (other booths have fans that clatter), and the clock on the main departure board is visible. On my third visit, the phone center customer rep behind the desk asks if she can help me. She has observed my experimental efforts to fit The Valise into one of her phone booths. I explain the problem, probably distractedly, without thinking that countless other portfolios poured countless dimes into her phone center before me. Her name badge declares "SUSAN—MAY I HELP YOU?" in Microgramma Bold Extended. The Microgramma font—perfect for, say, a sumo wrestler or a bouncer in a biker bar—is incongruous with her soft voice and demure manners.

"May I?" she asks, and demonstrates how to fold the handles back, ease the top of The Valise into the back corner of the booth, curve the monstrosity just enough to rest a bottom corner on top of the phone, slip one's person in, and carefully slide the bifold door closed; meanwhile pressing the bottom of The Valise into the hinge corner, so it stays diagonally in the top third of the booth, out of the way, adequately supported yet protected from the outside world. She steps out of the booth and hands me back my career in cowhide. I feel like an unsuspecting participant in a clown act.

"Try it," she says with a glimmer of a smile, but not a trace of irony. She had listened to my explanation of the problem so patiently, even though she had seen it all before! I do try it, and amazingly, it works. With The Valise thus suspended above me, I settle into cold calling.

Dan Small is no longer at the number I have for him. I also learn that the number I have for Papillion is actually that of his traffic manager, whose job is to protect her boss and his department from a flood of wannabes like me. Gottschall, I am told with the great cordiality afforded card-carrying, unemployed AIGA members, sees portfolios on Tuesdays and Fridays, and can see me at 10:30 a.m., three Tuesdays hence.

Having transcribed some of the more promising want ads onto three-by-five cards, I begin calling. Susan Microgramma passes by while I am on the phone. She does not wave, but she does gesture ever so slightly with her nose at my suspended portfolio; her look seems to say, "Others made it through here, you can too."

Somehow, I expected my arrival to have more impact. But the city sees ambitious kids wash up on its shores like so many pebbles and shells. Train ticket filling up with punches, pockets filled with index cards, I work the want ads, most of which turn out to be from employment agencies. I begin to place great hopes on my scheduled appointment with Ed Gottschall.

Answering help-wanted ads does not vary much. One is expected to wait a lot, fill out forms a lot, and smile through utterly impersonal treatment. None of the employment agencies even wants to *look* at The Great Midwest Mounted Valise!

THE VALISE GOES AWOL

After three weeks of answering want ads and researching design firms I have wrangled an appointment—a real appointment—with an art director who is looking for design help and has agreed to review my portfolio. This may be my ticket out of the phone booth at Penn Station! I take the bus there, a bit euphoric.

Sixth Avenue, somewhere around 34th Street. I am frozen stock still, perhaps 12 inches from the brass door pull at the location of my appointment. Seeing my hand reach for the door brings about the realization that my other hand, which should be gripping my portfolio case, is empty. I have left my graphic design portfolio on the New York City bus that brought me here. My body is paralyzed because my mind is sprinting, darting from realization to conclusion.

If I were in Cleveland, I could go to the Transit Authority lost and found and probably get my portfolio back tomorrow. The New York Transit Authority may have a lost and found, but I know instinctively my portfolio will never get there. Without my portfolio I will never get a job.

After an eternal instant, I am able to move my eyes in the direction of traffic. There are several buses that might be the one I rode, now a few blocks away, merging with other buses into the immense river of Manhattan traffic.

The word "portfolio" means different things in different professions. For an investment manager, it is a selection of investment positions representing ideas about what will succeed at a particular price and time. For insurance companies, it may mean a pool of risks being underwritten. For people outside the creative arts, it is hard to understand the young designer's attachment to his portfolio. In many professions, the newly educated practitioner passes tests and gains a license. The license means they are like their peers, having a certified professional status. Singers and actors must pass through the fiery furnace of auditions, but at least their talent resides within them. Graphic design is different. You may have a degree from Mount Olympus University, but if your portfolio sucks, your credentials don't mean much. You may have no education at all, but if your portfolio is exceptional, well, come right on in! Of course, if your portfolio is exceptionally *missing*, you are really and truly naked.

My mind races to the inevitable conclusion: that Valise is my future. My body takes up the sprint. I cover the first block in a single step. The light at 35th Street is against me, but traffic is immaterial. Screech! Honk! Keep accelerating. 36th Street. I am wearing the Sunday-school clothing of a Presbyterian kid from Ohio: a blue worsted wool suit, black wingtip shoes with soles well worn but uppers buffed. The pain of sprinting in dress shoes is unable to make its way up my spine, drowned by the flood of adrenaline rushing downward. 37th Street melts behind me. If only my high school coach could see this performance! The street sign for 40th Street looms and disappears. I make the first quarter mile in what seems like 15 seconds. Twenty numbered streets to the mile in New York City. I am running after a group of identical buses. 41st Street. For an instant, my resolve weakens. I have, somewhere in my mother's basement in Ohio, a set of slides of my portfolio. I could forget about it and reconstruct The Valise.

But the danger and the oxygen have me thinking clearly: C-prints from those slides would be of disappointing quality, and it would cost a lot! Find overdrive and catch that bus!

42nd Street is a torrent of traffic. I pick up a bruise on the bumper of some vehicle. I play chicken with a bicycle messenger breathing through the police whistle in his mouth. I have no idea how I am going to recognize the bus I was on, but I will only have to worry about that if I am not killed by a cabbie. Running full tilt, yet drifting back in time, I'm searching for an answer. How long have I been building up my dependence on this bundle of paper? When did it start? Surely I was not born with one? I look back to interviewing for my first job in Pittsburgh, to assembling my college portfolio, then to the portfolio I carried to get into college. Running, I think back further, to *Avant Garde* magazine and emulating the paintings of Dalí.

From somewhere in the cosmos, help arrives: there is road construction uptown, and a couple of lanes are blocked. I pull even with a half-dozen buses and slow to a trot. Bingo! I recognize the graffiti on the advertising placard on the side of my bus. It is at a slow roll. I bang on the side of the door. The driver does not stop, but opens the door; I catch the grab bar and swing on board. She clearly has not read the transit authority safety rules!

"I thought we would see you!" she says cheerfully. "Behind my seat. You run good!" I seize The Valise, thank her, and jump off; she never slows her pace.

I have to figure out what to do. Clearly, visiting the art director in the thirties is out of the question. I would be an hour late by the time I made it back there. I'll dream up an excuse tomorrow in Booth 6. My next appointment is (Aha, I have not lost my prized three-by-five cards!) Ed Gottschall, at AIGA. I'm a twenty-minute walk from 63rd Street and Third Avenue, and I am due to see him in an hour. I sit on a bench, my pulse returning to normal. I am now the owner of The Great Midwest Mounted Dumpster. Its contents are scrambled; all the careful mounting and sequencing is askew. Whoever gave it to the bus driver must have pawed through it first—maybe looking for money? Worse, there are large gaps between the soles and the uppers of my wingtips, and they are scuffed and scraped. I am sweaty, and my suit is decidedly grotty. There is a rip in the pant leg where I grazed a bumper. I decide to push on. Maybe there's a men's room in the lobby of AIGA.

Ed Gottschall
NOT YOUR AVERAGE INTERVIEW

Edward Gottschall (1916–   ) is a lifelong enthusiast in typography and design. He graduated from the City University of New York in 1937, and received a master's degree from the Columbia School of Journalism in 1938. He served as editor of *Art Direction* magazine from 1969 to 1975 and executive director of AIGA from 1973 to 1976. Gottschall served for two years as president of the Type Directors Club, founding the TDC annual show, one of the longest-running exhibitions in the graphic design world. He was executive vice president of International Typeface Corporation for fifteen years, and served as senior editor of *U&lc* magazine, an experimental typography magazine founded by Herb Lubalin. Gottschall taught at New York University and Pratt Institute, retiring in 1990. He is the author of *Typographic Communications Today*, and coauthor of 18 other books.

JUNE 1974 There is not, it turns out, a men's room in the lobby of the AIGA offices. I arrive at the reception desk still sweaty, but cold.

In the shiny door of the elevator, I see reflected a parody of a stereo-type: a Midwestern stripling who got rolled in the Bowery. If they laugh out loud, it will be entirely understandable!

Ed Gottschall is a cordial, dark-haired man. He clearly loves people. I consider explaining my appearance and scrambled portfo-lio, but cannot begin. He does not bat an eye; in fact, he is incredibly gracious. He rotates each upside-down piece carefully and asks about it. He takes a full twenty minutes to go through The Valise, possibly a record.

"So, David, what are you in New York to do? Oh, book publishing, excellent. That I can help you with." He reaches across his desk to one of four large rotary address files and starts browsing. "Anyone in particular you want to see?"

I name some names: Glaser, Chwast, Rand, Lubalin. Never mind that I am naming the most sought-after names in graphic design, Gottschall knows them and their dues pay his salary, so he figures out ways to be valuable to them all.

"Paul Rand's phone is unlisted, and he says he doesn't see portfo-lios anymore, but I know he does—just don't tell him where you got his number. You may get lucky."

I feel as though I've used up all the luck—bad and good—allocated to me for the decade. He is writing on a yellow pad, line after line, single-spaced. Name, company, phone, sometimes an asterisk.

He explains, "These are the publishers that care most about design—many don't, you know. Whole art departments without a single AIGA member!" He rolls his eyes with a smile, without inter-rupting his writing. "Now mind, you can use my name with the ones with asterisks. You will get their gatekeepers, but you mention my name in the same breath as your own. If they don't call you back, I want to hear about it. I send them business, I send them talent—they should know the score."

Gottschall gets to the last line of the page, pauses to reread, adds another asterisk, and tears off the sheet. "Son, you have a ton of talent. You stick at it—you will have a great job. But mind, the town is crawling with talent. Where you are in your career right now, two years out of school, you have a lot of competition. Talent is a given; the jobs go to the persistent. Be charming, but by Jove don't stop calling till they say yes!"

> **❝ You have talent, and you also have a lot of competition. Talent is a given; the good jobs go to the persistent. Be charming, but don't stop calling till they see you. ❞**

He continues, "You have a right to ask for referrals. Everyone will say they aren't hiring—even if they're desperate to fill a job. If they don't ask how much money you want, don't bring it up. But you should have your price in mind and say it without hesitating. Figure what you need to live and double it. They will beat you up on price, so have something to give up." His advice is not exactly new, but there is sincerity and gnosis about him that makes him sound like the oracle at Delphi. He is about to hand me off to his receptionist, when I spot a page on his desk. It looks like an illustration made out of typography. I am unable to pass it by.

"Mr. Gottschall, what is this?" I have just hit the mother lode.

"Oh, Gottschall is working on a book about typography," he says, as though he were talking about the inexplicable activities of a crazy uncle. His excitement for the project is impossible to contain. "Been working on it for some time."

I am wowed, so I act wowed. "What's the title? Where did you get all these fantastic examples? This wonderful old wood type? These old cigar box tops?" He's delighted to talk about it; I am making his pet project come alive. A good 45 minutes later, he has given me a short course on typography, and in the process he has been reminded of all the people he knows who love books and typography. I now have a second sheet of names and asterisks, better than the first. My AIGA dues have delivered a jackpot payoff—just because I asked about something interesting on his desk!

I learn two things of great value: First, a good interviewer will zero in on the faults of a portfolio and rank the talent by lowest common denominator. A really skilled interviewer sees past the faults, and looks at the potential. If a kid shows up in tattered clothing with a ransacked portfolio, look at it carefully; you might see

> *A good interviewer will zero in on the faults of a portfolio and rank the talent by lowest common denominator. A really skilled interviewer sees past the faults, and looks at the potential.*

something really good that everyone else misses. I am fated to forget and relearn this valuable lesson numerous times. Second, when you finally get in someone's door, you are getting a glimpse of their life and their interests. It is the mirror image of my first interview with Jim Burke—there he saw something in my portfolio that sparked the interest. Here, I found it on Gottschall's desk.

Gottschall's two pages of names become my treasure map and talisman. As I leave his office he says, "Now, don't be a stranger. I want to know where you land!" What a great expression! It frames job hunting as a flight, as a trajectory. A newcomer to any profession can easily liken job hunting to being earthbound, stuck in the mud. Gottschall says, in effect, "You are a bird on the wing surveying the professional landscape—enjoy the view!" The value of this analogy comes back later, when I am employed and exploration is difficult.

COLD CALLING 101

I hear from other designers that Herb Lubalin has a stable of talent with whom he works steadily, and though it's well known that he never hires green talent, every art and design student who comes to New York wants to interview there.

Sitting in my office in Penn Station Booth 6, I make the first of many calls to Lubalin's office. The secretary tells me—in what is really a very humane voice considering how many times she must have had to recite her speech—that he is not seeing portfolios or hiring. When I sat in Ed Gottschall's office that first day at AIGA and he told me to be persistent, I imagined having to call back three or four times. I invest a call to Lubalin, Smith, and Carnase every few weeks. Lubalin's receptionist learns my name, so I think I am making progress, but after a while she leaves and is replaced by someone new.

As the summer wears on, my book begins to feel tired. Really I am getting tired of showing it and getting praise and referrals but no job offers. I find odd freelance projects, which are not much use for demonstrating my value to the larger marketplace, but at least provide sustenance. I take the train into town and dutifully sit in my Penn Station office with a pack of notecards. I am now polished at hearing "no" and asking for ideas, names, and referrals, so that I always have new three-by-five cards and new names to call. Hope. Each card is scrap of hope. I am burnished by each indignity. Interviewers stand me up. At first I am angered, but no longer—next time I call they apologize and agree to see me. Rarely do they brush off the same person twice.

Herb Stern
THE ONE WEEK HENCE TEST

Herb Stern (1930–) was born in Frankfurt am Main. His family left Nazi Germany in 1938, relocating to New York City. Despite a fascination for art, Stern attended Bronx Science High School, and later studied Advertising Art at the Insititute for Applied Arts and Sciences, New York. Stern began his professional career at J.D.Tarcher & Co., working for Harry Pritchett, a talented art director who had worked with Paul Rand and Lou Dorfsman. The Tarcher agency folded while Stern was in the Marine Corps during the Korean War. Upon returning to civilian life, he worked at the William Weintraub Agency under Paul Rand, and then at Mel Richman Studios. He also had his own studio, serving mainly magazine publishers, before joining Ziff-Davis, where he stayed for thirty years. During that time, he rose from art director to VP Creative, and played a pivotal role in the company's transition from magazines to technology and media. He retired from Ziff-Davis in 1999, and continues his work as a fine artist.

SEPTEMBER 1974 Two hours a day on the train gives me a lot of time to read. *George, Be Careful* is the autobiography of George Lois, a brash and highly successful advertising art director. Lois describes his process of interviewing new creative talent. Sure, they have a great portfolio, but which ones can think on their feet? Lois devises tricks to startle his job applicants. He will pick up a glass ashtray and toss it at his unsuspecting applicant. If the applicant catches it, that's a good sign. "Good hands!" A missed catch usually means broken glass. How does the interviewee react? Poised and snappy, well, OK, maybe the candidate is still worthy of consideration. If the reaction is embarrassment or anger, game over.

I begin to think about the interview process from the other side. What are the tests likely to be? What do I need to do to pass them? Suddenly I realize that I'm already being tested. Several people have taken my call, heard my pitch, and responded, "Sure, I'll look at your book. Call me one week from today, at this exact time, and I'll set up an appointment." Up until now, I had noted it on the prospect's card, figuring that I'd call them later. Nothing magic about that exact time—*unless this is a test.* I put down the book and flip through my index cards. I realize I have failed the test several times already.

An art director named Herb Stern, I notice, asked me to call back at 10:30 a.m., and today is the day! I make it to Penn Station and call, just a minute or two early. He picks up the phone. I remind him of his interest in seeing me if I called back. He says, "Sure, come in next Tuesday at 4:00."

Tuesday arrives, and so do I. Between George Lois and Herb Stern, I have learned a new trick, and I vow I will be on the lookout for ways to pass tests with every phone call.

Stern is visible in the design community as the promotions designer for the magazines published by Ziff-Davis. He is a dapper fellow, with hair that lays down straight across the top of his head then erupts in curls at the side. Ziff-Davis is a crisp, professional place and Stern's office is spartan, almost unnaturally neat. Stern looks at me intently, but the effect is not uncomfortable.

By this time I've learned that, as much as I want to control the interview, things work better if I sit back and let the interviewer go through the portfolio. I hand it over. He flips through it without a word, giving

THE ONE WEEK HENCE TEST:

❝Sure, I'll look at your book. Call me one week from today, at this exact time, and I'll set up an appointment. ❞

each item about two seconds. Then he looks at the resume, again a fast scan. He reviews the book again at about half speed, putting clips on three or four pages. It's not uncommon for art directors to keep copies of a few pages of each book they see, so I feel honored when he hands the pieces he wants copied to an assistant. I don't remember seeing anyone scan the book once fast, then a second time slowly. He turns his attention to me. He asks a few questions about the production details on a few of my designs: what font here, who printed that, who is the photographer, and so on. Those hurdles cleared, he asks about my career goals. I tell him publishing is the reason I'm moving to New York.

Stern raises an eyebrow. "Really."

I've already learned that publishing is not the best-paid field, nor necessarily the place to win the most awards. You go into publishing because you believe in it. He turns to me more directly in his seat and relaxes a bit.

"All right, then, I'll make a few suggestions." He goes through my book, removing half the work. "You need not show more than ten pieces." He continues with barely a pause. "Next, let me comment on your presentation. You kept your mouth shut while I was looking at the work. That's uncommon for a designer your age." I flash back to how many times I motormouthed my way through a portfolio showing. I manage to say thank you.

He asks if I have any questions, and I ask whether he is hiring anyone at my level anytime soon. He acknowledges the question with a nod, but continues his advice.

He is not hurrying, but neither is there a wasted word. "You should be here to interview me, too, you know. You should ask what we do, what we look for in new hires. You made it in here, so you have earned the right to ask for names. You should not leave without having harvested at least three leads. Ask, 'Would you mind suggesting some other shops where you think my work would be well received?' That way, you're asking your contact to call your work to mind, and match it with the work of other employers with whom they have personal connections. Always ask for permission to use the contact's name when you call."

Stern is paying me a high compliment, coaching me like a rookie coming to the show. His voice takes on a serious tone. "You know why I asked you about production details?" I decide not to wing it, and confess I don't know. He continues, "There are always young designers who want to break into the business so much that they slide a few pieces of finished work by other designers into their own books. They don't realize that an experienced art director picks it up right away; so the questions about things like fonts and production are a sanity check, a way to see if the portfolio you are seeing is for real."

> THE ONE WEEK HENCE TEST:
>
> **" It's an employer's survival skill. Ninety percent of the first calls can't make that second call. I don't want disorganized help, no matter how great a portfolio they may have! "**

I like this guy—he's got one trick after another—so I hazard a question. "You asked me to call you back exactly a week later. Was that some kind of a test?"

He replies, "Perhaps. Really, it's an employer's survival skill. Ninety percent of the first calls can't make that second call. I don't want disorganized help, no matter how great a portfolio they may have!"

"I can't make time to train you, but I want you to keep in touch, and send me new samples." He scribbles several names on the back of his card, shakes my hand, and with his left hand he gives me the card.

To show I have been listening, I say, "May I use your name?" He nods, and at the same instant his assistant appears to show me out. He is already turning away to review his phone messages, and in seconds I am back on the chaotic Manhattan pavement. I send Stern an occasional note or sample, but the opportunity to work for him does not materialize. Yet his coaching quickly becomes a permanent part of my self-presentation.

Seymour Chwast
BAD LUCK, SO GOOD LUCK!

Seymour Chwast (1931–   ) was born in the Bronx, New York, and educated at Cooper Union. After an early attempt at setting up a studio with his fellow students failed, Chwast worked at the *New York Times* promotion department, followed later by *Esquire* magazine and Condé Nast. He began soliciting freelance work with some fellow designers by publishing *Push Pin Almanack,* which showcased creative illustrations. (It was later renamed *Push Pin Graphic.*)

Push Pin Studios did for the graphic design what the electric guitar did for music. Their work seemed to proclaim "We are for pure, joyful expression: decorative, rich, inconsistent, polyglot, and exuberant! Design and illustration are inseparable, and by the way we can originate the font and write the headline if we feel like it. We can do anything for anybody; we can invent three new styles every day before breakfast!"

Chwast's versatility in drawing, design, and typography, along with the fruits of his collaborative work with more than two dozen other Push Pin members, was honored with a retrospective exhibition at the Louvre. In 1984 Chwast was inducted into the Art Directors Club Hall of Fame; he was named an AIGA Medalist in 1985. He is the illustrator and originator of many books, including illustrated versions of Homer's *Odyssey,* Chaucer's *Canterbury Tales,* and Dante's *Divine Comedy.*

OCTOBER 1974   Twelve weeks and counting since I stormed Manhattan, and still no job. I train into Penn Station, check the want ads, make phone calls, and shuffle through my three-by-five cards to see whom to call when.

I try to schedule portfolio showings in the morning, pick up the odd freelance job, grab an early afternoon train out of the city to beat rush hour, then finish my freelance work in the wee hours. It has the regimentation of a job, but without the regular pay. The

Presbyterian Sunday-school outfit gives way to a commuter's shirt and tie. The intensity of work on new portfolio pieces tapers off. I am getting interviews, but no job appears. My new shoes—bought to replace the ones ruined chasing buses—look very worn. The Great Midwest Mounted Valise, purchased when my savings were ample and my optimism high, looks weary too. Discouragement is setting in, and I have to find ways to fight it.

What got me here was enthusiasm for big design, Push Pin, Chermayeff, Rand, and Lubalin, but none of them are interviewing. Sifting through my cards, I come across Push Pin Studios. I have calls logged weekly for the first ten weeks, then a gap. They have a receptionist, and she has a waiting list: you leave your name once and she confirms you are still on it, but they are not setting appointments. Someone is peering in the phone booth door at me, so I had better make a call. Push Pin it is.

"Push Pin Studios," says a new voice, and hope stirs. Remember to smile before speaking.

"Hi, this is David Laufer. I'm on the waiting list to show my design portfolio."

"I don't see you, when did you call?" A nice voice.

"I called first in May, and have been calling on and off since . . ."

"Oh yes, I see you. You requested Mr. Glaser. He is still booked, but I just had a call canceling a morning meeting with Mr. Chwast. Can you be here in thirty minutes?"

What a combination of great luck and rotten luck. In my exhaustion from the previous night, I hadn't rearranged or refreshed my portfolio, and I would have liked to refresh my memory on Chwast's career and work. I have barely enough time to get there. An unhappy commuter mutters at me while I extricate The Valise from the phone booth and dash across Penn Station for the southbound subway. I stop in the men's room. I look crummy! I splash my face with cold water. The paper towel dispenser is empty, so I dry off with toilet paper from a stall and scram.

The office is not glitzy, but it certainly is busy. There are several rows of cubicles, the surfaces of which are covered with reference material, clippings, sketches, and photos. There are a half-dozen large, black portfolios similar to mine, leaning up against the side of a cubicle. Are these other applicants' work? I look closely, and see that the luggage tag has a Push Pin business card in it. Even the most published studio in the world has several portfolios ready to show to customers!

I announce myself to the receptionist, who appears to be marking up a large manuscript and monitoring a lot of packages coming and going. The workspace seems smaller than my expectation, but the atmospheric energy is immediate.

"Mr. Chwast says he will be with you in just a few minutes."

The reception area is full of envelopes and boxes waiting to be picked up by couriers, and there is a table for inbound packages. I recognize the labels of several typesetters.

The receptionist motions me into a cubicle. After a few seconds I realize this is not a spare cubicle—this is Chwast's workspace. It is crowded but orderly. There are project files laid out in envelopes, and a side table with markers, brushes, half a dozen swatch books for colored paper, film, and inks. These are the usual art supplies that I and everyone else have available, and yet what world-changing work has come from them.

"Hi. Seymour Chwast," he introduces himself, extending his hand for a friendly shake. I've seen pictures of this man in magazines, smiling with his latest creation, holding this award or that. In person, he has a quiet demeanor. He has an air of mystery, which may be a result of my admiration for him, but I think it is real.

"Keep your seat. Give me just a minute," he says, moving purposefully through the files on his desk. A young man with sandy hair dashes in with an illustration and pulls back the flap. Chwast locks his gaze on it. Without taking his eyes away, his fingers pop off a few strips of masking tape, and he attaches a piece of tracing paper on top of the illustration. I can't see it well, but it's a line illustration in gray, with the white areas filled in with flat areas of colored film, like pieces of stained glass shining around the metal frame. After lifting the tracing paper to view the work, he lays the paper back down and circles selected areas, then hands it back.

Chwast turns to me. Someone with that many projects in front of him should be stressed, but he seems quite relaxed. His manner is at once smiling and serious.

"Do we have a resume from you?"

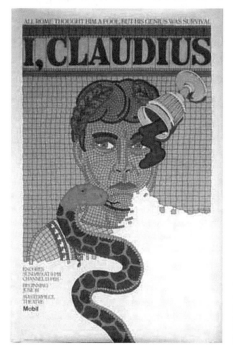

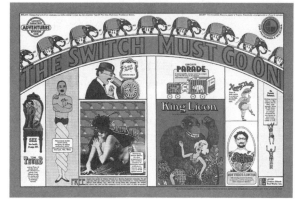

I probably sent one a few months back, but I reach in the back pocket of The Valise for one. Nada. I have a stack of them sitting at home, but The Valise has none.

"I am really sorry, I appear to have given out my last one—I will have to send you one. This appointment came open just today..."

I am feeling worse by the second, but Chwast is cheerful and unfazed.

"Sure, send one on. Not important really." He waves away the unimportant resume. "We use them to write notes on, is all," he says as he finds a legal pad and pen. "So, let's see your book!"

Here is a man who has probably seen thousands of portfolios, probably does not need to ever look at another one in his life, yet not only is he willing to see a drop-in, he still takes pleasure in the activity! He flips through the work quickly. My portfolio is loaded with watercolors and sketches as well as my finished work from Pittsburgh, and it is a bit of a hodgepodge. It does not look considered or organized, and I am cursing myself for not being better prepared. Note to self: Every day is your big chance!

In my mind I hear Herb Stern whisper, "Don't apologize. Just let him see what interests him."

Some interviewers engage their interviewee in small talk: where are you from, who have you been to see, how did you get my name. Chwast focuses intently on the work on his first pass through it, which takes perhaps 45 seconds. On his second pass, he makes a few comments without looking up.

"You draw well, but the mood of your work is very dark." He is reacting to the watercolors I made of a series of urban scenes, influenced by my commuting. "There is a place in illustration for every mood, but sunshine sells better. Your industrial experience—where did you work?"

"Pittsburgh." I give him a quick verbal resume. I am struggling to be cheerful and fighting the feeling that I have wasted the long-hoped-for opportunity of this meeting with this creative legend.

Chwast says, "When you draw for yourself, you can of course bring out your innermost feelings. When you draw for others, you must find expression for theirs." He is looking intently at me now. He is addressing me not as a student or a street kid, but as a peer.

I see in an instant that the intensity and authenticity of his illustrations are a natural extension of his personality, his disposition.

> 66 *You can draw anything you perceive, you convince me of that. Now convince me you can draw someone else's point of view.* 99

"There are a lot of times that we as hired guns have to feel an emotion or take a position that is not ours. I see here the work of a soul confronting raw truth with clear eyes. Not easy. You can draw anything you perceive, you convince me of that. Now convince me that you can draw someone else's point of view."

I don't have a good response. He is right. I feel bleak, and my work shows it. I am not sure why I came; maybe I should go back to Ohio. I hope I am not looking like I feel.

Then Chwast's voice dispels the cloud. "I want you to do something for me—well, for yourself really."

"Sure!"

Chwast picks up the steam engine, drawn with a compass and ruling pen. It is the same one Jim Burke liked. I keep it in my portfolio even though it is student work. Superstition, I suppose. Chwast holds it in both hands with a bit of ceremony and puts it in my hands.

"Go to your studio, and make a dozen new works that are not steam engines, but that have the same joy and simplicity and wit that are lurking here." He pauses to see my reaction. "I'm serious now—you have the skills to make this portfolio much more exciting, and the faster you prove it to yourself the more use you will be to the this community."

The sandy-haired man ducks back in with the corrected illustration. Chwast looks at it quickly. He removes the tracing paper. He makes a circular motion with his index finger over one area and says, "This area needs another layer of yellow, then flap it and it can go back to Forbes."

I have recovered my wits a bit and am able to remember some of the work of his that I especially admire. I ask him how he uses so many different media—most illustrators find a medium they like and beome expert at it. Chwast seems to be the master of a dozen.

> **The perceptions of the people who buy what we sell are more important than the truth.**

"Oh, speed, you know, we have to produce so fast, we are always looking for ways to get the right emotion on the page quickly." He talks about moving from wet media to flat, colored adhesive film, and then on to other media experiments, but it's clear he is less interested in media and more in the emotional effects he can get across. A phone call breaks in. Cradling the phone in one hand and shaking my hand with the other, he summarizes, as if stating a homily, "The perceptions of the people who buy what we sell are more important than the truth. So—good luck!" There is an elfish animation in his face as he says it, but I know he is earnest about his encouragement.

I can't help but wish I had I been better prepared for this meeting, but perhaps we get what we need. I make my rounds and head home to New Brunswick, New Jersey with the conviction that my portfolio needs a makeover, and Seymour Chwast has given me a powerful insight into how to do it. He has also added some clues to the art versus design dichotomy: something to do with expressing your feelings versus intuiting the feelings of others.

Ian Ballantine
A SHORT COURSE IN GENRE PUBLISHING

Ian Ballantine (1916–1995) was active as a publisher for his entire career. He attended Columbia College and the London School of Economics. He wrote his thesis on paperback book publishing. He brought Penguin Books to the US. Ballantine and his wife, Betty, were part of a team that founded Bantam Books in 1945. In 1952 they established Ballantine Books, which they sold to Random House in 1973. The Ballantines continued as freelance editors and consultants to many publishers. They are most famous for their commitment to promoting

science fiction as a literary genre. Their numerous awards include two
World Fantasy Awards, in 1975 and 1984. Ballantine published the first
authorized paperback edition of J.R.R. Tolkien's *Lord of the Rings*, the
H.P. Lovecraft series, and more than 160 titles on World War II. All told
the Ballantine publication list is more than three thousand titiles.

OCTOBER 1974 Interviewing involves a lot of waiting. Not infre-
quently I arrive for an interview only to be told that my interviewer
is in a meeting, out for the day, has been called away, might be back
in an hour. I note these things on my cards. I develop the habit
of carrying a book with me to read while waiting. I happen to be
reading Isaac Asimov's Foundation Trilogy the day I am to interview
with Ian Sommers, the art director for Ballantine Books.

"Let me see if I can find Mr. Sommers," says the receptionist.

So, I open Asimov and, within a few sentences, am engrossed in a
world far away.

"So, you are reading Asimov!"

The voice comes to me through a thick acoustical shield necessary
for reading against a noisy environment. I have never met Ian Sommers, so I assume this must be him, coming to look at my work. I
stand, and instinctively grasp for The Valise.

"You are young to be an Asimov reader. How did you get interested in him?"

"I—to be honest, I had heard of him, but didn't know what to
expect. I was intrigued by the illustration on the cover. I needed
something to read for the train. I had no idea what I might be falling into."

This answer pleases the gentleman and his smile broadens. "A lot
of thought goes into those covers." I am a bit confused, because he
makes no move to lead me anywhere. I decide to relax a bit and put
down The Valise. "He is one of our best authors—very fast, very deep."

I have to hold up my end of this conversation. I sense that some
sort of testing is going on, but different than that of Herb Stern,
since I am already in the door. My interviewer knows about book
jackets. I am interested in them too, so I go there. "The jacket of
this edition did not prepare me for the seriousness of the subject. I
thought it would be—"

"Oh, you are getting at the heart of the publisher's problem! How to make a sale with very limited information, very little time. There is no way to give the reader a full description of the narrative. We seize upon style, color, writing, typography, symbolism—absolutely anything we can use to get to the right emotional place instantly. The jacket has to be a window into the author's soul. So what made you decide to buy it?"

I consider. "It wasn't so much the investment of money as the investment of time, for me." I remember Heinz Edelmann talking about hooking the prospective buyer with curiosity.

"Yes, you are not alone there. We have to constantly look for a way to convince the reader that they will have a good read—that they will want to stick with it to the end."

I look at the cover again. "I think it was the unusual color scheme—it piqued my curiosity."

"Yes! Asimov is profound, but at bottom he is optimistic about humanity. We work to package him that way."

I need more information about where this is going, but I am not sure how to steer it. I gesture toward The Valise. "As a graphic designer, I am especially interested in those types of cues. I hate to quit a book in the middle, and I hate to invest time finishing something that isn't interesting. I feel an obligation to help people select what they will like and avoid what they won't like."

This apparently is a good thing to say. He begins walking, saying, "Let me show you." We enter a smallish conference room with bookshelves across the long wall. All the books are paperbacks. Some of the books are turned spine out; others are displayed face out, in layers, the way they appear in racks in stores.

> **"The heart of the publisher's problem: How to make a sale with limited information, very little time, and lots of distractions. We seize anything to get the reader to the right emotional place instantly. Design is like a window into the author's soul."**

"Each cover is a little poster," he says. He is animated, glad, perhaps, to have an audience for an evolving theory. "You have only the top three and a half inches to catch someone's eye. Title, colors, maybe a bit of the illustration.

So your first job as a graphic designer is to get the browser interested enough to give it a little attention, to pick up the book out of the rack."

This is a bit of a revelation. Even though I've lingered over paperbacks frequently, I have never thought to break down my decision-making process and apply it to my graphic design work.

I say, "So that is why titles are always at the top."

He looks at me carefully. "We're experimenting with that. With some genres we think we get more handling with only a picture visible at the top."

"Genres," I repeat, curious. "You mean like poetry, biography, reference?" I am parroting the categories of publishing from the *Literary Market Place*.

"Oh no, much more specific than that." He hands me a book. "You know the book *Jane Eyre*?"

I read *Jane Eyre* in high school and have forgotten all but the flavor of it. "Of course," I answer, a little confused because the book he hands me appears to be some sort of period romance, but the title is not Jane Eyre and the author is not Brontë.

"Hugely popular, so much so that publishers wish they had a dozen *Jane Eyres* every year." I look at the cover more carefully. There is a woman in a white nightgown trimmed with lace, her long, dark hair somewhat disheveled, running toward the reader, away from a large mansion, English—maybe eighteenth century. It is night in the illustration; the sky is deep blue, mysterious with brooding clouds. The mansion has a tower with a window high up, glowing dimly yellow. Is there a figure in the window, or is it a ghost? A flame? The story of *Jane Eyre* comes back to me. I look up at him.

"So this is like a *Jane Eyre* sequel?"

"A *Jane Eyre* industry! The cover of a gothic novel is a formula. It tells a certain reader what type of story to expect. If I put no light in the window, nobody buys it. Yellow is hope. If I put a man with the woman, it means she finds tempestuous love. If the man is chasing her, that means one type of plot. If he is running with her, the story is more about their struggle to be together. If the man's hands are touching her below the neck, then a handsome but mysterious stranger ravishes her. Of course, they both turn out to be royalty."
I am astounded.

He is telling me that there is a very specific set of cues that publishers use and that regular readers understand. "We know—after a lot of false starts—how to satisfy the many types of readers who want romance."

"The gothic novel." I repeat seriously. "That's what you mean by a genre?"

"This is how we solve the problem of helping the reader choose what they will like. Of course, it's constantly evolving." He hands me another book. "Western genre. You see? Indians in this one." He hands me more books. I hold half a dozen until I have to start putting them on the table to receive the next example.

"Here, weapons and a hangman's noose in a tree. Western lovers know that this plot has struggle, killing, heroism, but no romance. Here, spaghetti western-type plot. Here, more romance, less gun fighting. Here, the townspeople struggle against landowners and East Coast bankers. Townspeople win, of course."

He's very serious, so I hazard a joke. "That's why it's called fiction?"

He makes a knowing gesture, something like a wink and nod. "Now science fiction—completely new challenges here. So many types of writing, so many types of readers. Not as predictable as romance readers. That's why I was interested in why you bought your Asimov. Some readers like formulaic science fiction with hordes of little green men invading, being beaten back by plucky human heroes. Some want to be whisked away to other planets with fantastic machines. Your Asimov there, much too deep to be reduced to a formula. He defines new genres; other people copy his successes. But we are finding some cover imagery to help the buyer find their way."

The receptionist pokes her head in the door.

"Are you Mr. Laufer? Mr. Sommers says he has been held up at a photo shoot and can't make it back to see you. He asked me to make an appointment for next week."

I manage to reply, "Ah, OK, I will see you on my way out." In confusion I turn to my companion. "Sorry, I thought you were Ian Sommers." The spell has been broken, my lesson in the art of genre paperbacks ends abruptly.

"No, I should have introduced myself. I am Ian Ballantine. Pleasure to talk with you. I'll tell Ian we spoke." He is gone. The

Good packaging transcends decoration and sets an expectation that is consistent with what the product can deliver. A package both explains what is for sale and is part of the value of the item being purchased. In the case of cultural products—books, music, motion pictures, games, and so forth—the design challenge is to convey a highly nuanced idea of the cultural experience on offer. This requires an ability to empathize with many types of audiences. Modern cultural packaging can be traced to theater and circus posters of the 19th century; it developed into highly differentiated graphic languages in the 20th century. While genre marketing risks confining the appeal of a product that might otherwise find a wider audience, it can also be highly effective in cultivating a loyal audience.

Aha: Only in an economy where the consumer faces a staggering range of choice is graphic design a crucial service. Design is not just making things look good, it is making things look like what they really are, so that choosing and using are in harmony.

receptionist books me next week with Ian Sommers, and I am back on the street. I am never to see Ian Ballantine again, but he has given me a crucial scrap of publishing education at a crucial time, helping me think and speak like a publishing insider.

In college, it was fashionable to be suspicious of the dominant paradigm. Capitalism seems manipulative, controlling. And there are some people—capitalist or no—who do try to manipulate markets, to limit the choices, or to keep prices in their favor. But there are also capitalists whose success rests on their ability to see what people want, to differentiate slight variations in customer preferences, and to experiment until there is a profitable relationship. Ballantine's intense curiosity about the fiction reader adds a nuance to the design definition. Graphic design is rarely about selling people a product they don't want. It's about helping people avoid what they don't want and clearly presenting what's offered. This means developing a dialogue with the marketplace, so that buyers can distinguish, from among too many choices, the things they do want.

After talking with Ballantine, I tinker with my definitions. Design is the science of understanding how humans make choices. Art describes the consequences of our choices and perhaps lets us glimpse the choices we never made. I am not sure Ballantine would agree with this—we discussed nothing about art—but I find myself thinking that graphic design is largely unnecessary in an economy of scarcity. Only in an economy where the citizen/consumer faces staggering choice is graphic design a crucial service. Graphic design—all design really—is about making things look like what they are, so that choosing and using are in harmony.

SINGING TO THE GATEKEEPERS

OCTOBER 1974 Eighteen weeks in, interviewing has bogged down to a slow grind. Working from Penn Station Booth 6, I can reach out to perhaps two dozen people a day. I get more interviews than I did in July, because I have more names to drop when I call, but things are still not working right. I take on some modest freelance projects that I execute in the evening so I can make calls and go to interviews during business hours.

After my chance meeting with Ian Ballantine, I have a new appreciation for paperbacks, and I begin to work my way through the *Literary Market Place* (LMP) list of art directors for paperback publishers. There are paperbacks on sale everywhere. I browse their covers in Penn Station. Bantam Books has the most consistently provocative covers. LMP lists Len Leone as the art director. I mail a few carefully chosen samples, and, of course, call his office and leave messages—trying a few days, skipping a few days, trying again. This goes on throughout September. I try various tactics so the reception-ist remembers me.

She answers Leone's line with his extension number. "3313," she says. I decide she is probably a nice person, but saying that number a thousand times a week makes personalization impossible. I jot down my different lines each time I try one. They fill three cards, then four.

"Calling for Mr. Leone."

"David Laufer for Mr. Leone."

"David Laufer, graphic designer, freelance or staff." On and on.

She usually says, "Thanks, Mr. Laufer, may I take your number for Len?" After a while it becomes, "Thanks, Mr. Laufer, I have your number from yesterday."

Finally I try something new. She answers, "3313."

"Hi, is this 3313?" I ask, grinning.

She chuckles in spite of herself and says, "No, this is 2698, can't you hear?" Then I say my name. Variations of this game go on for a week. I try singing the number back to her using different tunes. Then, one day when I have dreamed up a clever new variation, I get:

"Leone here."

Rarely have I been so unprepared for success. I have to stumble through a sentence about who I am and why he should see my portfolio. He is incredibly smooth, even cordial.

"Yes, David, I have the samples you sent. Very nice work. Forgive me for not calling you back. Since the Macmillan bloodbath I've had calls from more experienced talent than I can see. But I heard Barbara Bertoli is looking for someone; do you have her number?" This is the first time I have heard "Bertoli" pronounced by someone who knows her (BEAR-toll-ee), but I manage to remember that she is Leone's counterpart at Avon Books.

The shock of getting through to Leone causes me to dump my address cards on the floor of Booth 6. Leone reads Bertoli's number and I write it on the back of my hand. I will probably never get another shot, so I go for the throat.

"Mr. Leone, you're the king of book jacket art directors, and you need to see my portfolio."

He doesn't disagree, but he doesn't lower the drawbridge either. "Well, in normal times it would be a pleasure—call Barbara, and if that doesn't work out, keep us on your list."

"What's the Macmillan bloodbath?" I venture.

"Oh, Macmillan laid off most of their art department. Rumor was they were trying to unionize—close to two hundred people I think." His voice has a remarkable quality of caring, calm, assurance, and relaxed sincerity. "Early June. I knew some of them, and, you know, we try to help as many as we can."

"Mr. Leone, I admire your work—I especially liked *The Sleeping Murders*—and I can't thank you enough for your time."

"Sure, David, good luck."

Aha! His gatekeeper is away for just an instant, and I reach The Man himself—and I have two transcendent pieces of information. First, the reason it feels as though I'm swimming against a torrent is that I *am* swimming against a torrent! The week before I arrive in New York, two hundred competitors begin looking for the same job I want, and they all have experience on their side—not to mention contacts! Somehow I feel much better!

Second, I have a warm lead. There is not a moment to lose, yet I waver, superstitiously looking for just the right dime, a shiny one, to put in the slot.

A TRIAL RUN

"Hi, Ms. BEAR-toll-ee, David Laufer here. Len Leone told me that you were looking for design—"

The effect is magical. I hear her voice smile. "Well, Joe Cool himself sent you! Let's see," Bertoli says briskly. "I have an 8:00 a.m. with my publisher. Can you be here at 7:40?"

The power of a name! No need to remind her what I do or that she has been receiving samples from me. Leone sent you, so come right on in.

The 6:02 is on time, and so am I. However, when I arrive at Hearst headquarters, it's clogged with people. There are several camera crews, and the crowd is bristling with microphones. Randolph Hearst has been in the news for much of the past year since his daughter, Patricia, was taken hostage. Then, the young Ms. Hearst shows up on the news robbing banks with the Symbionese Liberation Army and now has been missing for months. Maybe they found her, or—I hesitate to think of the bad news that could be breaking. A voice reaches me from below the crowd.

"Are you David?"

My eyes travel across the crowd, until I look closer and down.

"Barbara Bertoli." A tiny woman with dark hair and an exceptionally strong grip shakes my hand. "This way—we can go around the frenzy." As we circle, I see a silver-haired man, hatless in the cold, speaking into a circle of microphones and lenses, calmly but resolutely giving a statement. "Our owner. Everyone in the company feels so badly for his family," she says crisply. "His daughter gets kidnapped and they follow him around like he owes them a statement. And he owns newspapers! No professional courtesy."

Up in the Avon offices, she sets aside her great coat and I see she is even smaller than my first impression, yet her personality fills the room with confidence and purpose. Her office appears quite cramped. Even though there is space for a table and chairs, the room is closed in on every wall with book jackets laid side to side. They are in wire racks, just like those in pharmacies. It's a laboratory for comparing jackets. Even though my portfolio contains zero book experience, Ian Ballantine's crash course, obtained by chance just a week before, helps me say the right things. Like the

The Serendipity Theory: successful design interviews require—in addition to being on time and other basics—some unpredictable detail that gives the interviewer a premonition of good chemistry.

locomotive connection in my interview with Jim Burke, it is just enough of a hook to establish some dialogue. I develop a hunch now that design interviews require, in addition to the basics of being on time, not spilling the coffee, and having a reasonable command of language, a certain serendipity, an unpredictable detail that gives the interviewer a premonition of good chemistry. In neither case, so far, has it been factual—in both cases, it is an emotional bridge. I must work on systematizing and pre-arranging my serendipity!

Bertoli considers for a moment, then says, "I want you to come in tomorrow and work with us for a day. We'll see how you apply your thinking."

The next day, I'm shown to a drawing board that appears to have been salvaged from a Pacific island after an early nuclear test. It's in a windowless cubicle piled with collapsed cardboard boxes stacked to the ceiling. But it is downright roomy compared with Booth 6, and I am so happy to be actually designing something that I crank out dozens of different jacket comps. One of the four staff designers gives me a clipboard with half a dozen single-page synopses on it. Each one describes a book that Avon has in process, with a modest summary of the plot, key features, genre, audience characteristics, price, sell copy, and awards won.

Across from me, in a slightly roomier cubicle with a window, sits a tall designer with jet-black hair, quite a luxurious black beard, and blazing white teeth smiling out from under a curled moustache. Richard Nebiolo joins Bertoli to look at the pencil tracings I am taping on the cubicle walls. He seems like a giant next to her, but there is no doubt who's in charge.

Bertoli looks at my work and starts rearranging it. They discuss the merits of different ideas in a jargon I half understand. "This looks like a below-the-line title ..." "Not this, it sends warm and wonderful signals ..." "Too understated, too oriental ..." She stops to consider the first cut.

From under his moustache, Nebiolo smiles with a bit of mischief. "We got to get rid of this kid. He will put the rest of us out of work!" Bertoli spirits a few of my designs away to place on her racks.

Nebiolo says in a low voice, "I told her she is crazy if she doesn't hire you."

I am invited back for the rest of the week, but the following Monday I am back in Penn Station while Avon tries out some other designers. I tear into my remaining cards, determined not to sit around waiting for Avon to call.

James McMullan
WATERCOLOR WIZARD

James McMullan was born in 1934 in Tsingtao, China. He studied at St. Paul's School in Darjeeling, India, the Cornish College of the Arts in Seattle, and Pratt Institute in New York. McMullan is one of the most accomplished illustrators of his generation, combining a quick conceptual wit with an eye for color, pattern, facial expression, and gesture. His work is all the more remarkable because of his technical mastery of watercolor. He has produced more than fifty theater posters of exceptional quality, which are summarized in his book *The Theater Posters of James McMullan*. He has also contributed to magazines, books, and annual reports, and won numerous awards, including the Hamilton King Award from the Society of Illustrators.

OCTOBER 1974 I notice James McMullan's name among my cards and connect his name with an outpouring of exceptional illustrations I've been noticing in the media. I call his number and his assistant books a time for me that same week. I learn later that someone with whom I have interviewed recently sent him my name, though I never learn whom to thank. I'm torn whether to take my design portfolio or bring my paintings. I know I'm not in control of my wet media enough to sell illustration, but I want to paint and I want insight and encouragement. In the end I take two portfolios.

I gaze at the many examples of McMullan's work in his lobby, and realize that I've seen much more of his work without realizing it was his. I remark on this and he pauses momentarily, considering a response.

"You have to respond to the market, of course. I realized early in my career I could do caricatures, and that magazine and newspaper editors always needed them. I like doing more thoughtful, painterly work, so that's what I advertise—the work you have seen associated with my name."

I show him some of my urban environment paintings, and we talk about watercolor as a medium. I tell him I find it hard to go from a drawing to watercolor paper because tracing paper leaves marks that show through the finished painting.

"You have to sketch in a medium that dissolves as you paint." He shows me how he draws an outline of his subject with bright red watercolor in a crowquill pen and then paints right onto it. It explains the little flashes of bright red that appear and disappear like a thread sewn into the fabric of his work.

"Watercolor is a good illustrator's medium," McMullan tells me, "because it forces you to work at a furious pace. That suits the furious pace demanded by most clients!"

"What if it gets away from you?" I ask, referring to something that every watercolorist has experienced.

"Well, you do a sketch first. The sketch helps you get your composition, of course, and also helps you to decide in what order you're going to lay down your washes, and what colors are going to work. Here's a sketch."

McMullan shows me an illustration for a caricature of the comedian Don Rickles and the finished work next to it, which was commissioned by *New York* magazine. It's amazing how good the first one is; yet the second one, though not greatly different, has clearly benefited from the first.

"Sometimes the first one has more freshness. I'm taking more risk and working alla prima. Sometimes the second works better. I used to do a series, but now ..."

> **❝ It's tough to get started as an illustrator. There are very few places where you can earn a salary to illustrate. And when you find them, they want to control every aspect of your work. ❞**

Seeing his sketches next to his finished work is worth a dozen lessons in watercolor. He takes in the two portfolios and nods.

"I know your dilemma. It's tough to get started as an illustrator. There are few places where you can earn a salary to illustrate. And when you find them, they want to control every aspect of your work. You have to figure out a way to get your style and your name paired in the minds of the media community. And once it gets popular, people ape your style immediately. You have to be prepared to move on to something new quickly to stay valuable. Now I go after more complex, thoughtful work that's harder to copy."

That's the second time he's used the word thoughtful to describe his work. I know from experience that interviews as rich and valuable as this one never last long enough, so I decide to be direct.

"Are you looking for an assistant?"

"Yes, always. I get a lot of requests for projects that pay reasonably well and that with some coaching could be done by someone less experienced. The trouble is, they don't stay long enough to be profitable. Honestly, I think design is your most salable skill. You don't have to be an illustrator to be creative and influential, you know. A lot of designers can't draw. A lot of illustrators can't design. You can be a bridge. Your drawing will serve you well, especially when you're communicating with illustrators," he says earnestly.

This short interview helps me tremendously. McMullan, an illustrator's illustrator, uses a visual analogy—the bridge—to help me decide that I am probably a designer, not an illustrator. I keep drawing, but I begin to focus my portfolio toward design.

Barbara Bertoli
STRONG, YET VULNERABLE

NOVEMBER 1974 Richard Nebiolo from Avon Books calls me to tell me how much they can offer me. I know I should negotiate, but it is November 1, five vertiginous months after I arrived in New York. The savings my wife and I brought to New York are all but gone, devoured by 115 round-trip train rides, several thousand pay phone calls, two pairs of Presbyterian dress shoes, and countless three-by-five cards.

I enter a new phase of my career. I am immersed in mass-market, rack-size books. I must see every event, every emotion, every sales pitch in a 4 3⁄16 x 7 1⁄16-inch frame. I quickly realize that my salary covers rent, commuting, tuition, and taxes, but I must do freelance work for food and clothing.

Bertoli is very demanding, and she works for editors and a publisher who expect us to perform. A title might cost the company millions of dollars, and a packaging mistake can cause mass marketers to drop it from their coveted rack space—reserved for what they are sure will sell.

When Ian Ballantine described the design of paperback covers, it seemed complex but predictable. Now I'm in the thick of it, evaluating dozens of cues—fonts, colors, illustrations—to communicate with a harried reader who has certain needs and understandings about how their reading material ought to be presented. The jacket designs that Bertoli requests and I sketch are made and remade; sell lines rewritten; many color combinations tried; illustrations bought, modified, repainted, restarted anew. The floors are often littered with scraps and rejects.

Even after the first proof comes back from the printers, modifications continue. Bertoli is self-taught as an art director and has a very open-ended way of working, which at first I find baffling. She often senses where she wants the cover to go, but cannot tell her staff specifically how to fix something.

She says, "This design needs more depth, more atmosphere. But is has an intimate quality I like. Don't lose the intimacy."

Or my favorite: "The gothic novel heroine is strong, yet vulnerable. Explain to the illustrator that he needs to discover that essential gothic dichotomy in our heroine."

All this is to take place in the top half of the book jacket that is visible in the mass-market rack—a space less than 16 square inches!

Nebiolo, with probably ten more years experience than I have, becomes a valuable friend, teaching me shortcuts and introducing me to illustrators who come into the office. His best advice is about negotiating the creative process.

"When Barbara runs out of ideas, she yells. I find what she needs is dialogue. Give her the first wacky idea that comes to your head. She won't like it, but she will react to it. As long as the finished design sells, the success sticks to you. Be careful about falling in love with your own work. I'm not saying you never get your own ideas approved, but if the team hasn't seen it, I don't trust it. Somehow when the group mauls an idea—it breaks the dialogue open and then we discover the essence, the meaning, the indefinable something that makes the product good."

Nebiolo has a particular talent. He can take the title of a book, choose a font with a certain emotional resonance, and then exaggerate the letters to intensify the emotion. He works the letters in soft lead pencil on tracing paper, working back into the graphite characters with an eraser and a thin metal eraser shield until the grouping of letters has the right emotion. I watch in amazement as, with twenty minutes before a deadline, he lays a piece of treated acetate over his approved pencil drawing and draws the letters using India ink and a brush, then touches up with drafting curves and a technical pen. The result is typography with a special handcrafted quality. When I study the mass-market paperbacks on display in Penn Station, I see Nebiolo's titles setting Avon apart from the competition in a subtle yet persuasive way.

From the standpoint of hours worked per employee, Avon could easily be categorized as a sweatshop, but it is the opposite: the

> **" I'm not saying you shouldn't defend your own ideas, but if the team hasn't mauled it, I don't trust it. Somehow it breaks the dialogue open and then we discover the indefinable something that makes the product good. "**

atmosphere is so exciting, everyone wants to be there. That excitement emanates from the office of our publisher, Peter Mayer, and flows to every department. In my first weeks at Avon I hear Mayer's name breathed with the reverence with which the Lost Boys speak of their Peter Pan.

One morning, Bertoli hands me the briefing sheets, including a number of well-known Thornton Wilder books. Mayer likes to publish literature along with bestsellers. He has an eye for literature that can cross over and be big, and he picks up the paperback rights. And Bertoli has developed an eye for which of his pet projects he sees in this way.

I'm a bit intimidated by the assignment. Wilder is in print, so I stop into the public library on my way to Penn Station, pick up four of the Wilder titles in the series, and tear into them. I start to generate some designs and put them on my wall.

Bertoli scans them as she cruises by. "These Thornton Wilder sketches aren't in below-the-line format."

The meaning of what she is saying begins to sink in. The below-the-line formats are preapproved and therefore quick to design. I have screwed up, putting more time into them than was needed, and she won't be able to show them at the meeting.

But then she says, "I like your treatment, though. It's possible we could publish it outside our established formats."

"Wilder has personality," I venture. "I read the books before I started, then while they were fresh in my mind I started designing."

Bertoli looks at me sharply. "I think you should sit in on the cover meeting and present this series yourself."

Panic! I am going to have to present my ideas to Mayer, who chews up everything our department does and transmogrifies it. Even his failures work better than many publishers' successes. The only fortunate thing is that the meeting starts in a few minutes, so my panic has no time to escalate.

Barbara opens the meeting briskly. "I asked David to join us so he could explain his approach to the Wilder titles."

Mayer looks much different than I imagined. He has a boyish, casual stance and, underneath a head of unruly hair, a gaze so intense that it makes him seem closer to you than he is.

I put up my three series of Wilder titles. Out of terror, I say

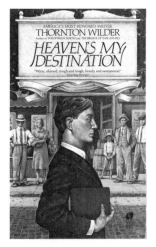

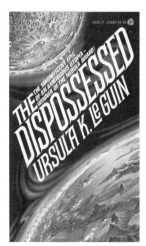

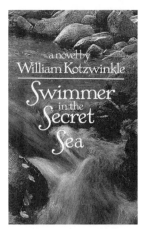

Paperback book art directors must be versatile, able to find the excitement in a subject and execute it within time, budget, and marketing parameters. Barbara Bertoli did not herself draw or make sketches, rather she used complex, emotional descriptions of the feeling she wanted, and called upon many exceptional illustrators and photographers to interpret her titles.

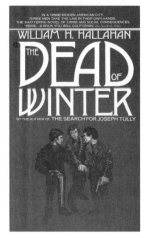

nothing, which is the perfect thing to do. Bertoli, four senior editors, and Mayer are looking at them carefully.

"David decided Wilder is too important to be lumped in under Bard format...," she begins for me.

"He has such a unique voice," I get from somewhere, "and we have four exceptional titles."

"Six, now," says Mayer. "Did you study Wilder?" I decide the folks in this room are too smart for me to bullshit.

"I read *Our Town* in high school, so I knew he was a writer of stature. When Barbara gave me this series, I got them out of the library and read these four. After a few chapters of *Theophilus North*, I became a fan; after *The Eighth Day*, a believer!"

Mayer has a dazzling smile, which I see for the first time now directed at Bertoli. "Where did you find a cover designer that likes to read?!" We all know this is unfair—everyone in the department loves reading—so he turns serious again; all eyes are back on the covers.

"So, David, you did three series, and they are different. Before I tell you what I am going to publish, tell me which one you like." Mayer leads by putting people to the test, and it's exhilarating.

I decide not to try to guess what he's planning, so I say a few words about each series, then turn to face to the wall those designs I am not recommending. Bertoli looks on apprehensively. Either Mayer is going to throw them all out and insist on a Bard format, or we are on the verge of a breakthrough.

"Good," says Mayer, studying them. "It's a bit risky, but I like the chutzpah. If we play our cards right, it may migrate above the line." I leave the meeting with a great feeling of accomplishment. In the past, I've had trouble explaining and defending my designs in group meetings—I thought I didn't like being in the spotlight. Here, with the acute interest of our cultural commanding officer—and no chance to prepare my remarks ahead of time—I discover a more intense spotlight, and I am suddenly able to talk about the designs with conviction.

Aha: *I didn't like being in the spotlight. I had trouble defending my designs in group meetings. Here, under the intense spotlight of our cultural commanding officer, I discover that I am suddenly able to talk design with conviction.*

Max Miedinger
GETTING HELVETICA RIGHT

Max Miedinger (1910–1980) was born in Zurich. He trained as a typesetter and attended evening classes in design and typography at the Kunstgewerbeschule, then went on to set type for the Globus department store in Zurich. His natural affinity for typography led to a position as a sales representative for the Haas'sche Schriftgiesserei, a renowned type foundry near Basel. In 1956, he began an independent consulting career. Miedinger is principally known for creating the Neue Haas Grotesk typeface in 1957; the font was redrawn (with Edouard Hoffmann) and released as Helvetica in 1960. Despite the presence of numerous other sans serif fonts, Helvetica achieved a balance between simplicity and emotional purity that made it a worldwide standard.

FEBRUARY 1975 Photo-Lettering, Inc., is a high-end typesetting company. They are the premier repository for unusual fonts, including many exclusives, and their craft is excellent. Their type specimen book is a treasure; they don't just give it out to anyone. Richard Nebiolo, who learned his craft working at Photo-Lettering, escorts me there on a lunch hour and introduces me to the owner, Ed Rondthaler, whom he describes as "a beautiful person."

I visit Photo-Lettering several times a month to pick up, drop off, or review work in progress. On one occasion, Rondthaler is just passing the pickup desk. He doesn't remember my name, but remembers we have met and associates me with Nebiolo.

Rondthaler says, with obvious satisfaction, "Guess who was just here?" and hands me a business card. The finely crafted card says "Max Miedinger." Below, in Rondthaler's handwriting, it says "Designer of Helvetica. Visited here," and today's date.

Just then, Miedinger himself comes back through the door. He asks Rondthaler if he might have an extra set of Photo-Lettering type books to take back with him. I am holding his business card.

While Rondthaler gets the books, I introduce myself and strike up a conversation. Miedinger is a personable, intense little man whose eyes are constantly exploring; he is very taken with Photo-Lettering, and with all things American.

Display type is set photographically, a couple bucks per word in most places, and the spacing is all manual. Photo-Lettering's work commands a premium, and Bertoli is so particular about type that I usually trace the book titles out in Helvetica on tracing paper to get the exact size and spacing. Then we send the tracing by messenger for them to follow. Bard format uses Helvetica; I use it so much that within a few months I can draw the entire font very precisely without tracing or looking at a specimen.

I show him some of my tracings for Avon titles, and Miedinger nods. "Americans like to set their headlines so very tight! I am used to the spacing of foundry type, where the letters cannot touch."

He tells me—not quite apologetically—that the foundry had made a mess of Helvetica. "They could not wait for us to refine our drawings. It does not look wrong to anyone until we show them something better. We designers are sellers of details too small to be seen—and that is precisely what gives typography its power. The average viewer does not see it, but they do *feel* it. The last little refinements are what make it sing."

I'm a bit shocked. "To most of the world, Helvetica looks like precision made visible. What could you possibly want to improve?"

He says in his clipped accent, "It takes so many tries to get it right. There was too much hurry to get to market when they expanded the offering to include many weights. The appearance of simplicity, you see, is a very complex thing to achieve."

I would like to learn more from him, but I have to rush off—Bertoli needs her type. Miedinger's frustration with the imperfections in Helvetica, so widely regarded as perfect, must seem unreasonable to his employers. Yet he keeps pushing

> **We designers are sellers of subliminal details that the average viewer does not see, but they do feel. The message is somehow warmer, memorable. That is precisely what gives typography its power.**

> **The appearance of simplicity, you see, is a very complex thing to achieve. It takes many tries.**

A B C
D E F G H
I J K L M N
O P Q R S
T U V W
X Y Z

Foundry Helvetica, as originally released, circa 1961.

It takes close obesrvation to see the problems with the original Helvetica that were so troubling to Miedinger. The C, G, M, P, Q, R, U, and W are the most "noticeable," though in truth every character is subtly redrawn and refined. Only a true perfectionist could have brought forth a font so durable and irreducibly simple as Helvetica, then revised it with such patience and attention to minute details of proportion. Many of the changes

A B C

D E F G H

I J K L M N

O P Q R S

T U V W

X Y Z

Helvetica Neue, 75 (Bold), released in 1983.

also involved drawing more weights of Helvetica and making the different weights as compatible and interchangeable as possible. The transition from foundry type, which was drawn with compensation for the "squish" of wet ink fattening the appearance of the printed character slightly, to photographic typesetting, where no squish occurred, necessitated the redrawing of most standard fonts, Helvetica included.

for a more precise realization! Sure enough, in 1983 Helvetica Neue appears. I study the refinements and conclude that, in Miedinger, I have met the most exacting perfectionist alive. He is right about details: I cannot say how, but the Neue version *does* look better!

Arthur Tress
THE DREAM COLLECTOR

Arthur Tress was born in Brooklyn, New York in 1940. An artist and photographer, he received his BFA at Bard College, studied filmmaking in Paris, and traveled extensively in his twenties. His work first became visible with his book *Open Space in the Inner City*, published with a grant from the New York State Council on the Arts. His work has been published in more than a dozen books and included in exhibitions and museum collections worldwide, including the Museum of Modern Art, New York; the Metropolitan Museum of Art, New York; the International Museum of Photography, Rochester, New York; the Center for Contemporary Photography, Chicago; the Bibliothèque Nationale, Paris; the Stedelijk Museum, Amsterdam; and many others. Tress's early influences include Duane Michals. His mature work is increasingly personal and visionary.

MARCH 1975 A few weeks after my success at the cover meeting, Peter Mayer calls me in and explains, "I bought the rights to a photographic book that the hardcover houses passed up, and I asked Barbara if she would allow you to design it. We have seen a few photographic books skip hardcover and sell well as original paperbacks, so we're going to test the waters." He hands me a bright yellow box, stacked perhaps two inches high with 8 x 10 black-and-white prints. Above the Kodak logo is written in black marker "TRESS/ SHADOW."

"Arthur Tress?" I ask, "Of *Dream Collector* renown?" Mayer nods.

"What does the photographer want the book to look like?"

"Exactly the right question! Please call him. He lives in town."

I flip through the photographer's work prints, and they are quite enchanting. Then I understand. Management is always looking for ways to delegate work that will run smoothly. I got involved in the Thornton Wilder content, and this needs a designer's involvement in the content as well as the cover. Mayer figures he can put a designer who likes to get involved in content together with a content producer, and things will run on wheels. He is gone before I can thank him. A light goes on: the designers I admire—from Papanek and Eames to Edelmann and Chwast—all seem to say, in their own ways, "Get involved in the content—design is about meaning." But as a young designer, the superficial aspects of appearance are all I am given. *Shadow* represents a small but exciting step toward participation in the content as well as the appearance.

The briefing sheet that accompanies every Avon title usually has a plot summary. The briefing for *Shadow* describes Tress as an up-and-coming young photographer. *Shadow* is billed as a "novel in photographs." Telling stories in pictures is of course a time-honored idea—as old as hieroglyphics, as popular as comic books—and one that will always be reinvented by each new generation. Tress's images are not a narrative in the strict sense of the word; they are more like theme and variation. The images are all square. He photographs his own shadow, trailing into each picture, and artfully hides camera and tripod. The images add to one another until a cumulative sense of mysticism emerges.

I order some copy prints of his pictures and make some test layouts at several different trim sizes and bind them into a dummy book. A thought, maybe more of an instinctive observation, occurs to me: Projects that do not fit the normal workflow, that somehow defy the usual means of description, often represent great creative opportunities, since there are no expectations, no established formats. Projects such as *Shadow*, I realize, require new ideas.

A few days later I visit Tress in his studio on the Upper West Side. He lives like a monk; a costly Hasselblad camera and lenses are his only visible concessions to the material world.

"I asked our publisher how you want this book to look, and he suggested I call you," I start.

Aha: Projects that do not fit the normal workflow often represent great creative opportunities, since the established formats don't apply; these projects require new ideas.

"What do you get out of it?" says Tress before I can go any further. I hadn't figured on this type of opening move from him, but I realize it is natural for a photographer to want to know how the work is being received, before coloring the thoughts with friendship or personal observations. He has an unusual countenance: a quiet, almost passive voice, yet the intense gaze of one whose mind is disciplined to capturing essence. It is not disconcerting, rather disarming. My short tenure in publishing has already made me more confident verbalizing about publications in progress, so I wade in: "I get a whole new direction from *Open Space in the Inner City*—less reportage, more mystical. There's a quality of spiritual journey."

Tress says, "*Open Space* is not really my style. It was done for the New York State Council on the Arts on a grant, so I had to do certain things to satisfy the grant. But it helped me arrive here." Here, I assume, means Avon. But it's bigger than that. Arrival means having his work published on its own terms: as *Shadow*, as an original cultural product, as art.

The old definitions game stirs: If art is work you create and put in the world on your own terms, design is work you create on negotiated terms—both the money and the creation. Actually, the money is negotiated on both sides of the fence.

I take out my sketch. I decide not to try to sell it; I just hand it to him. After a measured silence, I offer, "No numerals on the pages, no words appear on the same page with imagery. Your titles are isolated each on their own page."

Tress nods. "This is the size." He says it as a statement and a question.

"Yes. I could make the photographs larger and borders smaller, but after several experiments this seems like the right balance." I have the other variations I made of photo size and trim size in my envelope, but leave them there.

"Yes, it is. The cover has a black border, the inside pages white," he observes. I'm about to respond, but he adds. "It works. Black inside would be too ominous, but as a cover it sets the right tone." So Herb Stern and I keep quiet and let him look.

"Seeing a book take shape—reimagined by a designer—it's sort of shocking," Tress observes. His voice is quiet, detached. "I live with this idea of a narrative told in shadows. I can't predict where and

when I will find the right light, the right place; I have to be alert every waking moment. I can go a week, shooting every day, and not find a worthwhile image. Then I'll make six good ones in a day. I am so dependent on chance, finding the right light, being able to make a picture in adverse or ambivalent circumstances. At last, I can't see any holes. There is nothing more to add. So then the creation phase ends, and you go through this long journey of marketing, negotiating, administering. You begin to lose touch with the original spark. Even when I have all the work prints assembled, it still seems unrealized. But just this step of having you design it makes it intensely real. Like—" he pauses to search out an analogy—"learning you had a love child, and meeting her, all grown up."

Tress asks a few questions about paper and printing, and the design of *Shadow* is set. I send the design to the printer, and *Shadow* appears on the Avon production list.

The simplicity of this book is atypical. There are a few words for chapter titles, nothing else. The publisher puts designer and author directly together, and the simpatico makes the project happen. I think of Heinz Edelmann's description of the struggle to make *Yellow Submarine*. *Shadow* is of course far less complex than *Submarine*, yet still the contrast is remarkable. There is no single way; every project has a unique backstory.

An aha moment has arrived. What Tress describes as "shocking" is the transformational nature of design. I want to stay in the eye of that storm and make it my life's work. I like being an agent for the realization of ideas. Maybe this is what James McMullan was trying to tell me—illustration and design each have their own type of fulfillment. Authors, entrepreneurs, people of all stripes need to give expression to their ideas, but they can carry it only so far.

Aha! Authors, entrepreneurs, people of all stripes need to give expression to their ideas, but they can carry it only so far. Graphic design is a window between author and public. Transparent, yet crucial.

Graphic design is like a window between author and public, between content and consciousness. The window itself is invisible, yet without the transparency of the window, no illumination passes in either direction. I realize how much I like books—containers for cultural ideas. The design psychology of book jackets is very stimulating, so controlling the whole experience, cover to cover, seems a logical extension, and potentially much more lasting.

Tress and I do several more book projects together, including his *Theater of the Mind* and his limited-edition *Dream Collector* portfolio.

AHA: THE BERTOLI TOGGLE

Richard Nebiolo gets a job as an art director at another publisher. I am terribly sorry to see him go, but I take over his office and am delighted to inherit his window. Without his experienced eye, it's very difficult for me to interpret Barbara Bertoli's comments. Especially as release dates approach, more changes flood in. I am sometimes at a loss; the process feels like a guessing game. If I leave a cover design on my desk at the end of the day, Bertoli sits down and snips it apart, moving all the pieces around to see if more impact could be gleaned from the components. If she finds an arrangement she likes, she tapes it together. If not, I just have a pile of snippets. Sometimes I am able to gain an insight into her thinking, but it's an unpredictable process that also causes a lot of extra work.

On a Tuesday in March 1975, ice is forming on the inside of my little window at Avon Books. I need to run for the train, but all my press-ready art has been snipped apart; I am further behind than when I came in ten hours ago. I perform triage, so the desperately late can get first attention in the morning, before the urgently late. I look at the press-ready artwork not yet approved, knowing if I leave it out it may be taken apart by the time I come in the next day. I try to visualize what she would do. A cynical inner voice says, "Whatever takes the most work to fix, that is what she will do." I'm stuck in the mentality that my boss is an irrational creature, changing everything hundreds of times just to make life miserable. If I were the art director, I would not be concerned about the amount of repair work involved; I would just try to make the design more compelling. I arrive, quite unexpectedly, at an aha moment in my work as a designer. I divorce myself from how much work it requires, and just connect directly with the potential reader: seeing what she sees, wanting what he wants. As reader, I need to make the train in a few seconds, want something to read, don't want to be stuck reading something different than the cover promises.

Instantly, I'm able to grasp what Bertoli would want changed. I see what must be simplified, how I might trade a little line space here for a slightly larger illustration, how a darker sky makes the title of the book more legible. I even see that the sell copy could be expressed in fewer words. In an hour I fix half a dozen jackets and take them in to her office.

"Whoa. Much better!" She signs her initial block on the first one so that it can be sent to the publisher for final approval. The next one is also a hit. "Did Peter ask for this change?" Mayer would occasionally drop in unannounced and make a comment that enlarged everyone's understanding.

"No, I just figured out 'strong, yet vulnerable.'"

She nods, pleased that someone made sense of her verbal dichotomies. Rather than half a dozen rounds of revisions, we have six boards approved at that one sitting. It was as though I had discovered a toggle switch in my head. Toggle right, I'm the art director, engaged in an intense dialogue with my audience. I click through a thousand conversations with all different imaginary readers—young, old, male, female. Then I toggle left; I'm the technician, making the changes requested by the art director.

My job changes dramatically once I discover the Bertoli toggle—it's possibly the greatest labor-saving strategy I could imagine. I spend less time on mindless rounds of changes and more time critiquing ideas before they reach tangible form. I watch people in bookstores and observe how they reach for titles, how long they look at the front before looking at the description on the back, how they put books back in the rack, pick up another, go back to the first. One night, while waiting for several hours in Penn Station due to a train delay, I see a woman browse through the newest gothic novels and choose one of Bantam's covers instead of one of Avon's. She looks at the rack, grabs the book, opens it to the last chapter, reads a few

THE BERTOLI TOGGLE: *Toggle right, you're the art director, engaged in an intense dialogue with your audience. Toggle left, you're the technician, making the changes requested by the art director.*

lines, flips to the end, looks at front and back covers, and inside of 15 seconds heads for the cashier. Len Leone is one tough hombre!

To fill my two-hour daily commute, I always carry books. Bertoli observes my reading about design, designers, arcane stuff. One day she drops a magazine on my desk, one page folded over. No explanation. The article is about George Nelson. I had heard him speak at Carnegie Mellon when he came to show his film, *Planned Obsolescence*, and to talk to us about the design of everything. He is a great storyteller, raconteur, and charmer. The article surveys his career: writing for Time-Life books, designing pavilions for world's fairs, designing stylish clocks and chairs. Then a caption jumps off the page: Nelson teaches a class called Philosophy of Design at Pratt Institute. Pratt is nearby. It's tempting, but where will I find the time?

Peter Mayer
HOW TO RUN A SALES MEETING

Peter Mayer (1936–) was born in London in and immigrated to the United States in 1939. He received his BA in English literature at Columbia College on a Ford Foundation scholarship and in 1954 matriculated at Christ Church, Oxford University. He served in the US Merchant Marine before being granted a graduate fellowship in comparative literature at Indiana University, then in 1959 earned a Fulbright scholarship to study German literature at the Freie Universität in Berlin. In 1961 Mayer began as an editorial assistant at Orion Press, and in 1962 Mayer began a 14-year tenure at Avon Books, rising from education editor to editor-in-chief before becoming Avon's publisher.

In the late 1970s Mayer was appointed publisher and president of Pocket Books (Simon and Schuster). As the Penguin group's chairman and CEO (1978–97), he oversaw Penguin's companies in the UK, US, Canada, Australia, New Zealand, Germany, the Netherlands, and India. His numerous industry honors include the Foundation of Indian Publishers' and Booksellers' Association Award for Outstanding Contribution to International Publishing (1996) and recognition as a Literary Market Place Most Distinguished Publisher. Mayer was named Chevalier and Officier of the Ordre des Arts et des Lettres by the French Ministry of Culture (1996) and received the Poor Richard's Award for Lifetime Contribution to Independent Publishing (2007), a Lifetime Achievement Award from the London Book Fair (2008), and the Russian "Big Book Prize" for Distinguished International Achievement (2011).

Mayer is the president and publisher of Overlook Press, Ardis Publishers, and, in London, Gerald Duckworth Publishers, Ltd., and Nonesuch Press. He is the author and editor of four books and two translations.

APRIL 1975 Most publishers, Avon included, hold company-wide sales meetings at which Editorial (who makes the books) presents new titles to Sales (who sells the books). The style of the meetings varies from one house to the next. Editorial tries to generate enthusiasm for the coming titles, while Sales brings back news from the front: the book buyers, stores, chains, book clubs, universities, and other outlets. I have heard it gets pretty boisterous. Junior-level creative people are usually invisible, but in Mayer's organization we are each given a chance to introduce a few titles to the sales force. As a publisher, Mayer values articulate employees. He knows that the only way to become a good gladiator is to face the lions.

I'm asked to present at the meeting the book *Black Holes: The End of the Universe?* It's a cover design I quite like and Bertoli thinks would sell. I am ten words into my first sentence and feeling confident when I am unexpectedly shut down by a wave of blunt remarks.

"Vacuous!" someone says.

"Right subject, but the presentation trivializes it!" I am wholly unprepared for this onslaught, and it shows.

"Might as well throw in a few flying saucers," sneers a traveler in a blue Brooks Brothers suit.

Bertoli, who approved my cover, pipes up, "It is a very visible cover on the mass-market rack." She has on her auditorium voice, which contrasts sharply with her tiny figure, but there are a few other terse criticisms. When it's clear I'm in over my head, Mayer, from the back of the room, parts the waters. "About a third of our editorial staff is experiencing their first sales conference." His sound is not as loud as Bertoli's, yet he quiets the room. I imagine him as the revered guru in an ashram, bringing order among the disciples

Aha: Great bosses value articulate employees. They know that the only way to become a good gladiator is to face the lions.

merely by intoning "om." "For everyone's benefit let me explain that our travelers have heard every reason there is not to order the books we publish. They are not criticizing our titles as much as they are bringing us into direct contact with the people who decide which books go in front of the public. Those book buyers are opinionated, they have no taste, and we listen to them because nobody on Earth knows more about what will sell." The travelers are nodding, some vigorously.

"Many of you have experienced sales meetings at other publishing houses, where the sales force is expected to genuflect silently to the Great Editorial Acumen." General mirth ripples forth. Mayer is displaying his greatest gift, in fact the essence of leadership: getting everyone focused on what matters, and feeling good about it. "Avon, as long as I am here, will be a place where Editorial and Sales tell each other what they think, candidly, for the purpose of putting out books that people want to buy."

A mild applause arises and dies away quickly as he summarizes, "So, newcomers, this is possibly the most valuable and direct glimpse of the marketplace you are likely to get. Travelers, keep your own opinions aside and let us hear what you hear from the market. Editors, it is your job to provide an enthusiastic narrative that the travelers can use to overcome even their most skeptical buyers." He pauses. He has united the workers and ennobled the task. "We have about three hours before we break up. I suggest we spend it determining the selling strategy for the half-dozen titles that will pay all of our salaries." The meeting later devolves into cocktail hour, and everyone is mingling, renewing acquaintances. Since I am new and the *Black Holes* cover is my work, several critics seek me out, to add nuance and explain what they think would sell. Mayer glides by and adds to the discussion.

> **Having good ideas is important, but it's only half the battle. The other half is convincing everyone else your ideas are good.**

"You have to have good ideas, of course," he tells both me and the travelers. "The story has to be good, the author has to be a salable personality, and the cover and the PR have to nail it. But that is only half the battle. The other half is convincing everyone else that your ideas are good. This you do by convincing them you have listened to them, then convincing them why you believe in the ideas, unshakably." He makes it sound so easy!

Black Holes: The End of the Universe? was eventually published with the cover I designed. Although the cover had a few detractors, the subject was new, and, as Heinz Edelmann suggested, it made some readers curious enough to part with their money. It was not a best-seller, nor even the best-selling book on the subject. It was the last time I stood up to talk about my work without thinking about how to discuss its merits.

BOLDNESS IN THE FACE OF OPPORTUNITY

Peter Mayer is a whirlwind of activity, yet he still makes time to talk to many of his staffers. He does criticize some of my covers very bluntly, but it is always about insight, never power. Some of the covers Bertoli entrusts to me are getting good initial results; Tress is pleased with *Shadow,* and Thornton Wilder has started to sell in the mass market.

At one point Mayer asks me how I like working with Bertoli. I tell him gingerly that it took me a while to figure out how to interpret her directions, but now she is a great boss. Mayer is so goal-directed, I think I know where this is going, but not so.

"Avon had an art director when I arrived. Good work, no problems. He hired an assistant, a seemingly meek Midwestern girl named Barbara Koontz—she had not yet acquired her married name, Bertoli. Then, abruptly, our art director left. I called my friend Milton Glaser—you have probably heard of him—and asked him to recommend a few people for the job. Milton's office manager sent some resumes. Barbara figured out what was going on, and came to my office to ask for the job. She was bright and energetic, but I didn't think she was experienced enough. And I didn't want her there if she had been passed over. So I had to be very blunt. I said something like, "I will give you a

66 Managing creative people: When someone steps forward, give them a shot. You can pick up experience more easily than motivation. 99

try. But you have to sell books from the very first month. If things don't work out right away, I will have to ask you to leave.

"To my surprise, she was very confident, grateful for the chance, forceful enough that the editorial staff all respected her; and she turned out to be highly organized. So, I have to admit that to my further astonishment, she turns out to be terrific—the best Avon has had! So I've learned, when someone steps forward, give them a shot. You can pick up experience more easily than motivation."

Mayer is holding out a powerful leadership tool for my observation: using a concise narrative to explain his criteria for staff development and promotion. He seems to be saying: "Advancement needs more than talent—it needs boldness in the face of opportunity."

PENN STATION BOOTH 6, REVISITED

Because of the lack of privacy at work, I still visit Penn Station Booth 6 to work on my A-list of design greats, hoping for an audience. Why? The progress I've been able to make, I feel, has been built on insights from direct contact with towering figures like Eames and Ballantine and Chwast. Each new design example I add to The Valise makes me feel a bit closer to—to what? To attaining the flexibility and visibility that Edelmann described? To the body of work Chwast told me I was capable of? To the dream that one of them might scoop me up and teach me his secrets? Maybe it's because my goal still seems imperfectly defined that continuing outreach seems vitally important.

If I take the 6:28, I can get to Booth 6 at 7:30 and get in a half hour of calling before I go to work. I learn that many of the top designers get to work before their gatekeepers, and sometimes they will pick up. A few get angry, a few blow me off, but I get an appointment now and again. It is harder now to respond quickly; I have to try to slide my portfolio showings in around working hours and not be obvious about it.

Herb Lubalin's waiting list is still full. I call weekly, but it's eternally the same story. With Lou Dorfsman at CBS, the drawbridge is up. I get in to see one of John Berg's art directors at CBS Records, but he's on the phone while I am there—not much chance for rapport building. The receptionist at Vignelli Associates is very polished and polite but firmly not looking.

Chermayeff & Geismar is not looking, not interviewing, not keeping a waiting list.

I have learned that the search takes patience, a sense of humor, luck, and timing. On days when the process grows tiresome, I draw on the lembas bread of encouragement from previous interviews and mentors.

Frederick Schneider
TO BE RIGHT ...

MARCH 1975 In my deck of contact cards is one for Frederick Schneider, art director at Oxford University Press (OUP). He is listed in LMP, but is not on Ed Gottschall's list, so I have no introduction. I have left messages, let it ride, and called again. I settle into work at Avon Books when Schneider unexpectedly leaves a message asking me to come in. Someone has actually been receiving my many calls and samples!

My appointment at OUP falls on a particularly busy day at Avon; good sense would suggest postponing, but I decide to chance it. I sit in the waiting room at Oxford's New York branch at 35th Street and Madison Avenue. The lobby walls are lined with small wooden coats of arms, each for a different college at Oxford. There is a glass wall with a small but well-stocked library. An assistant carrying a stack of three-foot-long typeset galleys shows me to Schneider's office. It is very spare, with no decor, no plants. It is populated by several dozen stacks of paper in shallow boxes, manuscripts for books.

Schneider is neat and thin, and looks at me as though he has only one chance to remember everything about me. He has a slight hesitation in his speech; he purses his lips, then a few seconds elapse before he speaks.

There's something I like about this man immediately and deeply; I resolve to say less than he does. He looks at my work slowly. I watch to see what interests him, but my own attention is diverted. On his wall is a framed black-and-white photograph of a man with dark hair looking up, his gaze locked on the viewer with an intensity rarely captured in photography. Below the photograph is a quotation: "To be right is the most terrific personal state that nobody is interested in." The photograph, the typography, the printing, the frame, the white space, the proportions have a nice balance—nothing missing, nothing extra.

He sees me me studying the piece and says, "Franz Kline."

"Kline, the Abstract Expressionist? Where did you come by this photograph?"

"I took it." He continues looking at my work; I fight to keep silent so he can finish his pauses and continue his thought.

"In my twenties, I was determined to be a painter. Kline held court in a café I frequented. It took about eight years of very concerted work to realize I was not going to succeed as a painter. Kline's brilliance rendered that process bearable." He says this very simply. Here is a kindred spirit: someone who knows first hand of the struggle with definitions of art and design.

A definition presents itself, unbidden: "All creative people set out to make art; some of us end up as designers." I shudder and decide to reject this definition.

"I want to give you a jacket to design."

The galley-carrying assistant knocks on the door and strides in. She hands him another manuscript, saying, "OLI format, red sticker. 2,000 hardcover, 10,000 paper."

Just as the paperback world has cover formats, Oxford—and most university presses—has standard book design formats for certain subjects or series. This means a

TO BE RIGHT
IS THE MOST TERRIFIC
PERSONAL STATE
THAT NOBODY
IS INTERESTED IN.

certain successful book design has been chosen as a format—certain metrics such as page size, typographic styling, and printer are all predetermined and so the book is produced quickly with a minimum of effort and very predictable expense. "Red sticker" means "Drop whatever you are doing and work on this till so that project makes the fastest possible progress."

Schneider diverts his attention from me momentarily to the stack of paper. He fans through the pages, letting several hundred sheets flip by uniformly in several seconds. He looks at the last page number and hands it back to his production assistant, who is waiting expectantly.

"256 pages. Yankee can deliver galleys in three weeks." She nods assuredly and exits. Schneider is the most economical person I have ever met. Not a word, not a motion is wasted. He hands me a printed book jacket, a synopsis of a book, and a purchase order.

"Call me with questions. I need your sketch a week from today. Sorry, have to send you off. Do this well and we can use you regularly."

When I get back, Bertoli is furious, bellowing, "You picked a bad day to go AWOL!" I call Geri and tell her not to hold dinner, and by 9:30 p.m. Bertoli has most of the sketches and artwork she needs for her cover meeting tomorrow.

The book jacket Schneider assigns me is Wexley and Yukl's *Organizational Behavior and Industrial Psychology,* a thick paperback in an established OUP format, but there is still room to make the cover exciting. I know Schneider uses the Optima font family for his own work, and it suits the book's subject, so it is a safe bet. I have two colors to work with, no more. I execute four sketches that night and do a dozen more over the weekend.

My Bertoli toggle is tuned in to paperback readers, so working for a new art director and academic audience makes my decision making a little trickier. I've seen Oxford's line. Jim Burke's words pop into my head: Be sure to give Mr. Schneider a quart of milk along with all that milkshake!

I deliver two quarts of milk and a milkshake, two days early. I do not hear from Schneider, and as each day passes I am more convinced that I've missed the mark. Book editors are notoriously capricious, having their own preconceptions about an author and a book. How dare they!

I have not heard from Oxford for several weeks, and I'm reaching for the phone to call the next card in my stack when I get a voice message. He does not identify himself, but I recognize Schneider's voice. "I have another job for you. Can you come over after work?"

Wexley and Yukl is approved. A new portfolio piece, and I can toss a piece of student work out of The Valise! I do several more book jackets for him.

Tress's book *Shadow* comes out, and I show a copy to Schneider on one of my visits. Schneider studies it, pursing his mouth slightly, and begins, "Nice restraint. You like doing interiors?"

I say yes, thinking how best to elaborate.

Schneider saves me the trouble. "We are losing one of our designers. Would like you to sign on?"

He tells me how much he can pay; it's a 25 percent raise. My savings are depleted from my long job hunt. On the other hand, I feel great affection and loyalty for my tough taskmasters at Avon Books, even though I have been there less than a year.

I agonize for a day, discuss the situation with Geri, and conclude that the prospect of a raise and a chance to do more whole books is too good to pass up. I make a detour on my way to work at Avon to tell Schneider I am coming. He seems to know ahead of time, and hands me a weighty manuscript.

"This will be your first job—I made a copy of the manuscript, but don't lose it. Can you start the twenty-fifth?"

I like this style of communication. We read each other, we agree and discuss only what needs articulation. I'm not sure I can finish all that Avon expects from me by the twenty-fifthth, nine days away.

Bertoli scoffs, "And you really think you'll be happy at a stodgy scholarly press?"

"It's a 25 percent raise," I tell her, "and I'm eager to try the challenge of longer texts to design."

She says, with a good-natured exasperation, "Well, I don't understand that!"

I leave Avon after only nine months, during which I strengthen my portfolio, and the number of printed impressions bearing my designs goes from several thousand to several hundred million. The intense learning begun under Barbara Bertoli continues, in completely different ways, at the deft hand of Frederick Schneider.

TO BE RIGHT ... DECODED

I visit Schneider's office several times a day, and the Franz Kline statement that hangs on his wall seems by turns simple, utterly enigmatic, sarcastic, and alternately transcendent and nihilistic. What makes this saying important enough to hang on his wall? The fact that Schneider's office is otherwise devoid of decor puts a focus on it, like the effect of a gallery hung with a single painting.

Kline's enormous, dark, brooding canvases were so original and yet so universal that when they were first exhibited they caused shock and consternation as well as raves. They seemed to be land-scapes of boulders that had collided in prehistoric times, but had only just been discovered by humans. I decide that Kline isn't talking about being correct; he's talking about being right with oneself, about doing the work that is yours alone to do. Kline's work lets the viewer know what it means to be right. Yet his powerful sentence is ungrammatical! One could rewrite it: "To be right with oneself is the most important thing." Dud. "To be right is the most personal state in which no one is interested." Clunk. I have not discussed it with Schneider since my first visit to his office.

When I finally do bring it up, he remarks with characteristic brev-ity, "Be suspicious of any truth too plainly stated."

I try again, "Do you think the incorrect grammar is intentional?"

He squints at me. This is Schneiderspeak for "Oh, yes, I see what you are saying." He then answers.

"Kline believed that truth is so complex that it must be—can only be—stated as a conundrum, a collision of opposing forces. He's not talking about being right in the sense of using correct grammar or following the norms. He is talking about being right with yourself, knowing who you are, why you are here, and having the courage to be both ambitious about where you can go and content with what you have. So perhaps he would say the grammar serves a dual pur-pose: making the sentence seem more spontaneous and approach-able, and yet breaking rules to do so. It was there in his paintings: collisions, opposing forces, the struggle to be right. I would say, however, that colliding forces are great for painting, but best used sparingly in design."

I think about Schneider's decision to give up painting and earn his living as an art director. I had recently read, during a week of train rides, Somerset Maugham's great *Of Human Bondage*, which contains a very poignantly articulated description of this very category of decision. Schneider did not give up because he couldn't sell paintings, but because he realized, with the help of Kline's

> 66 *Kline believed that truth is so complex that it must be—can only be—stated as a conundrum, a collision of opposing forces. It's truth to use sparingly in design.* 99

mentorship, that he would not be a painter of the first rank. He gave up the opportunity to originate content and found a way to be at peace with being the form giver to the intellectual community of authors. Maybe Schneider has Kline's saying on his wall to remind him that doing design was the "right" path for him, even if it meant putting aside a more expressive set of tools he loved.

Schneider starts me off doing a half-dozen books that follow one of the OUP house formats. In that case, the designer does nothing original, but simply marks up the manuscript to conform to the style, then makes sure it gets set correctly as the proof goes back and forth from compositor to designer to editor to author, and then back again. Such formats also mean an experienced designer can handle about three times the workload.

Schneider can design books without making any sketches; he can go from a mental image to a set of specifications to the compositor. However, a mild nervous condition prevents him from drawing anything. Several times a day he asks me to handle something for him: drawing rules or ornaments, rendering ornate initials in pen and ink. One day he has me create a repeat pattern after the fashion of a William Morris textile to decorate the slipcase for the Oxford edition of Trollope's *The Palliser Novels*.

There are any number of disparaging terms in graphic design jargon to describe a designer who merely executes orders from others: "wrist" or "grunt" are two of the more polite such names. Applying them to one's self is a great confidence killer. I like helping Schneider, however, such tasks don't add immediately to my future, my legacy, my portfolio. I am impatient to grow, and I don't want to think I've left the energetic atmosphere of Hearst Corporation to become a grunt at, as Barbara Bertoli put it, "a stuffy old academic press."

After a few months of this, I am drawing a complex diagram and worrying about having to postpone designing the titles assigned to me. Schneider stops by and begins his characteristic pause that precedes his speaking. "I apologize for loading you up with production work just now. I ... appreciate the attention you give those details. You do them ... as if they were your own."

I am disarmed. I must think of the right response. In the spaces between his phrases, the nature of the larger bargain between us crystallizes before me.

"Well, Fred, it's a two-way street. I appreciate every opportunity to design something and I learn a lot by observing the way you work."

He says thoughtfully, "When you have experience, you have to barter it for access to young, nimble talent. The young talent takes the bargain to gain experience and opportunity. It's a creaky, lopsided sort of arrangement, but with the right matchup, it works remarkably well." Barter. I remember Ruedi Rüegg used that same word to describe his training under Müller-Brockmann.

That is just the cognitive adjustment I need: I'm doing wrist work, but there's a payout. Bertoli, by snipping up my work and struggling with the pieces, teaches me the Bertoli toggle. Schneider, delegating carefully proscribed pieces of his book, lets me bargain my small motor skills for participation in a large, complex workflow. Both mentors require me to rise to the opportunity. That's what he means by "the right matchup."

With that conversation, I see the way to channel my impatience. I have to anticipate what each book will need in advance. At production meetings I begin to pay attention to what each book is about, and offer to handle production details that might otherwise become outside expenses, no matter which team is doing it.

"Wrist" and "grunt" are two of the more polite terms for graphic designers who merely execute orders from others. Having them applied to one's self is a great confidence killer, and they miss the real point of mentoring.

Schneider notices, and pays me back in kind, announcing to me one day, "I'm assigning this book to your team. None of our standard formats are right for this, so you'll have to design a new one." He leaves me with a briefing sheet. Like the

Two covers produced under Schneider's direction. The transition to university press expectations meant the use of pattern and symbol rather than illustration. Schneider strove to make books that were memorable—both interior and cover—that would stay in the reader's mind as a residual pattern, to recall the reading experience months, even years later.

book *Shadow,* it is an outlier, a book that, because it does not fall easily into our workflow routine, represents a design opportunity. It's a book about the history of American show business. There is a chapter on the Ziegfeld Follies, one on minstrels, one on Vaudeville, and still another on the traveling circus. Each of these periods also has its own typographic tradition, though that is not mentioned by the author. I read the entire manuscript that night and sit down with Schneider the next morning to discuss it.

"How much am I allowed to do with this?"

I wait for his pause to end. Maybe he needs a more specific question. I try, "There's a lot of opportunity to express each chapter with the typographic tradition of its ..." Schneider makes a minimalist motion with his free hand, sort of like he is wiping dust off a window between us, so I can see more clearly.

With his usual economy of expression he says, "You may consider it a plum project." Without instructing me to do anything in particular, he seems to be saying, "Design what you think it needs. Show us what you

> **❝ When you have experience, you barter it for access to young, nimble talent. Young talent takes the bargain to gain experience and opportunity. It's a lopsided sort of arrangement, but with the right matchup, it works quite well. ❞**

can do!" I pour a lot of time into *On with the Show*, being careful to involve the author, making sure the team is OK with the "milkshake" instead of a "quart of milk." Schneider rewards me with another plum project, designing new branding for OUP to commemorate the 500th anniversary of publishing at Oxford. The quincentenary gets a lot of publicity, and my graphics are picked up in many publications. Schneider has made good on his implicit promise to "barter youth for experience." The wrist work pays off with projects that give my career visibility and momentum.

George Nelson
PHILOSOPHY OF DESIGN

George Nelson (1908–1986) was born in Hartford, Connecticut, and educated in fine art and architecture at Yale University. He worked briefly doing renderings for Adams & Prentice in New York. In 1932 he entered and won the Rome Prize, then spent the next two years traveling Europe, where he met many important designers of the day including Mies Van der Rohe, Walter Gropius, Ettore Sottsass, and Gio Ponti. From his early days, Nelson wrote often and with great clarity about architects, design, and modern solutions to the problems of living. He wrote for *Pencil Points*, the precursor to *Progressive Architecture*, and was instrumental in founding *Industrial Design* magazine (now published as *I.D.*) He wrote for *Architectural Forum* and eventually wrote or co-authored eight books, including *Tomorrow's House* and *George Nelson on Design*.

During his four-decade-long relationship with furniture maker Herman Miller, Nelson introduced to his client many other designers, including Charles and Ray Eames. This resulted in many exceptional designs. Nelson's wide-ranging interests led to the production of furniture, world's fair pavilions, branding systems, interior designs, product design, and several dozen playful designs for decorative modern clocks. His designs are in the collection of the Museum of Modern Art, New York. A strong believer in the power of design, Nelson wrote and spoke throughout his life with the objective of making design a natural, enjoyable part of life. Later in his career he became an advocate of "visual literacy," the idea that knowing how to experience beauty is as important as proficiency in reading and mathematics. This he outlined in his book *How to See*.

JANUARY 1977 I rediscover the article on George Nelson that Barbara Bertoli had given me. It takes a few volleys of calls to Nelson's office and Pratt to secure permission to audit Philosophy of Design, but it's a breeze compared to job hunting. Or maybe it's a breeze *because* of job-hunting boot camp. A new semester has begun, so it's a good time to start. The class meets in a modest-size, second-story classroom on Pratt's Manhattan campus. There are about twenty undergrad design students.

To my astonishment, several students sleep during the first half of his first lecture and disappear after the break, but Nelson keeps up a full head of steam. He has a great ability to take a question and elaborate on its meaning, weaving it into the rest of the discussion. I introduce myself after the first class. He remembers that his secretary mentioned someone wanting to audit his class, and suddenly he focuses sharply on me. I tell him about my education and career path in a sentence, and recall the article in *I.D.* magazine. "The title of the course, Philosophy of Design, really hooked me."

He feigns despondency, "Well, I'm glad it kept someone awake!"

Nelson's class becomes the high point of my week. Raconteur, storyteller, evangelist of good sense—here is a man who has assumed the role of spokesperson for the design profession, yet rarely mentions the word design. After several classes, I marvel to Nelson about his ability to talk about design so fluidly, to discuss complex design problems and make the solutions understandable. He squares his shoulders to me like Napoleon bucking up a scared young artillery-man before battle. "Public speaking is not an innate talent. It's just practice," he says matter-of-factly. I find this simple bit of mentoring very helpful. The extraordinary speaking skills of leaders like Eames, Bass, Fuller, and the more recent example of Peter Mayer make it look easy, but experience teaches otherwise. The idea that, with prep-aration and practice, I could become as eloquent as they about this profession lifts my courage. Nelson's mission as a design spokesman is to convince his listeners that world-class design is within reach for anyone with good sense and a passion for quality. Nelson can get up in front of an audience and talk about design extemporaneously for several hours without repeating himself. The class has no reading list, no advance lesson plan. The occasional outside assignments are very open-ended. I am under a spell listening to Nelson. He talks about the social impact of products and places. One evening he begins with a discourse on how the invention of the elevator is responsible for exacerbating slums.

A world traveler, he sells his services as an architect not by showing his own buildings, but by screening his show *The Civilized City*, which consists of several hundred visuals of amenities that make urban spaces come alive.

Another night he talks about great architects of his youth, how he met Frank Lloyd Wright. I feel a link, through this man, of mentor-ing relations going back through the generations of design leaders. At the beginning of one class, a young architect asks about stream-lining. Nelson pronounces it one of the master ideas of twentieth-century design, and proceeds to devote the rest of the two-hour lecture to that subject.

"Streamlining began as an engineering technique, but quickly became a driver for style. Even things that did not need to move through air or water were subjected to wind tunnels—furniture, appliances, even parking meters! A style begins with a philosophical zeal, proclaiming a new relationship between form and meaning. As it is assimilated into the mainstream, it becomes a vernacular, some-thing applied more and more carelessly. Even-tually it becomes a form of visual pollution,

> **66 Public speaking is not an innate talent. It's just practice. 99**

and some new innovation captures the popular imagination with a new, world-changing design philosophy."

Someone asks for another example. Nelson relates his own experience: Assigned to write for Time-Life the book that became *Tomorrow's House*, he filled chapters easily but got stuck on storage. He

Nelson is a captivating spokesman for design. His mission is to convince his listeners that world-class design is within easy reach for anyone with good sense.

recounts, "I found myself staring at the wall, idly wondering how thick it is. Six inches, maybe? Then, for no reason at all, it hits me: add three inches on either side and you have a cubic foot times the dimension of the wall, more volume than the average closet." This line of inquiry leads to some quick prototypes, and he writes a chapter about "The Storage Wall," which becomes the most influential part of the book and a signature of post–World War II interior design. As product designer and architect, Nelson is unabashedly consumerist. "I'm comfortable with my role helping people feel good about their material surroundings," he says, "about helping them find an identity in the things they need to live."

This contrasts sharply with Victor Papanek's philosophy, and with Buckminster Fuller's desire to redesign the world into a more harmonious system. I mention this contrast one evening, and Nelson momentarily stops in his tracks. I worry that I've offended him. But he reflects the question to the class. "Anyone have an answer for Mr. Laufer?"

There are a few good comments, which Nelson weaves together when he summarizes his thoughts. "Remember that design has only recently become an academic subject, taught in universities. It began as a survival skill, before recorded history. Design is a force for good, no one would argue with that. Both Fuller and Papanek rely on a large pool of students whose tuition pays for their theorizing, and whose assigned classwork becomes the validation of their theories. That does not mean it is bad work or that the theories are wrong. But industrial design is all about selling survival strategies—for countries, for companies, for products, but ultimately always for people."

Nelson never tries to explain the aesthetics of design. He has learned that "people stories" are the most powerful drivers of

> ❝ Remember that design has only recently become an academic subject, taught in universities. It began as a survival skill, before recorded history. Industrial design is all about selling survival strategies—for countries, for companies, for products, but ultimately always for people. ❞

clients' hiring decisions. He talks process with his students, but to clients and the public he likes to dwell on benefits. He rarely talks about style. He is more interested in how lives get better when the built environment is created "as if people mattered." That phrase he borrows from E. F. Schumacher's book *Small Is Beautiful*. Nelson describes this book as "a slightly subversive critique of capitalism that ought to be required reading for all citizens." Another evening, Nelson gets on a roll talking about Venice. "Venice was a unique collaboration. There were visionary designers there, capable of painting word pictures of things that had never been dreamt. They convinced their bankers that through design, they could establish a mercantile empire, drawing customers to their own, uniquely irresistible headquarters." One of the students in the class asks if there will ever be another Venice. "It isn't the bankers' fault that New York isn't as spectacular as Venice! Those boys down on Wall Street have the money to build Venice ten times over. If there's a reason, we have to bear the responsibility. We in the design community must not be making a compelling enough case for the power of visionary design."

One of the students asks Nelson how to decide which ideas are most worthy of developing. Nelson is emphatic!

"All the good ones! Often, you think you have too many ideas, but they are really variations on the same idea. Other times, you realize that of a hundred ideas, eighty have been done already and eighteen are original but on quick examination they fall somewhere between mediocre and stupid. That leaves you with two good, original ideas! You have an obligation to use yourself up! Don't die with a single good idea left in you untried."

Nelson gets started talking about the creative process, how one idea leads to the next. He is very animated on the science of heuristics, which he describes as an enthusiastic intellectual wandering.

I have heard that definition before, then remember Nelson is a close friend of Charles and Ray Eames. The mind, Nelson contends, makes connections between things seemingly unrelated. Why, he poses to the class, when you are working on a problem, do unconnected thoughts pop into your head? He believes that these thoughts, far from being disruptive, are gifts. The connection may obvious, or may require time to puzzle out, but it's there.

"Bucky Fuller describes [in *Nine Chains to the Moon*] his creative process as laying out a problem in his mind, then forgetting about it, and his 'phantom captain' solves the problem and leaves the solution lying on the table, for his conscious mind to pick up and execute. Charles and Ray Eames talk at length about 'finding the connections' as an enduring theme in their work." Nelson has a storehouse of information about creative people; I ask him about this. He "went through a phase" where he couldn't read enough biographies of famous creative people. He wanted to see the big patterns in their lives. This discussion period concludes with Nelson proposing a project: The class should undertake to do a visual demonstration of heuristic thinking. We are to try to explain how a creative idea develops. We will share them at the next class.

Oxford is in its busy season, right before the Frankfurt Book Fair, and everything is red sticker, front burner, short fuse. But this assignment is too good to pass up. Even though I'm auditing the class, I decide to do the assignment.

I assemble a slide show from my existing collection of photographs. There is no theme or outline, except that each slide must have some direct visual connection to the next. The first picture has a subject that is red and round; the next slide has round but not red, and has a face in it. The next slide also has a face on the moon; the slide after that no face but a lunar theme, and so on. I throw in a quick title slide—"Philosophy of Design/Science of Heuristics"—and catch a few hours sleep before it is time to get up for the train. I worry that it's too slapdash but I'm out of time, nervous that I may not show well against the other students, concerned that Nelson may decide I have no talent or am clueless. I worry that the other students will go first and there will

> **❝ You have an obligation to use yourself up! Don't die with a single good idea left in you untried. ❞**

be no time for my effort. At one point, I decide to skip it and go to class empty-handed. After all, I'm only auditing—no one would expect me to participate for no credit.

Nelson starts the class without mentioning the assignment, and the discussion meanders. At the break, Nelson asks me about the slide projector. I remind him of the heuristics assignment, and he is surprised I remember it. Oh, you have something? It turns out I'm the only one who took up the challenge! I'm astounded, but at least I have all the time I want. I screen my slides and make the first few connections verbally. The audience gets into it immediately, saying the connections out loud, racing to see who picks it up first. I'm surprised how many possible connections are latent in each pair of images. Nelson asks where I got the slides in the presentation. I tell the class cautiously, "I have this chronic photo habit. I have to shoot, sometimes without knowing why, except it's fun."

Nelson seems delighted with this. He exclaims, "Exactly! To succeed in design, you must develop your own resource library. Collect now, and make the connections later. The time you invest in processing the things you find intriguing will yield big dividends. You can, of course, begin with an intention to seek out and study certain things. But you can work the other way: keep your eyes open, and when something knocks you over, sketch it or photograph it or write in your diary. You don't think your way to creative work. You work your way to creative thinking."

I breathe a sigh of relief and click through the rest of the image chain, as the class continues to shout out ideas. It takes on the flavor of a game of charades. Although visual stimulation is a solitary event, it can also excite social interaction.

Nelson now takes an interest in me. The little initiative I put forward in the scrap of time I had available—combined with the energy stored in my random photographs—was enough to enlist his help. He invites me to visit his office so he can see my work.

The door to his office says "Nelson Design." Next to it is another door that says "Nelson and Chadwick, Architects."

> **" To succeed in design, you must develop your own resource library. Make the collections now, then make the connections later! "**

On closer examination, I see that the second door is meticulously painted on the wall, not a real door, but a trompe l'oeil rendering. The illusion is good—painted to match the lighting on the real door! Nelson's office is an open

> **You don't think your way to creative work. You work your way to creative thinking.**

plan. I'm surprised that it is not slick. No two chairs are the same. There are components of many different office systems. A menagerie of clocks and lamps can be seen. He sees me taking it all in.

"We do a lot of corporate interior design," he explains. "I never like to specify something as intimate as a chair unless we have lived with it ourselves to make sure it sits properly." I'm a bit puzzled. Here's a man who lives and breathes the philosophical movements of design, and yet his own office, while comfortable and organized, is unlikely to appear in any design magazines.

I venture, "Having taken Philosophy of Design, I thought your office would be filled with Rietveld chairs and Futurist paintings!"

A smile appears fleetingly at the corner of his mouth. "Try to snuggle with your honey bun in one of those chairs! Who wants to sit on a manifesto?"

I suggest to Nelson, "'Who wants to sit on a manifesto?' could be a paraphrase of Mies van der Rohe's maxim, 'It's more important to be good than to be original.'"

Nelson considers: "A wittier paraphrase, if I do say so myself! Both teachings hold across the whole range of creative activities. Design is first and foremost about serving the needs of the user; only then is it about expression. In the best design, the two appear effortlessly combined. But any seasoned designer knows it is rarely effortless."

We make our way to his office. The Valise is bulging—Herb Stern's advice notwithstanding, I have brought a lot to show Nelson, so he can help me pick my best work. It's about 7:30 p.m. A few of his staff members have left, some are still studiously bent over drawing boards. He looks carefully at each sketch and sample I show him. From time to time one of his designers hovers at the door and he waves them in. They say little, holding up a drawing for him to see. He tells them nothing specific:

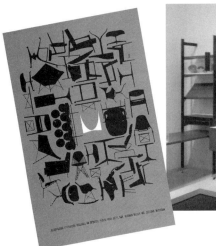

Nelson was trained as an architect, but came of age during the depression of the 1930s when, as he put it, "no architects were being called." So he maintained a flexible attitude, designing everything from furniture and packaging to world's fair pavilions and corporate headquarters. His clocks are a good example of the combination of playfulness and sophistication that characterizes his oeuvre. The storage wall concept–a category of furnishing now in use worldwide–was a Nelson innovation.

> **❝ Design is first and foremost about serving the needs of the user; only then is it about expression. In the best design, the two appear effortlessly combined. But any seasoned designer knows it is rarely effortless. ❞**

"Good, but simplify." Another time, "The patterns will be more effective if balanced by some quiet space." Then, on the next viewing, "Good, *finis*. Send it." He says little about my work, and I struggle to keep my silence while he concentrates. At last he says, "I'm glad you brought all this. Now I see you better." He offers to write a letter of introduction to anyone I might be interested in seeing. I have the sense of a door opening. I give him the names and addresses of my toughest and most desired targets: Paul Rand, Herb Lubalin, Ivan Chermayeff, Massimo Vignelli."

He nods. "Lubalin I don't know, really. Is there anyone else?"

Dang. "Lou Dorfsman, at CBS?"

"Good, now tell me why you picked these four." I have to admire this man. He is really a skilled mentor. His question forces me to articulate what I'll need to have on the tip of my tongue when I meet these titans. I do pretty well explaining the first three, but stammer when I get to Vignelli.

Nelson interjects, "Telesis. Massimo and Lella's work is all about planned progress... toward a future in which everything looks like what it means, and is uplifting to the human spirit. It would help if you were Italian. Since you aren't, you must certainly show an appreciation for all things Italian. Massimo believes very strongly that Italy is, if not the source of modern culture, at least its nucleus. He argues—very persuasively—that the Italian system of design education is the best ever devised."

A few days later Nelson's receptionist calls me to suggest I come by to pick up the letters. It is exciting to have them, yet at the same time, I need to keep my expectations realistic. Will the doors that have been shut for so long suddenly open?

PORTFOLIO TRANSITIONS, *or*
NEVER LET A GOOD CRISIS GO TO WASTE!

A week from the postmark of Nelson's letter to Vignelli, I have heard nothing, so I visit Penn Station Booth 6 to call.

The receptionist at Vignelli Associates, whom I have called numerous times over the past year, has the smooth voice of a classical radio announcer. She answers as though it was our first conversation and she is delighted I have called.

"Yes, Mr. Laufer. Mr. Vignelli will see you."

The appointment is several weeks away. I have got to do something about presenting my work. The Great Midwest Mounted Valise, as a presentation concept, is past its usefulness. I have some book designs and jackets of which I am proud, but the student work, industrial pieces from Pittsburgh, and small freelance jobs make an incoherent mélange. The oversize black case, purchased five years ago at the Carnegie Mellon Bookstore, is frayed from too many curbs, train rides, and from being stuffed into Penn Station Booth 6.

I am striding up Park Avenue, puzzling over how to solve this problem, when I see Herb Stern coming along. He is wearing his Big Apple blinders, seeing only what must be seen, probably thinking about his own career hurdles.

"Mr. Stern." No response. "Herb!"

"Ah, hello!" His face lights up with recognition. "David, yes?"

I tell him I'm still hoping to work for him at Ziff-Davis, and that I've put his advice into daily practice. He asks how things are going and if I'm still at Avon Books. I tell him I'm trying to work up a better presentation of my portfolio for a big interview.

"I would say come up and show me the progress, but I'm just about to go on vacation. But the key to a great portfolio is simplify, simplify, simplify."

He bids me call him in a few weeks, and continues on. Our encounter leaves me standing in front of a luxury luggage store. In the window is a leather briefcase: handsome, slightly larger than a standard briefcase, but also slightly thinner. I wonder how thick a stack of samples it will hold—perhaps two inches? I peer more closely to see the price: almost two weeks' take-home pay. I draw a long breath.

"May I help you?" asks the elegantly groomed salesman, who has ventured outside. "That case is a beauty, and Monday it is going to be on sale. The savings will be significant."

A thought stirs in the back of my mind. It would be really nice not to be dragging a giant case to the office; it's bulky and it screams, "Hey, I'm job hunting!"

"Can I look at the case more closely, please?" I have a color swatch book with me; I use it to match the colors of the exterior leather, the linen highlights, and the dark slub in the linen. I measure the maximum size sheet that can go in the case without folding. There is a laminated display on the counter; the salesman tells me they are made at a local supply company called Laminall.

I leave a card with the salesman and he promises to call me when the case goes on sale. A freelance check arrives at the same time as his call, and I take the plunge. Simplify, simplify, simplify. A tight deadline, Herb Stern's fleeting advice, and the leather goods store have intersected fortuitously. I spend several evenings figuring out the details of my new briefcase. The next few nights I painstakingly trim Pantone paper and mount a dozen book jackets and other samples. I get them to the laminator, and if their schedule holds true, I will have samples two days before I am to visit with Vignelli.

Several days later, a call comes from Laminall. The sound of the first few syllables foretells trouble. My samples have been ruined! It is apparently a problem with the adhesive I used to mount my samples; the Laminall rep is very matter of fact. If I bring them new materials, they will expedite, and so on. Brainfog! I am in trouble. It takes several seconds to think through the imperatives of the problem. There is physically not enough time to mount more samples and get them laminated. I have already paid for the case, and the old Valise is not an option. I have to put together something that can fit in the case and that will be of interest to Vignelli.

Fred Schneider cruises by. "Congratulations are in order," he says with characteristic reserve. "Your work for *On with the Show* won an award in the AAUP book show!" He puts a familiar-looking package on my desk. It contains the sample pages we submitted some time back, and a letter from the Association of American University Presses with particulars. I pull out a tape measure; the boards are about a quarter inch too big on one dimension, but can be trimmed to fit the new case. A vague feeling of encouragement scuttles about, like a prisoner trying to remain unnoticed. I take the boards home with me. I spend the evening salvaging what I can of my remaining samples. This setback *would* have to happen before someone important like Vignelli! Why couldn't it be any of the scores of interviews with less riding on them?!

With the interview a day away, Laminall calls, telling me my job is ready. What? Apparently they either misinformed me, or they figured out a way to salvage the first batch. I make the long subway ride and sure enough, there they are. I have a new confidence, and return to sort out my presentation once again.

As I leave Oxford and walk uptown to Vignelli Associates, I feel confident. By the time I reach my destination, however, I'm fighting a nervousness I don't want to carry with me into the interview. No more Great Midwest Mounted Valise—now I have a sleek new Valise Cruiser, the glossy laminated samples, and a brand new AAUP award, along with a few sketchbook pages, some ideation drawings, and letterform tracings. Without a deadline and the chance meeting with Stern, I could never have whipped this together.

Massimo Vignelli
THE AUTEUR SPEAKS

Massimo Vignelli (1931–   ) and his lifelong partner, Lella (1934–   ), are more often named together than individually. The Vignellis were both born and educated in northern Italy, he in Milan and she in Udine. Massimo's forte is graphic design; Lella's family tradition and training were "3-D"—architecture. They met at an architects' convention and were married in 1957. The couple opened an office in Milan, and eventually relocated to New York. Massimo was a cofounder of Unimark, an early leader in the modern discipline of branding. They founded their own design office in 1971, and became

AIGA Medalists in 1982. Charismatic and impeccably stylish, they find a startling array of emotional and intellectual effects with elegant simplicity. Their work includes premier-quality identity systems, maps, toys, tableware, furniture, and interiors. The Vignelli collection, encompassing all their papers and work, resides at the Rochester Institute of Technology.

MARCH 1977 Massimo Vignelli is visible in AIGA, but his work transcends classification as graphic design; his office can design anything. I am eager to know how he attained this exalted level. Sharing the same city with Push Pin Studios and George Nelson and so many other visible figures, Vignelli's work seems to my novice eyes to be utterly simple while retaining a definite point of view, a subtle personality. Hundreds of design firms have embraced the international style, standardized on Helvetica, and turned out clean, fresh, homogeneous work. Vignelli's oeuvre goes beyond: it is archetypal and it exudes optimism.

Vignelli's reception area has fresh flowers that still look perky even though I am visiting him at 5:30. The receptionist is still there, and her polished, media-savvy voice is matched by a news anchor-woman's grooming. Her smile is genuine and words few.

"Mr. Laufer, so good of you to come. Mr. Vignelli asked me to offer you a beverage?" She inflects the statement efficiently into a question and returns with water in a glass of perfect proportions. She observes as I lift it up to see the imprint on the bottom. It appears to be signed by Lella Vignelli, and its manufacture is of high Italian precision.

"You designers!" she says with a hint of affection. "You can't enjoy anything until you know the provenance of it!"

This starts me musing, here in the office of these masters of branding. She is right, but why? When we sense something speaking—fine surfaces, pleasing proportions, materials that are fit for their purpose—we sense the convergence, the rightness of the thing, and we question: how did this come to be made so well? We want to add to our knowledge of sources; like the hunter-gatherers memorizing leaf shapes and studying minerals for their utility, our latter-day survival instinct wants to understand the source of the good experience, to make it repeatable. That is the essence of brand.

Objects of fine art have provenance when their authorship has been confirmed and the chain of ownership is well documented. For design, being mass produced, provenance means something different; it has to do with being made under the supervision of the brand or designer name, and perhaps the client for whom it was created. High provenance is being in a design museum collection. The Vignellis are masters of creating branding because they have created brandable products.

"Mr. Vignelli will see you now."

There are enough people in the office to keep a definite hum of activity, but it is an after-hours hum. Vignelli rises enthusiastically from his chair and gives me a winning smile. His white teeth, salt-and-pepper hair, and perfect touch of tan all create the effect of instant friendliness.

"Forgive the wait; I had to finish briefing a sign manufacturer. The details are so critical. Let me give you a quick tour."

It is in fact a very quick tour. I am not introduced to anyone, and he points out a few of his more visible projects for Knoll. The cubicles are just high enough to protect workers' peripheral vision, but not too tall to peer above without standing. There is a sense of great intentionality about the placement of everything. Here are open spaces, punctuated by a single vase, or framed poster, or maquette. It is not a big office, but it feels spacious because the placement and proportion are so carefully balanced. I am struck by the contrast between the highly designed feeling of the Vignelli Associates office and George Nelson's studio of experiments. There are a few enclosed spaces, and it is to one of these that we retreat.

"Let me take a quick look at your file—yes." He has a wire caddy holding perhaps a dozen file folders: Last Name, First Name, then a space below on the tab. The space below my name says George Nelson. The receptionist's words come back to me, about "wanting to know the provenance of

Aha: *When we sense a product speaking—fine surfaces, pleasing proportions, materials that are fit for their purpose—we sense the rightness of the thing, and our hunter-gatherer instinct wants to know, "What is the source?" That is the essence of brand.*

everything." I am not able to read any other names, but about half of the folders have names or notes on the second line. I muse on how many calls went into each of those folders, awaiting Vignelli's attention, and how many hundreds of callers did not make this group. I begin to see the talent selection process from the other side. Such a flood of new talent, so few places.

He has my resume. "So, Pittsburgh, a good place to start!" He looks up at me with a scrutiny that is intense but somehow still very friendly. "The Bauhaus taught us much by beginning design training close to industry. It is ever so much easier to design well if you know how things are made! Hearst Corporation, then Oxford." He is nodding and takes a slightly longer look. I sense that this is a man who misses no detail of grooming, mannerism, or vocabulary.

"From one side of the literary spectrum to the other!" he quips. "How did you come to know Nelson?" The question takes on a larger meaning for me, knowing how hard it is to get to see anyone in the top ranks. Is he is asking "Were you born to the elite, or are you clever enough to get here by your wits?" He's already taken in my grooming, my best-you-can-do-with-no-money wardrobe, so he knows the answer; he must want to see how I tell the story.

"I worked for Barbara BEAR-toll-ee at Avon Books, and she gave me the *I.D.* magazine article about Nelson. He is teaching a class at Pratt called 'Philosophy of Design'. Nelson let me audit the class, and once I started going, I couldn't get enough. He makes the path to good design seem so natural, almost effortless!"

"Yes, it is rare and valuable to have a fine designer and an eloquent promoter of the whole design profession in the same person." I seem to remember Nelson said something similar about Vignelli. The timing of the interview, the pace says "Now"; I open my spiffy new case, and I set it facing him on his conference table.

"I brought a few examples of older work, but most everything here is in the past 12 months."

Vignelli now goes silent. He takes out the contents of the case, a stack of shiny laminated pieces, trimmed flush to a constant size, and flips through the deck in about ten seconds. He then begins spreading them out into several groups. His attention seems to gravitate toward the typographic examples in the Valise. "You like to draw your own letters!" he says. His voice is enthusiastic. I'm about

Vignelli's designs achieve a timeless feeling, in which functionality and style find a seamless integration. His system maps for New York City's public transit system were more readable than any that went before, and have been widely emulated worldwide. *About Time*, created for Champion International's Imagination Series #24 (left), is certainly one of the most perfectly realized printed showpieces ever produced.

to reply, but Herb Stern's invisible hand on my shoulder says "Don't interrupt when someone is paying you compliments!"

Vignelli continues, "But better still, you don't ruin the letters you change. You have studied typographic history. Your modifications are respectful of the origin and the aesthetics of the workmen who went before you."

I say, "I've been very lucky that Oxford has a longstanding relationship with the Pierpont Morgan Library, so I'm given a reader's ticket to study the old books. Seeing the Gutenberg Bible up close is inspiring."

My mind imagines an audible pop as Vignelli's intense gaze breaks contact with the portfolio; he looks at me with renewed interest. "You have certainly turned that opportunity into a great resource."

This man has a knack for saying what makes you feel good in your soul. His perceptive mind is matched with a gift for expressing what people want the world to see of them. I theorize this is also the source of his exceptional design skill.

"How do you do it?" he asks, motioning a passerby carrying a roll of blueprints as thick as a tree trunk.

Before I answer he says in a curt, specifying tone, "Our friend David here draws letters and ligatures that match their master fonts. He knows the work of the masters. I will get his card for you in case we need him. He works very close by."

The young man nods, looking from the work into Vignelli's eyes with a practiced precision. He is being briefed on a resource and it is up to him to remember it when Vignelli calls on him.

"He has been with us just six weeks. I saw his work in Milan and I knew we had to bring him here. He understands English quite well, and his spoken English is coming along."

I say, "I did not understand the reason why—" I almost say European, but Nelson's words come to me at the last minute, reminding me to focus on Italy—"Italian design is so different, so refined. For too many American designers who don't travel, Italian culture remains a mystery. In Italy, history is alive in every building, not just in books and museums. A week

> **" It is rare and valuable to have a fine designer and an eloquent promoter of the whole design profession in the same person "**

in Florence is, for an American, worth more than a semester in a classroom. In the old country, it seems that every building is revered for its heritage, and every archway, even if broken, still shows its noble origins."

He takes me by the shoulders for an instant, to add emphasis to his thought. "Yes," he agrees, "that is part of it. It is also education. Our intern, whom you just met, studied design the Italian way. In Italy, where—as you observe—the design standards are at least as good as anywhere in the world, all artists and designers are first trained as architects. Only then do they specialize. That is why we build nobly. That is why our graphic design has structure. Very few who study architecture can become great architects, but in this way we educate the future patrons as well as the practitioners."

He comes back to the portfolio, "So, how do you do it? Get your ligatures so close to the originals?" Surely Vignelli knows full well how such ligatures are created, but, like Herb Stern, he wants to know I'm for real.

"I studied under Richard Nebiolo, who drew fonts at Photo-Lettering, and ..." I pause to see if he really does want a full explanation. His interest appears to be gaining so I brief him on Nebiolo's technique of rendering letterforms.

Vignelli is listening intently, going back and forth between my face and the portfolio. He is stopped on one of the type posters in *On with the Show*. It uses the Bodoni family, a timeless classic of Italian origin; perhaps the redrawing of Bodoni has captured his attention? "I do not know this man Nebiolo, but I like him already!"

Vignelli seems pleased with the discourse. He makes no motion to go, but flips back through the work and asks for more detail on pieces he likes. Then, he asks permission to make copies of a few. "You have an amazing ability; I hope Oxford realizes it and is paying you for it." He probably knows about the pay in book publishing. Maybe he is testing me again somehow—like the flexibility of my salary needs?

> **In Italy, where the design standards are at least as good as anywhere in the world, all designers are first trained as architects. Only then do they specialize. That is why we build nobly. That is why our graphic design has structure.**

> 66 *The proximity to art and antiquities—things that move us aesthetically—is a form of riches.* 99

"They pay me in the access to their library and their antiquities. We have a Bruce Rogers pencil tracing for the Oxford Lectern Bible title page hanging on the wall outside my office."

Vignelli affirms, "The proximity to art, antiquities—things that move us aesthetically—is a form of riches." His expression changes, as though an internal timer has sounded. Vignelli closes with, "Well, it is wonderful to know you are so close by. We must find some ways to work together, and please tell George I send my special regards."

As I walk back to Penn Station, I feel that I have failed in that I did not ask Vignelli more about his process and his work, yet I am so bouyed by his enthusiasm for my typography, it still feels successful. It strikes me that so many of the people who are in positions of creative leadership have something similar—Stern, Chwast, Gottschall, Ballantine, Mayer, Leone, Nelson, Vignelli—all seem to share an ability to establish very quickly a bond that feels strong and deep. It is not that they make you feel how valuable they are, it is that they make you feel so valued.

So, Nelson's letter of introduction worked! And just as importantly the occasion forces me to make a new portfolio. I go away feeling that nothing went as expected, yet I feel I have crossed a great threshold in my design career.

James Craig
KEEPING YOUR POWDER DRY

James Craig was born in 1937 in Montreal, and studied fine arts there and in Paris before immigrating to the United States. He received his BFA from Cooper Union and his MFA from Yale University. Craig was the design director for Watson-Guptill Publications for thirty years. He lectured widely and taught typography and design at Cooper Union and at the Academy of Design in Ljubljana, Slovenia. He is a member of the New York Art Directors Club, Type Directors Club, Typophiles, and a past member of the American Institute of Graphic Arts. His publications include *Working with Graphic Designers, Graphic Design Career Guide, Production for the Graphic Designer,* and *Designing with Type: The Essential Guide to Typography.* The remarkable thing about Craig's books is that many have stayed in print and gone through multiple editions, a testament to his ability to simplify and communicate the essence of very subjective topics.

APRIL 1977 The success of my interview with Massimo Vignelli gives me new impetus. I return to examine the names of those on Ed Gottschall's list whom I have not yet reached. Some are famous, some are less well known. By others I have a few words of Gottschall's scrawled to remind me what to say. A few I don't recognize and have no note. One of these last, James Craig, I skip calling until I connect him with his book. *Production for the Graphic Designer* is neatly designed, restrained, and orderly. I see its bold Helvetica cover on many bookshelves in studios uptown and downtown. Finally, I just call, and am invited to visit.

Craig is the art director at Watson-Guptill. They publish quite a few visual books, and many bear Craig's stamp, which is to say they are orderly and easy to navigate, with the design always serving the content well. There is a school of thought that holds this approach as the zenith of design.

> **Many 'great' designers are hit or miss; some days their talent makes great design look effortless. Other days, their fastball just can't find the plate. Conversely, I'm not a great designer, yet I am capable of a great design. I believe we all are.**

Craig looks at my work. I look at his office for clues on how to relate. His workspace has no windows. Publishing houses in New York City usually reserve the window offices for editors. He has a lot of flat file drawers, all labeled in the economical block capitals of an architect's hand. I compliment him on his book. He acknowledges that he wrote it because other Watson-Guptill employees encouraged him to do so, and he figured that it might bring a little extra money. Very self-deprecating. We run through the obligatory questions. What are you looking for? Freelance book design, jackets, contacts with other publishing people.

"Why books?" he asks. "You have a flair for design that does not often find expression in books."

I have to acknowledge this compliment. "I do like variety, yet I especially like doing books. They are perhaps not flashy, but they seem like the most permanently important thing a graphic designer can do. He nods; we share a bedrock belief there, no need for small talk. This is a very purposeful man. We discuss whom I have already seen, and a few of the design studios that might like my portfolio.

Then he says, "I'm not a great designer, in the sense that everything I touch goes into a design publication or wins an award. I don't have the social connections or the oratory to sell. But many 'great' designers are hit or miss; some days their talent makes great design look effortless. Other days, their fastball just can't find the plate. Conversely, I—as a designer of no special talent—am capable of a great design. I believe we all are. You have to hone your work skills so you can do good work day in and day out, and watch for the stars to align. If there were a recipe for the ideal design project, it would read something like this:

- Just enough time, but with a definite deadline.
- A budget that gives you a bit of running room.
- An encouraging client who trusts your abilities.
- A subject that hooks your personal interest.

And—*here's the important ingredient*

• A designer to observe that the right ingredients are all there.

"Combine ingredients in an atmosphere of excitement and optimism, serve hot.

"It may still not win awards, but you'll know the perfection of your design the moment you get it roughed in. If you throw yourself into every project as though it were a gold medal candidate, you will dash yourself to pieces. Discipline yourself to do good, clean, sensible work day to day and keep your powder dry. Opportunities for great design come along in unexpected places. Be alert—live for those projects."

This is not what I expect to hear from Craig. It does not fit the pattern of Heinz Edelmann, or Charles Eames, or Seymour Chwast. Craig is matter of fact, but he may have given me the single most practical piece of advice to come out of my New York years. Rarely do I begin a new project without thinking of Craig's recipe and doing a quick inventory of the elements necessary for great work.

We talk a little further. Great clients are not the ones who spend the most money; they're the ones who figure out they get more results with less control. Edelmann's quest is for the flexible client, who may not always pay well but trusts his genius to let him do his flamboyant work. Craig's work is completely different than Edelmann's, maybe opposite: disciplined and spare, to the point of invisibility to the lay reader. Yet he too is alert to the right working conditions. Edelmann relies on an audacious self-confidence, walking away from relationships that don't give him room to be explosive. Craig is willing to do orderly and professional work and wait for an opportunity for exceptional work. Yet both Craig and Edelmann are attempting to describe the same thing, something that can't be fully explained—something personal yet universal. What is the common thread? I wonder, as I leave the Watson-Guptill offices. Both are seeking work that fits their criteria for success, but Edelmann fires his clients, burns his outdated

> **" If you throw yourself into every project as though it were a gold medal candidate, you will dash yourself to pieces. Opportunities for great design come along unexpectedly. Be alert—live for those projects. "**

Craig's suite of books for graphic designers is valuable for both individual professionals and for the profession as a whole. They establish the idea that there are core disciplines for the communication process, ideas and relationships between form and content that apply, regardless of the medium. Craig has continued to reinforce this idea with updated editions as technology changes.

samples, and does spectacular work. He does throw himself into every piece as though it were a gold medal winner. Craig goes with the flow, and waits for opportunity. As I swim in the sea of New York traffic, it hits me: it has to do with the number of opportunities available. A staffer cannot choose clients, and so the opportunity flow is relatively finite. Craig writes his own books to improve the odds. The independent designers who have been able to generate enough opportunities can uphold their quality by turning away the work that does not fit their personal recipe. Nelson uses public speaking and publishing; Edelmann uses motion pictures; everyone who succeeds in a big way has mastered the art of increasing the number of opportunities that flow his or her way.

Aha: It's disheartening to try to produce good design where it's not wanted or remunerated. It is also wrong to let your expectations be lowered so that you miss the opportunity to do exceptional work when the time is ripe.

It's disheartening to try to produce good design where it's not wanted, not remunerated, sometimes not tolerated. Craig's remarks suggest that the opposite is also true: It is also wrong to let your own expectations to be lowered, and thus miss the opportunity to do exceptional work when the time is ripe. Craig has—perhaps unintentionally—given me a vital idea. I can't increase my native talent. I have limited control over opportunity. I can, however, adopt the discipline to make the most of the talent I do have, and to maximize those opportunities that do come my way.

TIPPING POINT ON A TRAIN

MAY 1977 New York is in a raw emotional state; there has been a bloody accident that is all over the news, involving a helicopter shuttle from Kennedy Airport to the top of the Pan Am building in midtown Manhattan. I am very familiar with this shuttle, because from my north-facing window at Oxford I feel the percussive whump, whump, whump as the copter settles several times a day onto the rooftop heliport ten blocks away. During a recent rush hour, one of the choppers had malfunctioned, and there was terrible carnage. People standing by were cut to pieces. The part of the story that gets the most buzz, though, is the tragedy of a commuter walking down Madison Avenue. Fifty-nine stories below and several blocks away from the accident site, she is struck by a piece of the helicopter's rotor and killed without ever knowing what hit her. Numerous others are injured by what was described as a hailstorm of broken glass. I even hear that Ed Gottschall sustained an injury from this glass while walking in the area, though fortunately not too serious. In Manhattan, everyone is a pedestrian for part of the day, everyone identifies with this commuter. Everyone's inner voice says, "That could have been me!"

I am in a muddle. I shuttle daily between New Brunswick and New York City. My job at Oxford pays for food, rent, and my train ticket. I make up the difference by staying up all night designing book jackets, so I am always exhausted. I calculate that I am making enough by freelancing to quit my day job, just barely, but letting go of the security of a regular paycheck is terrifying.

If I can get out of the shower by 5:20, I can catch the 6:02 Metroliner out of New Brunswick and get to Midtown between 7:00 and 7:30. Oxford starts at 8:30, so this gives me an hour to deliver freelance projects or make calls from Penn Station Booth 6. The blue bloods from Princeton are on the 6:02 heading for Wall Street, and on one particular morning I sit behind a Princeton banking executive and his boss, the very picture of a British aristocrat, visiting the operations in the States.

My work at Oxford has attuned my ears to the fine points of the King's English, so without intending to eavesdrop, I find myself drawn into their get-acquainted conversation.

The Princetonian is explaining, "No, I don't come from a banking family; in fact I read economics with the intention of teaching, but a college chum convinced me to help him for a year at his start-up company. I became the bookkeeper and CFO and liaison with their bank—Rodney was our lending officer. After it took off, I decided I liked the thrill of companies in their go-go growth years. Rodney had just gotten kicked upstairs and I talked him into letting me start a unit to serve that market. I didn't realize at the time how risky that was, but fortunately my friends brought me enough business to make my quotas until I learned what banking really is. So I fell into it because of enthusiasm, not training or competence!"

His British counterpart nods as if he knows this narrative, and responds, "You know, I'm in banking because it's what my father's family has always done, and I had to do what was expected of me. If I had announced that I wanted to be a soldier or a choreographer, he'd have discouraged me. If I did as you did, following my own interest, the Pater would have given me a stern thrashing. If I persisted, it would go without asking that I'd be disinherited.

"But here in the US, you have this amazing agreement amongst yourselves—you can just declare yourself to be whatever you want, and everyone says, 'OK, fine, jolly good, carry on!'"

He turns to look his American counterpart squarely in the face. *"Do you have any idea how extraordinary that appears to the rest of the world?* How like an impossible dream? That anyone at any station in life can just decide their destiny and enjoy the support of family, government, and even get a tax incentive to do it? Is it any wonder that people are risking their lives stowing away in cargo containers, crossing oceans to immigrate to your 'land of the free?'"

It seems this little paean to American exceptionalism is put in my ear by Providence for me to hear, at this hour, at this juncture in my career. I can't really keep burning both ends of the candle, that's for sure. The newsstand in Penn Station is a wall of tabloid photos of the recent helicopter crash. The sudden feeling of everyday danger somehow puts me over the top. The risk of freelancing seems small compared to the risk of doing nothing.

I must find a way to tell Fred Schneider, who has become like a second father to me. I stammer my way through a sentence or two, but it seems he has expected to hear it for some time. In words remarkably like those still fresh in my ear from the bankers on the train, he tells me, "Well, OK, fine, go ahead. I'll give you as

> **❝ Here in the US, you have this amazing agreement amongst yourselves—you can just declare whatever you want to be, and everyone says, 'OK, fine, jolly good, carry on!' Do you have any idea how extraordinary that appears to the rest of the world? ❞**

> *The feeling of everyday danger puts me over the top. Suddenly, the risk of freelancing is small compared to the risk of doing nothing.*

much freelance work as I can—get an office close by." He writes a recommendation letter that is as humbling as it is useful. It opens many doors. To complicate matters, I break my foot playing squash racquets the same week I begin freelancing, so I hobble to meetings with my leg in a cast and the Valise in a backpack. It generates a lot of sympathy, and work surges. Nevertheless, I don't recommend the old "Break a leg" as a marketing strategy for a new business.

Hermann Zapf
YOUR SOUL'S MUSIC

Born in 1918 in Nuremberg, Germany, Hermann Zapf survived a dangerous period in German history to become one of the greatest font designers of the twentieth century. Germany was struggling to rebuild after World War I. The Spanish flu pandemic took two of his siblings, and a great famine in Germany also hampered his education. Zapf's father was sent to the Dachau concentration camp during the Third Reich; he was later released. Due to this political and economic hardship, Zapf was unable to attend a university, but rather was apprenticed as a retoucher. He was self-taught as a calligrapher, and was influenced by Rudolf Koch. Conscripted into World War II, he developed heart trouble and shuttled around various military roles, finally working as a cartographer. He taught calligraphy and became the artistic director for the Stempel foundry, where his excellent font designs became known worldwide. Zapf's work includes many trademark designs, hundreds of lettering styles, and 30 font families of exceptional quality. His work is widely published in books, periodicals, and featured in a short film, *The Art of Hermann Zapf.*

Zapf was an early proponent of computerized typesetting and held the first professorship in the subject, at the Rochester Institute of Technology. While Zapf's business ventures were sometimes hampered by theft (and by the long-standing legal bias against intellectual property protection for fonts), his creative endeavors were always world class. His classicism is a countervailing force to the ubiquity of Helvetica and the Swiss school, yet his typefaces are more modern than traditional. His writings have been translated into 18 languages. In 2010, Prof. Zapf was awarded Germany's highest civilian honor, the Order of Merit.

MAY 1977 The person who booked the room for Hermann Zapf must have been unaware of Zapf's global reputation. I arrive early and stake out a seat in the third row. Zapf, a highly polished lecturer, starts on time and leaves the seating problem to his hosts. Soon after he begins, I turn and see forty or fifty people standing shoulder to shoulder. More are milling about in the hall.

I give up my seat to gain a better view of Zapf's demonstrations of lettering on the chalkboard. He is so experienced at teaching about letters that he's mastered a technique of breaking chalk sticks into pieces of similar length then drawing calligraphic letters with the broad side of the chalk. Standing at this board he makes extraordinary O's and Q's half a meter high; each stroke is fast and the curves are more perfect than if they had been traced with a French curve.

"The secret is the speed," says Zapf. "If you take time to think, to aim, to guide, you will wobble." He makes his hand go at half speed and circles the few wobbles in the resulting letter. "Of course you have to go slowly and concentrate when you are a student, but when you get serious, you push for speed. If your eye is on the pen, it cannot see where it should be going. The eye should be visualizing the whole word—the complete calligraphic thought—and leading the hand."

Everyone is spellbound. His English is definitely that of a German; his grammar is occasionally bumpy, but his expressions are well studied—delightful companions to his enthusiastic personality.

> *When you get serious about your craft, you push for speed. If your eye is on the pen, it cannot see where it should be going. The eye should be visualizing the whole word—the whole thought—and leading the hand.*

"Yes, you are a very good class and very quiet, but you know, there is no test today and I cannot give you any academic credits—not even at a German school—for listening to me. So I am happy to draw letters for you, or you may ask questions." Without waiting for any questions he continues his rhythm of drawing a few large characters, turning to address his audience first to the right and then to the left, often without lifting his chalk or missing a stroke.

"I learned most in my early years by looking at stone inscriptions. Here in the US you love your billboards," Zapf says, waving his arms to indicate the overpowering size of Times Square graphics, "but in Germany we prefer carving letters on stone. Gravestones, cornerstones, cathedrals, public buildings, even flat rocks in the countryside—anywhere we can get a little space."

The audience laughs at the contrast, as though even the German graffiti artists carved in stone. He motors on, drawing, warming us up with a sly remark while he mesmerizes us; a few large characters fill the board, are erased, new ones appear.

"So, I come across a stone when I am very young, with shapes like this," he draws from memory a replica of the stone, "and they become the basis for many drawings that turn into my font Optima." We applaud quietly in support of Optima as, with facility approaching legerdemain, he renders the full set of Optima capitals in three rows on the chalkboard, perfectly centered.

Now I see why Zapf is so successful. He is not only an artist, he's a showman. He can make creativity appear effortless. I'd pay a hundred bucks for that drawing, which is erased as fast as it appears. I decide he is just entertaining us because we are not giving him any direction about our interest.

Since he gave us leave to ask, I venture a question the next time he turns in my direction. "Professor Zapf, would you mind talking about the business side of being a font designer? How do you present your ideas? How far do you have to develop the design of an alphabet before it is approved?"

He is nodding and stops drawing mid-character. "Ah, here is a gentleman who gives his seat to ladies, and asks questions like a practical fellow!" he says good-naturedly, finishing his

I see why Zapf is so successful. He is not only a gifted artist, he's a showman. He can make creativity appear effortless.

character without looking. A pregnant woman took the seat that I vacated, and Zapf, who controls the pace of the evening masterfully, gives me a very slight nod of approval and continues. In addition to drawing letters and lecturing, he is watching his audience's every move! How many things can this guy do at once? My inner theorist suggests, "A designer demonstrates extraordinary skill. An artist convinces you that *you* have extraordinary gifts and that there is nothing preventing you from using them—starting today."

Zapf answers my question: "For us, on the wet end of lettering, it is an art and we know when something looks right. But if you want to make a font, you work with rooms full of hardboiled business-men." Zapf pauses to consider his tale, then continues, "When you start out, they think you are a pair of hands, and they make you draw things their way. I could never tolerate that and I had a hard time with some bosses. I had to be double good to get them to trust me. That is where I learned the speed, I suppose. But for metal type, your designs have to be cut into metal punches, and for linotype the design of the letters is even more complex, because the brass matri-ces have mechanical limits. And now the photographic fonts require a new way of thinking, because they do not have to allow for the spread of the ink in letterpress. So there is a lot of decision making, and money tied up in the release of a new font. The foundry wants a return on its money!

"And me, you know, I have these needs. My wife is nicely dressed, and we have to have food—" he pauses to allow the audience a second of mirth—"every day, so I need to be paid. I worked on some fonts that were the designs of others, but when the first font of my own design was released it sold well. As soon as you can demonstrate that your work will sell, you need to press your advantage.

"You can't let the hardboiled businesspeople change your idea. If they want me to hold the pencil for them, I tell them, 'You have a good idea there—you should develop a font around that!'"

All the designers I meet who are at the top of their game talk about this tension between their world and the struggle for control. "Yes, I insist on ownership," Zapf continues, "but I always listen to what they say. You know, if you let the hardboileds run everything, the work looks like dung. It makes a profit, but only an average profit. They know this, so they need what we do, but they hate to

> **❝ If you fight just for control of something unimportant, you are 'temperamental.' If you have strong opinions that don't make sales, you are 'unfocused.' But if you fail to insist on something really crucial, then they will say, 'Why didn't you speak up?' ❞**

give up control." Now Zapf proves he is a genius, as both an artist and a teacher. "But you know, we need them, too. If you don't have them, counting your hours, reminding you how expensive everything is, you—well, me anyway—I will dally about, making a hundred variations of the smallest thing." Here his chalk arm blurs to almost invisible speed as he dashes off a dozen ampersands, each a slight variation in design. He uses this superhuman display of virtuosity to drive home his point. "We need them to help us get down to what is really marketable, and get it out the door." He stops drawing and looks around the room, seeming to make eye contact for an instant with every onlooker.

"So you have to learn—it takes time and there is no way to train for it—when to fight for what is right and when to give way to the talents of others. If you fight just for control, for something that does not really matter, you will be thought of as temperamental. If you have strong opinions that don't pan out, commercially, they will dismiss your ideas. Worse, if you fail to insist on something that really is crucial, then they will say, 'Why didn't you speak up?' For example, I did a font based on my own handwriting. The foundry was eager to release it, but they wanted to give it a different name. I called it Norse after my home region, but they were adamant and I decided that as long as I got to do a good font, I should let them handle the marketing."

Zapf has not given the type of answer I wanted, but now others begin asking questions, and the session goes in a dozen directions. The soon-to-be mother raises her hand shyly, and Zapf coaxes her to ask her question by holding up his chalk hand and leaning toward her. She says something very softly, and Zapf nods, drawing a breath. "Our friend asks what advice I have for someone entering the working world who," he thinks how to summarize, "wants to use her artistic talent to make money." He looks back at her. "Yes?" She nods vigorously. Zapf pauses his lettering to give this answer his full attention.

"Nobody can give you specific advice about this. Talent is, by its nature, unique to each individual. There is a young lady, one of my first students, who has amazing gifts. Her portfolio has just a few pieces in it, but they are exquisite. She can draw and letter and play piano and sing, all beautifully. So what does she pick? None of them; they come to her too easily. She drops out of my class for a few weeks, then expects to be admitted again. I have lost touch with her now, but I hope she concentrates on something." For an instant Zapf has a faraway look of compassion and loss, then he continues, "Another student applied to the same advanced-level class—good manual skills, but not gifted. In fact, the first two times she applied to my class, we did not admit her. But the third time, her work had improved, and there was a lot of it. She proved that she was very industrious and committed. I said, 'This student does not give up easily—maybe my teaching will not be wasted on her as it was on the other, more gifted student.'"

Zapf is offering a keen insight here; I jot in my notebook. It isn't only about portfolio. People size you up in a great many ways. They want to know that their investment in you—whether as teacher or employer or client—will bear fruit. But Zapf is not done. He is building, one stroke upon the next.

"If you have talent, you have to decide what to do with it. Concentrate first on the thing that is most important to you. If making money is the most important, use your talent to take you where you can make the most money. Your expression will not be your own, but you will be comfortable sooner.

"If your muse insists that she must be first, that what you have is unique, and must be heard or seen on its own terms, then you must seek the employment that gives you the most room to grow and

> **66** One of my first students has amazing gifts. Her portfolio has just a few pieces in it, but they are exquisite. She can draw and letter and play piano and sing, all beautifully. So what does she pick? None—they all come too easily. **99**

> **Aha:** People size you up in a great many ways. Portfolio is only a part of it. They want to be sure that their investment in you—whether as teacher or employer or client—will bear fruit.

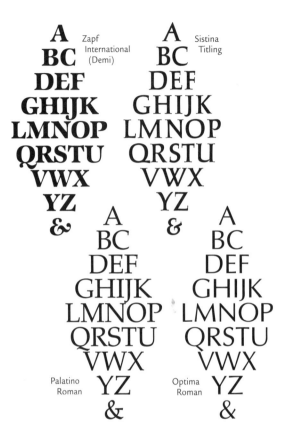

Zapf created several hundred exceptional lettering styles and fonts, as well as logotypes and books for an elite international clientele. Zapf lectured and taught widely; his chalkboard renderings, like the example below, demonstrated his virtuosity and enchanted many audiences. The sheer beauty of his designs revitalized interest in the classical history and practice of calligraphy as a basis for modern design.

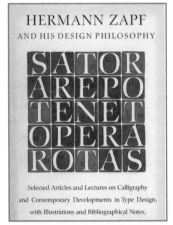

HERMANN ZAPF
AND HIS DESIGN PHILOSOPHY

Selected Articles and Lectures on Calligraphy
and Contemporary Developments in Type Design.
with Illustrations and Bibliographical Notes.

develop. You need a mentor who values your skill and who will teach you. They will still need to make money on you, but a very few places will place emphasis on developing talent. You find these places only by searching diligently, by talking to others—not by taking the first thing that comes along. You will have to live on what you can earn, and forego many things. If you have a talent for living cheaply, if you avoid debt, you can afford to wait for the right situation. Once you get good, then you can earn more money, and then it will be because your mastery of your talent draws opportunities to you."

An adult student asks for clarification. "Professor Zapf," he says, raising his hand and speaking at the same time, "do you mean it is better not to take the highest-paying job?"

Zapf smiles at this simplification—he has heard this question before—then answers deftly, "What I mean is that you should be aware that every decision you make about your work determines something about your direction. If a job is offered to you, but the work coming from the employer is not exciting, if it is commerce but nothing more, you have a choice: 'Do I take this money and learn what I can here and move on? Or is there nothing here for my talent, only a means to feed my body?' It takes great courage to pass up a job that does not feel right. Finding a place where you can do the work you feel is most valuable, that is a bit of a holy grail. You may get lucky and find it early; you may search—as I did—for many years. I did not know where my career would lead, and there are always wars, depressions, inflations, illnesses. I initially thought I wanted to be an engineer, but politics prevented that. I was lucky to know what made me happy—I loved to draw letters. I went where I could do that. Work on what makes you happy, and the money will come, though never as fast as you need it to." He paused, as if realizing he had meant to give the young man a simpler answer.

"You need to be clear about your goal, and then, like my second student, be steadfast in the pursuit."

"Professor Zapf, please," asks a tiny woman standing to be heard. "How do you know if your talent is really good enough to be worth so many sacrifices?" The room goes stone silent.

Zapf finishes a group of letters with a flourish and puts down the chalk. "The best answer I have for you is not mine. I think it is maybe Bach who says, 'If going for a single day without giving expression to your soul's music makes you miserable, then music is your calling.'"

I checked to see if any of the Bachs really said anything like this, but have not yet found the source of this impressive piece of wisdom. Whether it is Bach or Zapf himself, it stands as a challenge to confront every morning. *What music does my soul yearn to play today?*

Paul Rand
THE DESIGNER AS BRAND

Even people who know nothing about graphic design have heard of Paul Rand (1914–1996). His logo for IBM is probably the most copied—and the most impossible to copy—of all modern brand marks. His client portfolio included Westinghouse, El Producto, Cummins, UPS, and numerous others. Unlike most other designers in the top echelon, Rand worked alone for most of his career, utilizing at most an assistant or student intern. His work is characterized by a powerful directness, sometimes leavened with a disarming whimsy.

Born Peretz Rosenbaum to Orthodox Jewish parents in Brooklyn, New York, he studied at Pratt Institute, the Art Students League, and Parsons, yet described himself as "a self-taught designer." In his early twenties his work for *Esquire* magazine attracted worldwide attention, and he built a portfolio by designing magazine covers—sometimes for no fee, in return for a "no alterations" agreement. This allowed him to do fresh, experimental work before a large, influential audience. An articulate spokesman for design, he is credited for giving graphic design, and particularly branding, legitimacy as a strategic business tool. He taught graduate-level classes in graphic design at Yale and and continued working until shortly before his death in 1996.

JANUARY 1978 I hold George Nelson's letter of introduction to Paul Rand in my hand, rereading its four sentences, and decide to walk out of my way to use a good-quality Midtown copy shop, then post it. A week goes by and I receive a phone call from IBM.

A crisp, youthful, military-sounding voice begins without greeting or identification, "Mr. Laufer? Mr. Rand will be at the Manhattan office on Thursday next week. He can see you at 10:30 for about twenty minutes." He is not asking for a reply; it doesn't matter whether I can be there or not.

"Very good, thank you." In a moment of lucidity, I remember to ask for the address and how to pass security.

"Just tell the guard you are visiting Paul Rand." At IBM, Rand's name is a security clearance! I take my gray Presbyterian suit to the dry cleaner, put the Valise Cruiser in order, and shine my shoes. I reread his writings and review everything I know about his clients and his work. I also call my classmate Geoff Fried, who went on to get a master's at Yale and study under Rand.

"Rand," he says in a tone of considered reflection, "has definite opinions about everything in design—and," he pauses to choose his words, "his opinions are never wrong. He explains the way design is—conclusively. You know his work?"

I play back what I have just been studying: "Westinghouse, IBM, UPS, some of his magazine work. The stuff that is published regularly. Not in great detail."

"Well, you will learn the most if you ask him about his decisions. You have to understand that he believes there is a best way, and that he alone knows it. Don't make the mistake of dropping names with Rand. He's a bit like Frank Lloyd Wright: he knows he's great and he can't bear the work of other famous designers, with the exception of a few great predecessors. Herbert Bayer, he likes. A. M. Cassandre."

The security guard at IBM shows me to a small meeting room furnished with a Knoll table and a few chairs. Rand comes in with the confident stride of an impresario on stage. He is wearing a gray suit, a red tie, and black shoes. His close-cropped, salt-and-pepper hair and his glasses look like all the publicity pictures. I am seated, but rise to shake his hand. I stay semi-bent over and sit back down, conscious of the difference in our height and not wanting to tower over him. He is very commanding in his carriage, but he is short!

Rand has a mild tic that causes him to squint frequently, but he is relaxed and businesslike.

Rand begins, "So, you are a student of Nelson's; he thinks rather well of you, and you are working at Oxford. I have a few minutes before my next meeting. How shall we spend our time together?" I notice he has a folder with my name on it, with the resume I sent and Nelson's letter in it. I'm on.

"I went to school in Pittsburgh, so I spent quite a lot of time watching your Westinghouse animated sign, waiting to see if it would ever repeat."

His mouth curves up, almost imperceptibly. *Print* magazine did an article about the large outdoor installation Rand designed, a series of large neon Westinghouse logos set on one of Pittsburgh's prominent hillsides. Each stroke of each logo could be illuminated independently. The article said that the sign was programmed with so many variations that it would not repeat for at least a thousand years.

"I studied under Dennis Ichiyama [also a student of Rand's at Yale], who made no secret of using many of your assignments. We did a proportion book, a series of type posters, and we drew a Roman alphabet from scratch."

"Ah, time to change my lessons again," he says, matter-of-factly, "or there will be no reason for anyone to pay Yale's tuition!"

"I brought a portfolio, and I would be happy to have your insights." I put it on the table. "But I have to confess, that what I am most interested in is, how you ..."

"Became Rand?" he fills in.

"Just so!" I am glad he understands.

"Well, I publish. My books are my best marketing. I do shows of my work. The shows are also good visibility, though it is hard to measure how much they really benefit me. As far as how I came to be, I didn't have a grand plan. I was working for a guy who stopped paying me, so I got a job in an agency, I learned as much as I could about advertising, then I left. I'm too opinionated to make a tolerable employee. I needed to know about ads, but I gravitated toward work where I could get involved in the subject matter as well as the form. Editorial work, especially magazines, and design."

He looks at my design for the Oxford title *On with the Show*, set in linotype Caledonia supplimented with hand lettered chapter titles.

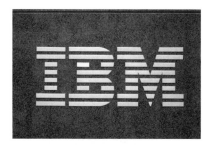

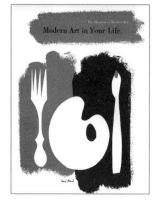

Rand's design aesthetic is deceptively simple. One design utilizes a strict grid, the next design is casual brushwork. Many of his designs feature loose components or fragments of something familiar, and let the viewer's eye assemble them. He can find meaning and emotion in small details and extract humor from the most elemental forms. Rand thought of himself as an artist, his quirky signature becoming a sought-after brand in its own right. In his writings, *Thoughts on Design* and *Paul Rand, A Designer's Art,* he is as articulate and forceful in his prose as he is in his designs.

"You shouldn't waste your time with Caledonia." Fred Schneider uses the Caledonia font as a mainstay for some of Oxford's most established formats, and I am about to ask why. "It's just a mish-mash of shapes from other, more successful fonts. Lacks clarity. Not in the same league as Bodoni, Garamond."

He flips through my work, moving at a brisk pace, but very atten-tive. He lingers a minute on a jacket for *Many Dimensional Man*, an Oxford hardcover that uses a moiré pattern to define a human head.

"That's good." Note to self: call Schneider and tell him *Paul Rand* likes our cover!

He stops at my identity package for the Oxford quincentenary, and his jaw tenses.

"Mmm. Optima, problematic choice for an identity system."

Hermann Zapf, the creator of Optima, is a European rival, commanding high fees and wielding influence similar to Rand's. But where Zapf is a classicist, Rand is a modernist; Zapf is known primarily for his calligraphy and typography, Rand is known for identity systems and startling, symbolic statements. Fred Schneider loves Optima, so I use it a lot.

"It's so classical in its origins—" I start to explain why I use it, why it is such a good choice for Oxford, but Rand will have none of it.

"I already said I don't like it." Right, Geoff Fried had warned me that Rand doesn't discuss design. He moves on smartly. "Now this makes a good layout," he says, holding Arthur Tress's *Shadow* out at arm's length to flip the pages. "You stay out of sight as designer, and let your photographer shine. Important skill—augurs well for you that you learned that so young. Futura would have been a better font choice, but since you are using only the Avant Garde capitals in a light font, this works. Looks like your publisher changed your title page, though. You have to choose your battles, but when you come this close to perfec-tion, it's important to win." I'm dismayed. He has picked up on exactly what happened: an editor threw in a single line of extra copy on the title page in a different font. It doesn't look bad—I told

❝I'm too opinionated to make a tolerable employee. I needed to know about ads, but I gravitated toward work where I could get involved in the subject matter as well as the form.❞

myself at the time—but Rand sees immediately that it's inconsistent with the rest of the book.

Remembering Geoff Fried's advice, I decide to ask about his decisions. "I understand that you work mostly by yourself. How do you accomplish so much?"

"Well, I usually have a grad student or two assisting, setting up content and managing the workflow for me," Rand explains. "But I'm very direct with my clients. I tell them that I will work out precisely what they need, and it will be excellent, but I don't change my work and I expect them to implement exactly what I do. If they want to dink around, they can hire someone else. That scares off the dilettantes, and allows me to work faster."

> **I'm very direct with my clients. I tell them that I will work out precisely what they need, and it will be excellent, but I don't change my work and I expect them to implement exactly what I do. If they want to dink around, they can hire someone else.**

The Rand aura sinks in further. His designs are nonnegotiable, even before he is hired. He dictates the terms of the relationship at the outset. Compared to Schneider's soft-spoken give-and-take with his editors, even compared with Barbara Bertoli's forcefulness, Rand is a commanding presence.

He is looking at a few of my illustrations. "You draw well," he says, flipping through my sketchbook, "but you rarely use your drawings in your designs. Seems like a missed opportunity. In fact, your work is still a bit polite—maybe it's your employer. But you should be more aggressive about becoming 'Laufer.'" He says this with an eyebrow raised.

A young man in a dark blue suit pokes his head in the door. "Mr. Rand, two minutes." Rand's nod to him is barely perceptible. He continues in a smooth manner.

"Two minutes," he reiterates under his breath, as if he wished for more time to go into detail. He flips back through my portfolio quickly. "I want you to send me a few samples. I have to take care of my students first, of course. I can't make any promises, but things come up." We shake hands and I try to express the type of gratitude I feel toward him—not just for seeing my work, but for "being Rand." Rand nods with a silent cordiality and steps briskly out the door.

I came to New York thinking that if I could meet famous designers and find out how they planned their careers, I could follow their plans and be as successful as them. The interview with Rand is the beginning of the end of that youthful misconception, yet the insights gathered from my dialogues with creative legends are among my best navigational tools. Creative careers are difficult to map in advance. I learn later that Rand was born Peretz Rosenbaum, and that he "rebranded" himself Paul Rand. So ambition is a crucial ingredient—talent and drive too, certainly—yet neither Rand nor any of the heavy-hitting creative professionals I interviewed professed to have a career plan—at least not one that actually worked out. If there were any common threads to their stories, it was their ability to recognize their own shortcomings as well as their strengths, to act quickly on creative opportunities, and to employ strategies to build the trust and respect of their clients.

Rand represents one extreme in client relations: an autocratic style that insists on his control as a precondition. Nelson's style was perhaps the opposite extreme: charming and storytelling and joking his way to his client's trust. But both arrive at the real goal: the deep trust of their clients. Successful design requires control, and gaining control comes when the client *willingly relinquishes* control, entrusting the designer with the decision making, the budget, and the positive impact of the design in question.

Ivan Chermayeff
A SEARCH FOR ESSENCE

 Ivan Chermayeff was born in 1932 in London. His father, Serge, was an influential architect, industrial designer, and writer. Chermayeff met Tom Geismar while studying at Yale. They began their partnership in 1957, and would go on to design such pervasive brands as Mobile, NBC, and Chase. Their firm has for decades occupied a unique position in design—with a handful of other design firms, they set a standard for how modern corporations control their public image worldwide, and how such identity systems can evolve.

Chermayeff and Geismar shared an AIGA Medal in 1979 and have collected numerous awards worldwide. Under a new generation of leadership, the firm continues to lead the profession. Chermayeff participated in leadership positions at many cultural institutions including the Museum of Modern Art, New York; Yale University; Harvard University; and the Aspen Design Conference.

FEBRUARY 1978 Walking to Chermayeff and Geismar, I reflect on the time and effort invested in George Nelson's Philosophy of Design class. It was one of many efforts at self-education that could have been a dead end, but instead became a portal to the future. Design would be a much easier career if each day, each phone call, provided some evidence of progress. Instead, it often feels more like purchasing lottery tickets—all or nothing.

Nelson's letter has worked its magic again; Chermayeff appears promptly to wave me through the C&G lobby. He's impeccably dressed, has a ruddy, handsome quality, patrician yet personable. He has the almost hypnotic ability to give you the full breadth of his attention: hearing every word, meeting you where you are, and lifting you to a higher understanding. I wonder if this is an innate gift, or if, like Nelson's public speaking, it can be learned with practice.

The interview with Rand is less than two weeks past, and the size of the Chermayeff and Geismar operation stands in sharp contrast. Chermayeff shows me hastily through their bullpen area, introducing me to one or two people in passing, but there is a buzz to the hive, and leisurely conversation seems out of the question.

"Thanks for coming to see us," he says even before I can thank him. Could he be unaware that I have been calling him for several years? It's more likely an acknowledgement; perhaps he is thanking me for thinking well enough of their work to persist so long. No way to know. Chermayeff sits down at a circular table in a small, white room with an original Saul Steinberg drawing on the wall.

"I consider your seeing me personally a great honor." After I say it I wince—too formal, or fawning, or something. I take a sip of the water the gatekeeper has brought unasked. I open the case and pass it to Chermayeff. He spends two or three seconds on each piece of work, nodding as he goes.

"We are waiting on several large projects that we expect to be awarded. This might open up several new design positions," he says with a confident air. "What we always look for is a solid basis of production experience—we find it is essential to know what process one is designing for—and an innate curiosity that leads to a robust background knowledge."

"Do you mean background knowledge of design?" I ask.

"Actually, I mean everything else. Virtually every designer has learned about design—that is a given for anyone with a degree. We look for those with broad knowledge of business, culture, sports, politics—the world," he clarifies, nodding his head slightly to each of the different compass points to convey wide knowledge. He is speed-reading my resume now. "Foreign residence and foreign languages are a plus." I know now from experience: elite interviews are short.

> **Virtually every designer has learned about design. We look for those with broad knowledge of business, culture, sports, politics—the world.**

Rand stated up front his twenty-minute limit; I was in and out of Push Pin in under half an hour. I have a few burning questions I want to cover before an abrupt ending.

"Mr. Nelson was kind enough to give me an introduction to Paul Rand, whom I have just visited." Chermayeff does not acknowledge my name dropping, and I hasten on. "He can maintain a personal vision by working alone, but how does an operation the size of C&G maintain such a recognizable style?"

Now Chermayeff sees where I am going, and responds, "You have to look at design from the client side, always. Rand is—" he pauses diplomatically—"a difficult guy. It takes a particular and patient client to work with someone like him." He shifts direction. "We strive to make great design accessible. We don't have a mystique. We don't wrap it up in a personality cult or intractable processes. Our clients can call us, explain a problem or objective, and we take it from there."

There is no hint of irritation, but it occurs to me for the first time that Rand may be a burr in the saddle of many firms. Without the overhead of large staff or offices, Rand cherry-picks certain high-visibility clients.

"Besides," he continues, relaxing a bit, "you can't take on a major identity campaign as a lone ranger, or do government work. You just can't. Our work for the post office takes a lot of staff just to respond to the volume of their requests, let alone do the work."

"And how . . . ," I begin, but Chermayeff grins broadly now. He sets my samples back in their case, giving me full attention.

"I'm getting there," he says, smiling amiably at my impatience and giving me a glimpse of the personal charisma that his clients enjoy. "Everything depends on having great people. I try never to hire anyone who isn't a better designer than the previous hire. Rand may or may not have a personal 'vision' as you put it, but we certainly don't. When my staff delves into a design exploration, my job is to be a transparent window to the client and to the larger audience beyond. I weed out the overly personal work. What you may see as a C&G 'style' is really just a search for essence. That essence always originates with the client's audience relationships." He motions to the Valise. "Your work is very influenced by the expectations of the publishing industry. Nothing wrong with that, but you will need

> ❝We strive to make great design accessible. We don't have a mystique. We don't wrap it up in personality cult or intractable processes. Our clients can call us, explain an objective, and we take it from there.❞

some additional client perspective to grow into the fine designer I believe you can be," he says. How different can design and publishing be? Maybe he means the scale of book design is smaller.

I decide to pursue this. "I'm used to design projects being given to small teams: one editorial assistant, one designer, one production artist. How do you structure a project with multiple designers working on the same problem?" I am not sure I am scoring any points by directing the interview toward him, away from his attention to my work, but I want to take advantage of the moment. I've waited so long to see into this rarefied world.

"Ah! A crucial question. I used to think there was a single method, but now I know better. We have to be flexible, and suit our teamwork." Another midsentence change of expression signals a coming insight. "Tom and I look for ways to deliver the maximum value to a client. The trick is, every client has a unique value matrix. One client needs a good design in a week—miss it by a day and the design has no value. For that client, putting three people on a project and structuring their assignment so they cooperate is the ticket. Another client may be selling against a very sophisticated competitor. They can be a little more flexible on time, but good design won't do it, they need spectacular. For that assignment, we might put five designers on the very same task, and foster some internal competition. This gets a lot of results, but requires the account manager to be a very judicious and sensitive referee. With five excellent designers, you can't afford to have a winner and four losers. The competition has to build to joint ownership. I try never to say 'the client picked this one'—that is a weak resolution; it abdicates my responsibility for overall excellence. I want to look at a wall of designs and be able to articulate exactly what makes a winning design."

"Does the client see the wall?"

"We rarely give the client a lot of designs. It's confusing to them, and they pay us to remove confusion, not generate more. They pay

> **When my staff delves into a design exploration, my job is to be a transparent window to the client and to the larger audience beyond. What looks like a 'style' is really a search for essence. That essence originates with the client's audience relationships.**

Chermayeff & Geismar's designs are characterized by timeless simplicity and elegance. Many of their brandmarks are so familiar they appear not to be "designed" but rather seem to have always existed.

C&G's oeuvre includes virtually every aspect of visual design: posters, exhibitions, interiors, publications, branding systems, packaging, architectural murals, and interactive. Their star design for the American Bicentennial is possibly the only brandmark ever to appear on 100 million postage stamps as well as on interplanetary spacecraft!

> **❝One client needs a good design in a week—miss it by a day and the design has no value. Another client can be a little more flexible on time, but good design won't do—they need spectacular. Every client has a unique value matrix.❞**

us to recommend one design that will work." I'm about to ask how he knows which is the winning design, but he has probably had this discussion many times. He knows this territory and takes the reins of the interview back firmly.

"I know instantly which design will work best. But—to your question before about the firm's vision—I know that providing the client and audience perspective to my design team is the most likely way to build consensus around the strongest design. There's a difference between strong leadership and autocracy. There are design firms where an autocrat reigns, but they lose their best talent regularly."

The interview will be over soon. This is my last opportunity to go for the throat. I stand and square my stance to him. "You've been generous with your time, and these are invaluable insights. I would be honored to be a part of the C&G team. How soon can I sign on?"

Chermayeff acknowledges the correctness of asking the question directly, responding with a smile of his own. He extends his hand for a vigorous shake.

"I think you are better than this portfolio. We will certainly keep you in mind, but do send us new samples when you stay in touch. And please tell George we hope he will stop by for a visit. He is such a brilliant fellow."

I thank him and he leaves me to pack up my case. His gatekeeper appears to show me out. Chermayeff's parting words—you are better than your portfolio—offer a multifaceted insight. It could be an insult: a suggestion that the portfolio falls short. It could be a challenge: You need to get in gear and do more and better work. It could be encouragement: I like you and I think you are capable of more than what I see here. It could be a dismissal: You are not ready to work here until your portfolio is. I leave as I arrived: thinking about what it all means. I reject any intention of insult, and

> **❝You are better than this portfolio.❞**

think of it as encouragement, a challenge to be worthy of Nelson's sponsorship. The heat reflecting from Manhattan's pavement blasts my nostrils; a sharp contrast to the cool, oxygen-rich C&G atmosphere. I remember Robert Lepper saying "everyone is always worrying about portfolio." Is anyone's portfolio ever finished? When the portfolio is better than the designer, is that a triumph or a danger sign?

I resolve to respond to Chermayeff's challenge by always being better than my portfolio, and never showing a portfolio that isn't at least a little better than the last presentation.

Lou Dorfsman
I JUST TRY TO MAKE IT LOOK GREAT

Lou Dorfsman (1918–2008) was born in Manhattan and graduated from Cooper Union in 1939. His early experience included making signs for his father's business and displays for the 1939 New York World's Fair. Dorfsman served in the US Army during World War II, and after the war started work at CBS Radio. There he worked under the legendary William Golden, a self-taught designer who pioneered CBS's persuasive visual style. Dorfsman became friends with Frank Stanton—also a strong believer in the power of a well-designed brand—who later became president of CBS. Dorfsman's career at CBS spanned many world events, including the first moon landing and the assassination of President Kennedy, which gave him the designer's most important raw material: electrifying subject matter.

Dorfsman's successes led to increasing influence at CBS, until he eventually oversaw almost every aspect of advertising and corporate identity. In 1987, after more than 40 years with the network, Dorfsman retired from CBS and started his own design studio.

FEBRUARY 1978 The CBS branding is in millions of households every night, and it is always in the design annuals. CBS is the first major interview I have had on the corporate in-house side of the equation. Between attending Nelson's Philosophy of Design class and reading design books on the train, my head is brimming with high-minded questions for Dorfsman.

CBS has an expansive lobby with glass walls, and people move about briskly, carrying things of great importance. I am shown to Dorfsman's office. He has a long side table that spans the whole length of one wall. Above and below it are shelves. He has a large desk. He motions me to a chair and I sit. A large television is off to one side, showing a live feed of the current programming. The sound is audible, but does not interfere with conversation.

Dorfsman notices me looking at it. "I have it on all the time so I can see what we're doing. I am always seeing things that don't mesh, that need refinement or reversal."

I open the Valise and hand him my lead sample. He opens a manila file folder an inch thick, extracts my resume, folds back Nelson's letter, and scans it for ten seconds.

"Oh, right, you worked at Oxford. Because of your letter, I was thinking you worked for Nelson." He rises, moves the case to his side table, and takes the work out of the portfolio. He leans each piece up against the wall, forming a continuous line along his table, and then steps back to review the whole. I do a quick mental inventory of dozens of interviewers; no one has ever done this before, and I realize this is the way a TV art director thinks: in sequences, storyboards, looking for connections between takes. Since I have no television experience, I put in as much variety as possible, and have more than twenty pieces in the case. Dorfsman walks up and down the line, saying nothing. On his third pass he moves in closer to look at typographic details.

"Well, David, I see you've had a chance to do some important individual pieces—jackets and journals and things. You have a fine eye for type. Nelson recommends you. Where do you want to take it from here?" I try to frame a big-picture question respectfully.

"Mr. Dorfsman, you are perhaps as influential as anyone in setting the direction of our culture, visually. In this century alone, we have had such a lot of major design philosophies competing for attention—Art Deco, Futurism, De Stijl, Bauhaus, International style, on and on. What's the style that will carry us forward?"

Dorfsman shakes his head ever so slightly for the last half of my question, in consternation.

"The philosophical questions on design, that stuff embarrasses me. No disrespect to Nelson, but TV, you know, moves fast. The folks I work for—and those who work for me—don't often have the time to theorize. If they see something they don't like, I have to make a snap judgment whether they are reacting to content, which is outside my control for the most part, or the appearance, and what I can do to address their concern. I have to reassure them that what we're putting in print and what we put on-air will be harmonious. The bigger questions, philosophy, pure design ..." He pauses, thinking about how to frame his feelings. "I just try to make it look great."

> **The philosophical questions on design, that stuff embarrasses me. The folks I work for, you know, we move fast, we don't theorize. I have to reassure them that what we're putting in print and what we put on air are harmonious. I just try to make it look great.**

He sees me looking at his wall of awards. "The guy I learned from, Bill Golden, used to say 'the visual environment of advertising gets better when you and I do a good design—*and in no other way.*'" He picks up my jacket for *On with the Show* as an example. "You were given this book jacket to do. You couldn't change the title, the author, the trim size. You had to work within the area open to you—visual design. You could propose colors, fonts, the layout, the style. You didn't stop to think 'How would the Futurists do this?'"

"It's a book about a specific period in show business history, so it had to be a historical design," I offer, trying not to sound apologetic.

Dorfsman brightens. "Exactly! Design has an audience and a message, a historical context and a purpose. You did what you could to help your publisher and your author develop an audience, and sell books. You helped your reader get an idea of the subject. How your book jacket—or my media kit" —he picks up a presentation board with a design on it, covered with corrections in red pen, from his side table and gives it a little huzzah— "may impact civilization is probably beyond us. At least, I can't let that complicate my workflow."

I realize I have asked a show-off question instead of answering

Dorfsman's use of black and white as a house style continued for some years, even after color television became standard. The ultrasimple layouts, startling changes of scale, and masterful typography—especially their CBS Didot font—made the station's communications among the most arresting and recognizable of the twentieth century.

Dorfsman's question, so I retreat to safer ground. "You asked where I want to take it from here." Dorfsman nods. "I want to work in a place where design is valued, for someone who really knows how to get great work done."

"If you find one, let me know."

"You're kidding, right?"

"I think it's very rare to find a company that values design for its own sake. When you do find an organization with excellent visual image, it is usually because someone there has demonstrated to mangement that they can achieve management objectives. You make design valuable by understanding your boss and, most importantly, by demonstrating that good design grows good audiences."

Dorfsman takes a sidelong glance at his TV. "Who else in town have you seen?"

I name a few of the most important names; this might be a tacit offer to use his name to open a few doors.

"I've been wanting to see Lubalin, Smith, and Carnase, but their dance cards are always full."

Dorfsman nods knowingly. "That is one I can probably help you with, in terms of an appointment. In terms of getting hired, I need to think for a few days about where you would be a good fit."

"I'm interested in how the designers of the first rank get their approvals," I tell him. "I feel as though, in spite of encouragement from some quarters, my best ideas are too often getting shot down. I'd like to be in an organization where I don't have to haggle."

Dorfsman looks at his TV and says "Ah, yes." I'm not sure whether it's to me or to the set. "I know what you mean. It's especially difficult when you're younger. Once you get a few big successes, people trust you more readily. A big turning point for me was when I realized that I needed to engage with and win over my detractors as well as my supporters. The natural tendency, if you're presenting to a group, is to seize on the first person that gives you positive

> ❝The natural tendency, if you're presenting to a group, is to seize on the first person that gives you positive comments. A big turning point for me was when I realized that I needed to engage with my detractors as well as my supporters. ❞

comments. But the ones who are silent, or who say something menacing or inexplicable—it's important to cultivate their criticism. You never know why someone takes an opposing stance. They may feel threatened by the 'creative types.' They may have an axe to grind against the person who hired you. They may look at design as a frivolous expense. And they will rarely tell you the real reason.

"Their comments will come out in the form of sabotage like, 'When I squint at it, it reminds me of a cow pie.' Or 'We tried something like that last year and it was a total flop.' You have to try to figure out what that person's real concern is. It may take some research into who they are and what they do in the organization. Now my old boss Bill Golden, he thrived on confrontation. He would go up against his detractors and try to flatten them. He had the support of management and he didn't like to waste time. People said he got his way because he had the protection of Frank Stanton. But really it was the other way around: Golden believed so strongly in his work and in the power of good design that Stanton supported him. Sometimes he won, sometimes he didn't, but people learned not to make idle criticism of what he was doing. TV is different now, the committees are larger and we..." Something on the TV screen has stopped his train of thought. He continues, as though perhaps a sentence was dropped.

"I have an idea in my head of how CBS should appear. The shows will change—must change—with the season. What I got from Golden and have—with management's blessing—built on is that the station has an identity apart from the shows, apart from the news anchors. It's an emotional space, really. I try to stay true to that, and I invest a lot of time in soliciting opinions from all quarters, to get their ideas before I present. When I present, I incorporate their language. It makes them feel part of the process. It's slow. Not everyone has the temperament for it!"

Dorfsman's phone rings; he answers, studying his TV while listening. "You're right, I don't like it," he says and hangs up. Turning to me, he says, "David, forgive me, we have a design issue that I have been harping about that has got to be addressed." I look at the screen, trying to figure out what has caught his attention.

I am puzzled. "What about this is amiss? Looks like vintage CBS." He does not have time to explain the details, but he stands tall and addresses me as though he were going off to war and might never have another chance to impart all his wisdom. "You can get a design ninety-five percent of the way there, and it still doesn't pop the way you see it in your mind. Then, you nudge the last few details into place. Bam! It doesn't just look five percent better, is starts ringing all the bells. I have a reputation for being demanding, for wanting to fix details that are too small for other people to see. Bu we see it and we put it to work for us

> *You can get a design ninety-five percent of the way there, and it still doesn't pop the way you see it in your mind. Then, you nudge the last few details into place. Bam! It doesn't just look five percent better, it starts ringing all the bells!*

We do it because those subliminal details give a design its punch, its staying power! Every font, every letter, every picture and sound, they are like the instruments in an orchestra. It is our job to envision how great it could really be, and to convince, to cajole, to demand, to coax until—I mean, you know instinctively when your design is working or not working. When you finally get all the details aligned, something extraordinary happens—the message bypasses the brain and goes right to the heart." This is another speech in praise of perfection. It is similar to Miedinger's and Zapf's comments about their respective crafts, but never have I heard it said so convincingly.

Dorfsman shakes my hand and leaves the room abruptly. I put the Valise Cruiser away, jot a note to Dorfsman on the back of a business card, and depart. Dorfsman's parting insight is far-reaching. He is saying, in effect, "Insist on high standards: It is better to have a reputation for being a demanding perfectionist who does great work than for being an agreeable schlub who does ordinary work."

Another striking realization arises from this interview: Dorfsman considers good design *innate*; he thinks people who are oblivious and uneducated as to design are still affected by it. He believes—without theorizing—there is something about a harmonious presentation to which the brain responds below the level of conscious thought. Criticism and theory are valuable for learning and selling, but, at least for Dorfsman, creating visual communications is very visceral—you believe in it and you fight to make it visible to all.

Dorfsman is as good as his word; the next time I call Lubalin's office, the receptionist puts me on the interview calendar, as though it was the easiest favor in the world.

Herb Lubalin
SUPERLATIVES AND SCHLOCK

Herb Lubalin (1918–1981), though he traveled widely, was born, lived, and died a New Yorker. He attended Cooper Union, and he scuffled after graduation, eventually getting a toehold working for Reiss Advertising. In 1944 Lubalin began working at Sudler and Hennessey, an advertising agency where he became a partner. In 1964 he started his own shop. He is best remembered for his expressive facility with type, his ability to find illustrative meaning and emotion in almost any word or headline. An irreverent and inventive magazine designer, Lubalin found a kindred spirit in editor/publisher/bad boy Ralph Ginzburg. The two pioneered richly visual magazines such as *Eros*, *Fact*, *Avant Garde*, and *Moneysworth*. Eventually Lubalin cofounded the International Typeface Corporation (ITC) to distribute their new generation of photographic and computer-generated fonts.

In 1971 Lubalin began publishing *U&lc*, a smart, sassy tabloid publication that became a playground for Lubalin, a showplace for ITC fonts, and a way to promote the design work of Lubalin, Smith, and Carnase. It also became one of the most avidly read design publications of the day; when the new *U&lc* arrived in the mail, work in design studios around the world stopped for everyone to savor Lubalin's latest profundity and pranks. Lubalin won numerous awards from the Type Directors Club and the Art Directors Club, and he was an AIGA Medalist in 1980. He collaborated with Lou Dorfsman on many projects, including the celebrated "gastrotypographical assemblage" in the CBS lunchroom.

MARCH 1978 It is winter by the time my appointment with Lubalin finally rolls around. I have spent the day working on freelance projects at my apartment in New Jersey. There is a major event at Madison Square Garden, colocated with Penn Station, so I take the bus into Manhattan at about the hour I am usually commuting in the opposite direction. I reach the curb outside Port Authority to catch a cab south, and make a shocking discovery. My wallet is not in my pocket! I'm a bit early for my appointment with Lubalin if I catch a cab, but I am late if I have to walk it. Today of all days! Either I've left my wallet on the bus, or my pocket has been picked. Without ID I can't get cash. Port Authority is a mad throng of commuters beating a retreat out of town. Most of the phone booths are empty. Phone booths! I wonder. I step into a booth and check the change bin. As if to repay my many months of patronage, this phone yields a quarter and a dime. The next two are empty. In ten minutes I visit a couple dozen pay phones, collecting about $4.50, which is certainly enough to get me to LSC. I can walk back at my leisure. Based on that take, I could make $12 an hour doing this—20 percent more than my starting freelance rate at Avon!

I pay the cabbie with a handful of dimes and bound up the stairs to the Lubalin, Smith, and Carnase studio. I'm finally buzzed in, and I am pumped. I feel I have overcome every possible adversity and am finally going to stand in The Presence! I have shown the Valise Cruiser so many times now that I have honed it down to just the work that gets consistently high praise.

Lubalin accepts my handshake with a nod, and says, "Welcome."

He sees all the best portfolios that come through New York, and it is 6:30 in the evening, so he breezes through mine, pausing only once or twice. I have an idea of this man as a warm, chatty guru, and I'm prepared for some insights and war stories. He says nothing about my work.

"So, why did you want to come here? They told you we aren't hiring." His bluntness is unexpected.

"Because, you are the greatest living graphic designer, and ..."

He raises a hand gently and wags two fingers, as if erasing an unnecessary phrase. "You think that because I spend $80,000 a month publishing a stupid magazine."

I'm trying to apply my praise with a trowel, but the mortar just isn't sticking.

I persist, "Herb, it may be a stupid magazine, but it's still a lot smarter than anything else out there. I was a charter subscriber to *Avant Garde*, and that magazine is what got me started thinking about a graphic design career."

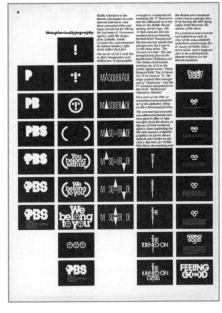

U&lc is by no means Lubalin's only claim to fame, but was perhaps his most visible project, dedicated to the creative interplay of word and image. Like *Graphis*, *U&lc* was a showcase for award-winning work and a spotlight on new or special talent. But where *Graphis* provided the cool, neutral environment of an uptown art gallery, *U&lc* was more like a visit to a boisterous art festival. *U&lc*'s tabloid newsprint and exuberant layout proclaimed, "Rules are made to be broken!" *U&lc* made no secret of its connection to the International

Typeface Corporation, giving exciting demonstrations of new ITC fonts, but always made room for anyone creating exciting or experimental typographic visuals. Editorial hijinks and humorous uses of language suffused every issue. *U&lc* began when typography was in transition from the rigidity of metal type. Much of the experimentation and freedom of expression that first appeared in *U&lc* influenced the highly nuanced typographic controls that became standard in the user interfaces for digital typography.

Lubalin softens slightly. "Look," he says, "how many of my designs have you seen?" I start naming them, grasping a different finger for each one like a disciple reciting catechism: "*Avant Garde*, the SH&L logo, *Moneysworth, Eros, U&lc, Mother & Child* magazine."

He nods slightly with each one. I stop at ten, thinking I have acquitted myself well enough to earn some pearls of his wisdom.

"Right." Lubalin shifts his weight a bit, and I see that he looks more tired than he appears in his press photos and films. "Those are the only ten pieces I ever show." Where is he going with this?

"Look," he repeats. There is a pattern to his expression, a cadence. He uses a single-syllable word to focus your attention on his point to follow.

"Look," he says again, this time gesturing behind me toward multiple banks of flat files with a hundred drawers, maybe more, neatly labeled. "I show only my best work. People never see the drawers and drawers of schlock work I have done all my life to pay the bills."

In disbelief I hop off my stool and open a few drawers. They are full, although I am not really able to see the finished product. There are a lot of pencil roughs on tracing paper.

I can't tell what's wrong, but the interview is ending too soon. A couple years wait—hell, I have to learn something before I am shown the door.

"What's the most important thing ..." I have a complete sentence cued up, but it seems he's heard it many times.

"*U&lc* is important to me, because it's the only project where the client, the designer, and the reader are the same person. I've been on a quest for years to eliminate the client from graphic design. I have created an environment where I can make up editorial content just to provide an opportunity for an inventive design, rather than having the design be the minion of the content. It's very expensive, and what it comes down to is basically self-promotion."

A voice comes from the back room: a project is ready for his supervision. He shakes my hand hurriedly, but looking me full in the face for an instant, with

> 66 *You are doing good work. You are probably capable of great work. But it's a fight. The world will tell you 'that's good enough.' Don't give up. Keep moving. Get faster.* 99

warmth, he says, "Don't spend too much energy chasing people like me. There's nothing I can tell you that you don't already know. You are doing good work. You are probably capable of great work. But it's a fight. The world will tell you 'that's good enough.' But of course, the world has its head up its ass. Don't give up. Keep moving. Get faster." Then calling over his shoulder, "I hope that helps."

I gather up my portfolio and leave a resume on his table. After such a long anticipation of enlightenment, I now feel a bit dazed. Since he's given me leave to look through the flat files, I drift back and open a few more drawers. There are not many finished works, but the pencil sketches are amazing. Here is a fellow for whom even quick graphite scribbles on a piece of bumwad have poetic potential! There are a dozen sheets with minor variations of a single arrangement of type, taped together in sequence, each set out in minimal, purposeful strokes. I linger perusing the mother lode, hoping perhaps he will come back. After twenty minutes, I have seen all the Lubalin pencil tracings my brain can hold, and make my disappointed retreat.

Outside, a blast of cold night air hits me, and with it a shocking question: *If the great Herb Lubalin does schlock work most of the time, what on Earth is going to be left for me?*

The word *schlock*, derived from Yiddish, refers to something inferior, cheap, or shoddy. Like a lot of slang, it is very versatile, describing merchandise, literature, food, even neighborhoods. Shlock has an especially nuanced meaning in graphic design: Lubalin used it to describe design projects that have no potential for quality, often being for a customer that is more interested in fast and cheap than good. Therein lies a trap: in applying a label like "schlock" to a new project, one signals defeat before starting. Shlock is what Rand and Edelmann say they turn down, and what other designers say they handle with minimal effort. I know all this intellectually, but the sight of all those flat files—and the thought of my towering immortal hero having such a high schlock factor—it's just too much to bear.

> ❝ *I only show my ten best pieces. People never see the drawers of schlock work I have done all my life to pay the bills.* ❞
>
> *If this towering immortal hero does schlock work, what on Earth is going to be left for me?*

For a while the future seems very bleak. I am at the New York Public Library looking for a picture source when I hear my name.

"Hey, David, how's it going?" I look up to find Ed Gottschall radiating his boundless optimism. Seeing his smile reminds me of our crazy first interview that started my odyssey in New York. I realize that the smile I am seeing reflects his personal pride in my progress. I have heard that he has left AIGA, and we talk about his book and his new role at ITC.

"I finally got to see Lubalin—thanks for all your help in setting it up." It was really Dorfsman who set it up, but Gottschall brightens.

"Congrats—he doesn't see just anyone." Then he looks at me more closely. "*And?*"

I replay the gist of the conversation with Lubalin, now a week or so in the past. Gottschall can't quite suppress an avuncular chuckle.

"Well, I'm not sure what you expected." I guess I'm not sure what I expected either. His receptionist only told me *five hundred times* that he was not looking for help! Gottschall puts his hand on my shoulder reassuringly: "Look at it this way. Lubalin paid you perhaps the highest compliment he knew how; he skipped all the pleasantries, assumed that you're going to have a career worth fighting for, and tried to prepare you for harsh reality. The life of a topflight graphic designer is a continual search for flexible clients who trust you enough to give you the control you need. It requires merciless self-appraisal and relentless self-promotion. And, yes, probably it does include doing some schlock work, some near misses, some things that aren't worthy of your talent but that pay bills."

> **The life of a topflight design professional is a continual search for flexible clients who trust you enough to give you the control you need. It requires merciless self-appraisal and relentless self-promotion.**

I gradually warm up to this compliment, and eventually conclude that I caught Lubalin at the end of a hard day, when he really needed to finish up and get home. By the time I hear of his passing, barely three years later, I am grateful to him for every word.

AN ARTHUR TRESS SNAPSHOT

Arthur Tress asks me to visit his new publisher, Morgan Press, with him. We meet in Grand Central Station for the train ride to the town of Dobbs Ferry, about an hour upstate from Manhattan. Tress is carrying his Hasselblad, and looks at everything with a prescient intensity, as though he were on the verge of a great photograph. Frequently he peers through his viewfinder, yet he shoots nothing. It is a mile or two from the train station to Morgan Press; we decide to walk along the tracks. Near the station, we come upon a sign with an icon of a man walking. The icon man's head is tilted forward and the legs are straight. Originally, the sign read "Pedestrian Crossing." Now the R in "crossing" is missing, and the adjacent O is damaged and rotated, so the sign appears to say "Pedestrian Cussing." The crowding of the trains, their frequent delays combine with the stiff, almost bristling pedestrian icon to give "Pedestrian Cussing" an unintentional irony. Arthur smiles but walks by without touching his camera.

> **When you get to a certain point in your career, you are defined as much by what you don't do as what you actually do. You have an obligation to the things that you alone can do.**

"Aren't you going to take that?"

He shakes his head without losing stride. "There are 50,000 new photographers every year—buying cameras, taking classes, having shows, and publishing. Every year! Most of them would come upon that sign and have the skills to make an amusing shot." He pauses to reflect. "When you get to a certain point in your career, you are defined as much by what you don't do as what you do. You have an obligation to the things that you alone can do."

TRANSITIONS

My interviews in Europe and New York help me shift from the desire for a concrete career path to a more flexible, spontaneous mapping process.

Viewing Atlanta from the air, there is very little city to be seen. Its neighborhoods are covered by trees, with a very few buildings poking up every now and again. On the ground, the streets are a fairyland of dogwood and azalea blossoms. It's enchanting and the people are friendly.

The town has been through a severe crash of real estate prices, I learn, and a number of real estate developers, banks, design firms, and advertising agencies have also suffered or closed. Agencies that have survived are very cautious. It's against this backdrop of extreme caution and rebirth that I begin my contact process all over again. I carry a newly brushed up Valise Cruiser to design firms and corporate design departments, where I hear different variations of the same story: "We don't have any staff positions, but could you design this for me by Monday?"

Thus I find my dialogues shifting. I still enjoy learning from creative legends, but increasingly find that entrepreneurs and business leaders also have a lot of wisdom to offer—as buyers of design, as stewards of their brands, and as people who must lead by inspiring.

Don Trousdell
GROWING A STYLE AND OUTGROWING STYLE

Don Trousdell (1937–   ), born in Newark, New
Jersey, attended Arts High School, majoring in graphic
design. As a student at Pratt Institute he majored in
advertising design. Trousdell left New York to work at
Pitt Studios in Cleveland. There he started an in-house
design studio and worked with many talented illustrators. There he also met his future partner, designer Ron Mabey. The
Mabey Trousdell studio started in Atlanta in 1969, working for clients
such as *Playboy* Magazine, the NFL, and the US Army. Over the span of his
40-year career, Trousdell won more than 500 design awards, and along
the way helped establish nine different design groups serving clients
including Coca-Cola, Turner Broadcasting, CNN Headline News, IBM,
Marriott, Kimberly-Clark and World Carpets.

Trousdell taught at Syracuse University and the University of Kansas,
and lectured widely; he also judged numerous design competitions.
Trousdell retired but never stopped working, producing numerous
paintings and mounting more than 35 solo shows. With characteristic dry
humor, he remarks of his later work, "The art establishment has been
quick to tell me often, 'You're not an artist, you're a graphic designer.'
Known for my themed shows and exhibits, I guess in the end I am still a
graphic designer—just with a different client base."

OCTOBER 1978 During my student and early professional years,
the Mabey Trousdell design partnership was very much in the
limelight, winning numerous awards. They were among the few
American firms to be featured on the pages of *Graphis*. When I arrive
in Atlanta, visiting them is one of my first priorities.

I find that Ron Mabey and Don Trousdell have parted ways and
are working independently. Mabey has his own shop and Trousdell

is working for an agency. I call both and start my call tracking, settling in for a long siege. Mabey's gatekeeper calls back and says they aren't hiring but I can show my work in September (some months ahead). McDonald and Little's gatekeeper takes my information and promises to let me know if Trousdell starts seeing portfolios again. I mail a resume to both and go on to other calls. Imagine my surprise when Trousdell's voice on my answering machine asks me to come in the following week.

"You're the guy who worked in Pittsburgh." He is walking fast, looking quickly at the resume I sent and leading me to his office. It has a great view and is crowded with bookshelves and a table on wheels, with orderly piles of projects in progress. After a few more questions we realize we both know Pat Budway, an illustrator with a great talent of his own as well as a fantastic ability to mimic classic illustration styles. I toss out a few other names, trying to think of other acquaintances we might share. Trousdell becomes more animated, eager to hear about his old friends in the Burgh.

"Budway does Leyendecker better than Leyendecker himself!" he exclaims. His demeanor changes again rapidly as he sits down. "I'm on deadline, so this is going to have to be pretty quick."

The phone rings, and he answers before the first ring is complete. "Jeez, yeah, I thought I had till 4:00—OK, right now." He returns to me. "Really quick!"

I know the feeling of too little time, so "I can come back later..."

"Nah, it will be the same drill no matter when you come." I open my sample case and set it before him. I hand him the first piece and sit back. He speeds through most of the work, but looks at it with intensity. He stops at *Sexual Secrets*, a book I designed that surveys many of the ancient Eastern "pillow books" on sexuality.

"Wow, you did this? How many times in life do you get to do a book like that! Great subject matter! I mean, we hint around about it in advertising all the time, but you just got to air it all out!" Trousdell jumps up. "Look, stay here and we will talk. I have to punch out this ad, but don't leave." His tone changes again, becoming apologetic, almost conflicted.

"Nobody realizes how much time it takes to design. At agencies, they fired all the people who could design and consequently the clients want to tinker with everything. Design it right the first time and don't let them screw with it." The old control issue. I guess it will be an issue with every design interview I ever have! He is cutting apart a copy of an illustration, cutting off the head and neck of a turkey. "Here I am cutting apart a Bill Mayer. Mayer is one of the great illustrators, and they don't give me time to send it back to him to make it fit the layout. What am I supposed to tell Mayer? I tell you, the integrity is gone from the whole craft."

He is saying this partly to me, partly to the turkey, working rapidly. It appears that the illustration is too tall for the space, so he has to take some sections out of the neck to fit it into the collar of a shirt.

I venture, "I don't know Mayer's style—is all his work like that?"

"Oh, Mayer, amazing kid. Your age, and he's already done more than most of us hope for in a lifetime. He changes his medium and his approach constantly. Not like Budway, who is very controlled, and knows all the great illustration styles, but Mayer—he just has a way of capturing what you mean."

I remember discussions with Pat Budway, thirty years my senior, talking very candidly about his work. "Budway didn't really like imitating other people's styles, he had to do what art directors wanted. He was really a good illustrator on his own," I venture.

Trousdell looks up at me sharply, remembering I am there and quickening both the pace of both his work and his voice. "Yes, the whole notion of style, it gets in the way of real expression, makes it harder to make your work truly communicate, especially when clients have preconceived ideas."

He is trimming, looking, trimming, looking again, getting closer and closer to the exact size he needs.

"There are so many styles out there I don't like and would never use," I say, trying to segue into a compliment of his work, but this sparks another change in his face.

"The only style I want to get rid of is my own," he says.

I'm a bit puzzled—here is a guy whose work has dominated the trade pubs, always walking off with top honors in New York and Europe. The Mabey Trousdell style was so recognizable, yet so fluid. Apart from Push Pin, Mabey Trousdell's style is probably the most decorated—certainly one of the most admired—within the American design scene. And Trousdell says he wants to avoid it!

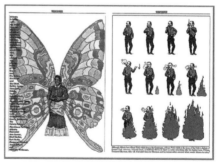

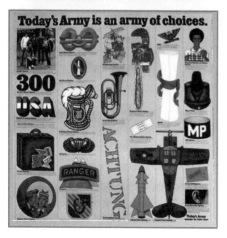

Don Trousdell's work varies widely, but is characterized by a love of illustration, and unusually tight integration of the visual concept and writing. His compositions are by turns simple and complex, orderly and chaotic. His work stood out against competing messages; its richness of illustration and painstaking layouts kept readers engaged long enough to appreciate the theme and intent of the client's message.

Trousdell developed his famous style by trying to have no style; by being true to the needs of each project, his style grows richer and broader. What looks so effortless is really a struggle to keep exploring, to resist repeating past successes.

"You start getting work because people want what won an award for someone else three years ago." He changes expression for the nth time, and now is talking to his illustration, which has become the embodiment of the customer he is describing. "Get over it, turkey— that was then, we are working on tomorrow, not yesterday!"

Suddenly, I remember the conversation with Heinz Edelmann and I get what he's trying to say. I'm building a portfolio and trying to make a style, or something that people will recognize and buy. Trousdell has done that and succeeded with it, and at the same time found it constricting. It's more about finding the right formal aspects for the immediate message than about building a style. I'm struck by this conundrum—trying to build a coherent style is self-defeating, like placing arbitrary limits on the imagination. As soon as your style gets hot, it becomes confining, and you start trying to outgrow it. Trousdell has developed his famous style by trying to have no style; by being true to the needs of each project, his style grows richer and broader. The style that looks effortless is really a continual struggle to explore, to resist repeating past successes.

Trousdell puts a black paper flap on the artwork, puts an agency sticker on the cover, and pulls out a burnisher, leaning hard on the illustration to make sure his paste job does not come loose before it can be photographed. A young account executive in impeccable agency dress strides in as if on cue, and Trousdell hands him the work. The AE flips up the flap, nods, looks at me without curiosity or acknowledgement, and strides out.

"Was it like this at Mabey Trousdell?" I ask.

"Nah, there we took the time—I'd go back to that way if I could, but I have alimony." Trousdell exhales, sits astride a chair with the back against his chest, and flips through my work a second time. He pauses to admire a David Willardson illustration on one of my Avon covers. "We are blessed with so many great illustrators here, and I wish I could keep them all busy. Me, I can't draw worth a hoot." His walls are covered with his skillful concept sketches, so I take this more as an homage to his illustrators than as fact.

"How do you tell your illustrators what you want?"

"I'm like an illustrator's therapist, sometimes. When I'm not getting what I need from them, I go to visit them, to see what they're doing. Often the work is too tight, too rigid. I go through their wastepaper bins and pull out the stuff they have thrown out—little sketches, things torn apart in frustration, where the medium got away from them—and I say, 'Hey, what about this? This is a lot fresher, more exciting. Start over and give me one that's designed like the tighter version, but is fresh and fast.' By then there is no time left, so they have to work fast and loose, and it comes out better than any of the previous tries. I think it comes from the pressure.

"Then sometimes the illustrators are my best therapists. If my concept is struggling, they help me figure out what really needs to be said. Things are due so fast, you have to start rendering immediately, which is too soon. Budway used to say, 'Spend 80 percent of your time designing the illustration, and only 20 percent rendering it.'" Trousdell pauses, remembering some past conversation. "Of course, he was so good, so accomplished, he could pull that off. For me, it's more like half and half!"

Someone walks by and shoots Trousdell a look, without breaking stride. Another change, and stress knits over his brow.

"Hey look, I want to get together with you and talk more. Can you find your way out?" I speak with Don again on other occasions, and he is helpful in getting me networked in Atlanta. I remark on the similarity of thought about style between Trousdell as designer-art director, and Edelmann as designer-illustrator. Both find that their success at expression creates expectations in the marketplace that add additional challenges to their creative process.

> **❝Style gets in the way of real expression, makes it harder to do work that truly communicates, especially when clients have preconceived ideas. You want to tell them 'Get over it, turkey— that was then! We are working on tomorrow, not yesterday!❞**

Dave Condrey and Bill Duncan
WELCOME TO THE GREATEST MARKETING ORGANIZATION ON EARTH

Any new arrival in the Atlanta business community, in any line of work, is quickly drenched in the Coca-Cola corporate mystique. It's not a conspiracy, nor is it mass hypnosis. There are a few dissenters, of course, but virtually everyone in Atlanta loves Coca-Cola, the organization, if not the beverage. Usually it is both; Coca-Cola is Atlanta's vin de pays—the vintage of the region. As a little boy, it was my duty to bring a cold Coca-Cola to my dad while he was working on his car. I heard his "Aaah!" of satisfaction after the first swig; I felt I understood the brand. Even so, within a few days of my arrival, I'm surprised by the reverence for the beloved brand. It's not until the appearance of an unexpected mentor that I begin to drink deeply.

OCTOBER 1978 I begin calling on Coke soon and often for design business. Newbie that I am, I dial the main number, get the operator, and ask for the person in charge of buying graphic design. On five different days, each operator gives me a different name. By the end of the week I reach each of them at least twice, and figure I must have the whole organization covered. They begin to respond; I get a few chances to show my samples, but not much work. I know from my time in Penn Station Booth 6 that this is just a matter of persistence.

Waiting in the lobby at Coca-Cola USA for an appointment, I strike up a conversation with a big-framed man in a tailored gray suit with an equally outsized sample case.

"You must be new to Coca-Cola," he observes. He puts out his hand. "Dave Condrey. Let me welcome you to the greatest marketing organization on Earth!" His smile is genuine, yet not without a trace of mischief. I hear his elevator pitch, and give him mine. Condrey comes across as a sort of cowboy-poet turned salesman. The company he represents, Colad, manufactures custom-imprinted

ring binders. His commanding size contrasts with his courtly manners and willingness to help.

"Who have you seen so far at Coke? Really. You haven't spoken yet
to Bill Duncan? Let me introduce you. First thing you have to know
about Coca-Cola is, no matter how long you have been calling on
the company, no matter how many people you know, there is always
more opportunity. Bill Duncan is where you need to start. Let me
give you some background."

"Mr. Condrey, Fred says you can come on up."

Condrey goes to the receptionist and says a few words, and
returns to the waiting area.

"Duncan has been here a long time. He may not be at the top of
the pay scale, but he has a dotted line to the CEO. Bill handled all
of Coke's internal advertising needs for a long time, but as fast as
he and his department are, the volume has grown so much that it
is now decentralized. But anything that comes from Mr. Woodruff
goes to Duncan. Robert Woodruff, you need to understand, is a
merchant prince masquerading as a good old boy. His daddy led the
investment team that bought Coke from the Candler family, and
Bob Woodruff built this thing"—here Condrey waves his arm casually to encompass the Coke campus—"from a little regional business
to a global marketing powerhouse."

I feel as though my fortunes are taking a turn for the better!

Condrey is getting warmed up, and continues: "You talk to a
banker, a lawyer, an accountant in Atlanta. If they're established in
business here, the first thing they're going to tell you is that they do
work for Mr. Woodruff. They won't say 'Coke'—every hotdog stand
does business with Coke. They will say 'Mr. Woodruff.' He is the
genius, the leader, the fountain of profits, and The Boss."

Condrey pauses to think what he might have missed. "At most
companies, marketing is just a department. Here, look at this
building. The five or six windows on the top floor, that's where
they count the money. Every other window, on every other floor, is
marketing. Bottling, that is done at the bottlers. HR, legal, all that
is there, but this is an organization built by the smartest marketer
alive. David, I'm telling you to keep your ears open every time you
step in an office here. You will get an education in marketing second
to none."

I meet many other Cokevangelists, though few are so eloquent.

True to his word, Condrey makes an introduction that rapidly results in an appointment. The Coca-Cola headquarters building is designed and appointed with understated extravagance. There is fine art and big-name designer furniture throughout the lobby and common areas. Yet Bill Duncan's office is modest, without windows, and filled with projects in progress. It is orderly, but it is obvious that this is the engine room, not the guest hall. There are people coming in and out with constant questions, updates, and needs.

Duncan begins by saying, "So, I must thank Dave Condrey for sending you my way. I don't often get a chance to see new talent. What have you got?"

I hand him the Valise. I keep my mouth shut except when he asks a question. Every sentence is punctuated with instructions to someone who comes in the open door.

"So, David, on this photographic book, tell me about your role—*Shelley, this goes to Grizzard by rush courier*—what part did you do on this book?"

I respond, "The publisher had no staff at all, so I took a shoebox full of prints. They gave me a handwritten manuscript in Lakota Sioux, and I trafficked the translation and gave it back to them, ready to print. There were a few bumps, but there always are."

Duncan looks up from the portfolio as though I have said something profound.

"There sure are! *Dana, do we have type back from Swift Tom? Get it to Shelley the moment it walks in.* Always bumps!"

The conversation continues. Duncan is jovial and makes detailed observations. "Oh, you use Deepdene! Everyone knows Goudy Old Style—*Susan take this to legal, and tell them you will wait there for immediate comment*—everyone knows Goudy Old Style; hardly anyone knows Deepdene. *You need me, Fred? Come on in.* Deepdene, it's the best thing Goudy ever did!"

Duncan closes the Valise. His desk is a haystack. I have my card out to hand to him, but it is too far to reach. He navigates around to take the chair beside me, and then thinks better of sitting.

"David, your work is very professional and Lord knows we need all the good talent we can get. Let me give you a few insights on how-de-do at Coca-Cola." He walks to the door.

"You are still holding your business card in your hand, and the interview is almost over. I am telling you that by the time you got to here"—he is one step inside his door—"you should already have smiled, handed me your business card, and said your name clearly and cheerfully." He pauses. "Come over here and do that for me." I comply, and he says, "Why do I ask you to do that?"

"Good Southern manners?" I venture.

Duncan laughs. "Good answer! But understand: Every executive and manager here gets a hundred vendors a week flooding through. No way to remember all those names. I want your business card in front of me where I can call you by name three times during the meeting, so I remember who the hell you are. Simple as that. If I have any use for you, I'll want to make a note on your card about something I saw."

It is great to work with someone who wants to see you succeed in their organization!

Duncan motors on. "Now, you got an appointment here. That gives you the right to ask me for my card. Don't you ever leave any office at Coke without getting the occupant's card. There are hundreds of us, and we don't like having our names misspelled or our titles wrong. Titles matter here. If you don't ask for my card, you must think I'm unimportant. Write my name in stone above your desk and get it right. Pronounce it right. Remember who reports to whom. You don't want to ask me"—here he gestures to mean any of my potential clients at Coke—"who I report to. But it's fine, once you are working for me, to ask me who else reports to whom. Get it?"

Duncan strides back around his desk for the next lesson.

"Your friend Dave Condrey, he is a master at this organizational stuff. You know how many competitors he has here? Selling pretty much the same products he sells? Must be two dozen. You know how many of them I give business to?" Duncan pauses for emphasis, but not long enough for me to hazard a guess. "All of them, David, all. You know why? *Susan, have we got proof back from Swift Tom? They're sweating bullets upstairs.* We have enough programs needing that product here to swamp any factory, including Condrey's. But you know who gets the best projects? You got it. Why? Condrey any faster? Nope. Lord knows he isn't cheaper! It's because he knows the people here, the structure, the unwritten rules. *James, you need me? Sure, let me see it. Case-Hoyt printing it? OK, get going.* Dave knows about relationships here that I wouldn't have guessed, and I've been here for centuries! *You got the courier here waiting for this? Go, Jamie, go!* When your 'bumps in the road' come along, I want my work in the hands of someone who will know."

Duncan is holding my card and he looks at me emphatically.

"David, understand I am not always around to give my vendors the answers they need. Even if there were five of me here 24/7 my vendors would still not get all the answers they need. So I want my work with Condrey, who knows not to call my boss to ask something basic. *Hey, Will, tell the boss he will have his storyboard a day early.* The work goes to the people we can trust to get it right. Your 'bumps in the road' aren't just expensive in money. They entail risk for me. Mistakes made in haste can take a very long time to repair. I can get a hundred projects right, but I get one crucial one a little bit wrong or a little bit late, and things get ugly." He shakes his head ruefully to finish the sentence.

Duncan's pace escalates; he exhales and smiles. "You get the idea. Condrey watches my back. He will get the information from an assistant or, Lord knows how he gets it, but he never"—knocking on the only square inch of wood visible on his desktop—"lets us down. You learn what he knows and you will be invaluable to us, just like he is. I'm telling you to ask him to coach you."

"Now I'm not telling you all this because I think you are an amateur designer. On the contrary, I think you're a hell of a designer and you have a fresh perspective that we need. I do think you are a bit of an amateur salesman, and that is a sin people here won't tolerate. We work for the greatest salesman that ever lived. You can have the best design in the world, but if you don't storm in and sell it to me with enthusiasm and finesse"—here I flash on Condrey, welcoming me to the greatest marketing organization on Earth—"I won't trust you with our best work." A bell goes off in my head. For what seems like a hundred interviews, designers have been telling me how client trust is the key to doing great work, and agonizing over

> **❝You can have the best design in the world, but if you don't storm in and sell it to me with enthusiasm and finesse, well, I won't trust you with our best work.❞**

how hard it is to gain that trust. Here is a guy who buys hundreds of creative assignments a year, and he is telling me how to get his trust! Quality+Enthusiasm+Finesse=Trust. Could it really be this simple?

"I want you to do a project. We gave this project to someone new who used up all our time and didn't understand the project. I want you to take this sketch"—without a bit of rummaging, he pulls a manila folder out of the haystack—"and read this creative work plan. Then get me something that proves to me that you really did all the great work in this portfolio. If you have questions, call Condrey and get him to explain. Call me and give me a price—someone will call you with a purchase order. You can't bill me without the PO. I needed these designs yesterday." He's down the hall and gone.

I decide to park in the lobby and make notes. Dave Condrey appears from the elevator bay, a supersize man trailing an even more supersize sample case on wheels. I flash on a Jim Burke image—a switching engine pulling a loaded freight car.

The engineer wheels up and smiles, "So, how did your meeting go with Mile-a-Minute Duncan?"

"He gave me a project. And he sure thinks highly of Dave Condrey!"

Condrey feigns exasperation. "He had better! All the times I have dumped our factory upside down to meet his impossible deadlines!" Still smiling, "Duncan is a prince of a fellow. I have a crisis to quell now, but I want to hear about your project."

Condrey meets me for coffee the next morning and gives me some of the unwritten rules. "Start with the obvious. To most of the world, Coke and Pepsi are like, you know, Laurel and Hardy; rivals who can't live without one another. Their employees meet on a golf course, they are cordial. But inside the Coke organization, you never mention beverages that begin with P! You also never forget they are the elephant in the room. To them, it's thermonuclear war. You never mention that organization by name. You always say 'The Competition.'"

He moves on. "You're a designer, so you know the Coke colors?"

"Pantone Warm Red and white."

"What's the one color that does not exist within Coca-Cola HQ?"

"Pantone Pepsi blue?"

"Pantone anything that even smells a little bit like anything close

Aha: An inherent contradiction: buyers are always looking for a fresh perspective, yet they want someone who knows their company like an insider. As creative providers, we must quickly develop an insider's instincts—yet keep the wide-eyed wonder of a newcomer.

to blue! My factory makes swatch books of all the colors of binding materials we offer. But before I hand one out at Coke, I remove all the blue swatches." He winks. "A word to the wise."

Condrey *could* dismiss his customer's mania about "The Competition" as an amusing customer foible. Instead, he makes it an article of faith—even to the point of modifying swatchbooks so that the odious color blue does not exist! Condrey has grasped an essential truth: *Competition is an important driver of brand excellence.* He reels off other job-related details; my breakfast is cold but I have an outline for a Coca-Cola encyclopedia.

"Now, what's your first objective?" he asks me.

I'm about to say something about the design process, but Condrey answers his own question, "*Purchase order!* You can't get paid without a purchase order, and if you submit an invoice without one, you make Bill look bad. Duncan likes your work, and he is short of fresh talent just now. Show him you can deal with their paperwork, and you will get more work from him than you know what to do with." Condrey continues, "By the way, Coke people are in such a hurry, they can give you the impression that the cost of things doesn't matter, but it does, greatly. It's OK to talk money early, often, and whenever they change the mandate you have outlined on your proposal. Which," he winks, "has been known to happen! All this is doubly true when starting a relationship. Every person at Coke is a new relationship. The pricing expectations for Duncan may differ from those for the guy in the office next to him. Even if the project is so open-ended that you can't price the whole thing, give them a price to get to the next step. Got it?"

❝Talk money early, often, and whenever your client changes the mandate you have outlined on your proposal—which has been known to happen! ❞

I'm about to ask something else, but the waitress is clearing the table and Condrey the switching engine is revving up to move cargo. "What's your next objective? Deliver fast! I have no idea how long it takes you to come up with an idea, but if I were you I'd try to get him something less than twenty-four hours after you phone in your PO."

Condrey's coaching proves to be the start of a variety of projects. There is an inherent contradiction to all this: Duncan—and many buyers of design like him—are always looking for a fresh perspective, yet they want someone who knows their way around the company like an insider. As creative providers, we must quickly develop an insider's instincts to avoid blunders, yet keep the freshness and wide-eyed wonder of a total newcomer.

Robert Woodruff
TAKE OUT EVERYTHING BUT THE ENJOYMENT

Robert Woodruff (1889–1985) is known for the leadership that built Coca–Cola from a struggling regional enterprise to a global marketing powerhouse. Born in Columbus, Geogia, he moved to Atlanta. He was an indifferent scholar, but his exceptional skill as a salesman at White Motor Company quickly resulted in promotions and leadership roles. His father, Ernest, as president of Trust Company Bank, led the syndicate that took Coca-Cola public, and the fledgling company needed a dynamic leader. Both Wood-ruffs had invested in the stock offering, and it was underwater. At age 33, Robert Woodruff became CEO and began one of the most amazing growth stories in American business. He not only grew the business, he established a culture of competition, civic involvement, and marketing prowess that attracted top-flight talent. A philanthropist of almost unimaginable generosity, Woodruff and his wife, Nell, gave away hundreds of millions of dollars over their lifetime, benefiting Atlanta and many people worldwide. Woodruff was involved in shaping Coca-Cola's brand image and often personally reviewed advertising campaigns for content and design.

1982 For my first few years in Atlanta, I make the rounds to the major ad agencies, design studios, and printing companies with the Valise. My portfolio consists mainly of book designs. There are few book publishers in Atlanta, but because so many companies have cut their staff, it's a pretty good time to be an available free-lance designer. My contacts result in a stream of freelance work that grows steadily.

The amazing thing about making direct calls is how long people remember you. I get a call from Case-Hoyt, a printing company I called on two years ago. Their art director remembered I had done books, and they have a book to design, about none other than the Coca-Cola magnate Robert Woodruff. Actually, it is a biography of his wife, Nell. The Nell Hodgson Woodruff School of Nursing wants to publish a biography about "Miss Nellie," as she is affectionately known, and give it as a present to all the students at the school. Equally important, I learn, the book is to be a present to Robert Woodruff, who is 92.

Even though Dave Condrey has briefed me on the Coke orga-nization, I have only a northerner's understanding of Woodruff's importance. Only later, after the book circulates with my name on it, do I understand the mythic quality of the man: a tough yet charismatic boss, an aggressive and opportunistic businessman, and a philanthropist of great generosity. There is a mythology surround-ing his extravagant lifestyle, his hobnobbing with presidents, his devotion to his wife, and his vocal claim that he never read books. I decide not to remark to my client on the irony of creating a book for a man who claims not to read.

The art director gives me the name of his chosen biographer, Doris Lockerman Kennedy. "You'll like her. She's written half a dozen books. She is a contemporary of Mr. Woodruff, but don't let her age fool you, she is sharp as a tack. She has outlived several husbands, including the man who shot John Dillinger."

Ms. Kennedy is indeed delightful, and it turns out her manuscript is done as professionally as any by an OUP author—and more quickly. Ms. Kennedy has an amazing memory for historical sub-jects, and many of her insights find their way into the design of the book. She takes me on a guided tour of the School of Nursing.

"Nell was trained as a nurse before she married Bob and became the spouse of the richest man in Atlanta. It was her passion for nursing that lead the Woodruffs to donate so generously to the Emory School of Nursing. Here is her portrait, one of several Mr. Woodruff commissioned. It's an Elizabeth Shoumatoff—you know the name? Of course not, you are too young. She was *the* high-society portraitist. After Nell died of an aneurysm, Mr. Woodruff purchased this wall-mounted vase and paid for a fresh pink rosebud to be placed in the vase next to her portrait—*every day*."

This is the type of insight designers seek as a way to personalize design. So this story becomes a foundation for the book design, and a rosebud ornament to be used on the chapter titles and binding of the book. It turns out to be an important detail.

Some days later, I get a call. Case-Hoyt likes my design, and I am to show it to Joe Jones before it is presented to Emory. I've heard of the Jones brothers, Joe and Boisfeuillet, who have their names on buildings at Emory University.

Kennedy explains that Joe Jones is Mr. Woodruff's man at Coca-Cola, now that Mr. W is retired.

Despite my coaching by Condrey and project experience with Duncan, I feel I am being admitted to the inner sanctum. I am shown into a calm, richly appointed office, greeted cordially and offered refreshment. Since I was hired by Case-Hoyt and Emory is the client, Mr. Jones does not know me; so I take time to do a little verbal resume, being careful to include Oxford and my work for Duncan along with recent projects. We review visuals for the design. I explain the choice of font and paper, but see that he is not interested in the technical details.

"The binding is navy and white, to match the uniforms worn by the undergraduate nurses." Jones perks up. I realize I just have to talk about the emotional connections. I replay Doris Kennedy's story about the rosebuds, then point them out on the binding design and pages.

Jones nods more vigorously. "Robert will like that. He is not really that much of a reader, but he will like the subject, the photographs, and the rosebuds. It's too bad there's no color in the book."

"The Elizabeth Shoumatoff portrait of Nell that hangs in the lobby of the Nursing School is in color. We could use it as the book's frontispiece," I suggest. Jones nods.

"You have done well. Please proceed. Will we be able to have this before Mr. Woodruff's birthday?"

Design approval, proofreading, and printing move ahead on schedule. I go on to other things.

"David, Joe Jones here. I have the first copies of *Devotedly, Miss Nellie* back from the bindery. Do you want to see them?"

Again I am in Jones's office. "This looks great," says Mr. Jones. "I want you to accompany me when I show the book to Mr. Woodruff. Ms. Kennedy and Dean Grexton want to be there, but they're both tied up, and this should not wait."

The Woodruff mansion holds a commanding position in Atlanta's Buckhead neighborhood. The sight of it brings a bit of apprehension. Woodruff personally oversaw many of the ad campaigns that put Coca-Cola at the forefront of American business. What if he has strong opinions about typography? What if he rejects it?

Jones says, "This should be a cakewalk. Let me do the talking unless there are questions about the design."

Woodruff is seated, a newspaper and a humidor on his desk. When we enter, Jones and Woodruff embrace cordially, like wartime heros at a peacetime reunion.

"We have brought you something special—a memory of Nell," Jones tells him.

Woodruff's eyes light up momentarily. Jones is holding the book in his hands. Woodruff has not reacted yet, but is paying attention. I have heard he attends board meetings even now. Is it true that he never reads books?

"And, look at this," Jones continues. He opens the book to the color portrait of Mrs. Woodruff, and the title page with the decorative border of rosebuds. "It has your rosebuds! On all the pages!"

Woodruff takes the book in his hands, looking intently, finds the pages of photographs, and turns a few pages with a wistful air. He returns to the frontispiece, and browses a bit more.

Jones nods at me approvingly. This is why I love designing books. Books can contain a story, a person, an epic, a tragedy. They can transport us to our best places.

Woodruff speaks up; his voice is thin, but the air of command is unmistakable. "Be sure to tell Edna that Nell and I—how much this means to us."

Jones, who is possibly the most diplomatic person I have ever witnessed, intones, "Of course, Bob, of course. Edna was to be here today but had to leave on urgent family business, and asked that we not delay giving you the book. And I want you to meet Mr. Laufer, who designed the book."

I come forward, Jones's hand on my shoulder. Woodruff shakes my hand, and for an instant, I am in the gaze of this man—full of years, commander of millions, and stuff of legends. In that instant, a voice inside whispers, *This is your only chance, learn something important!* Dave Condrey's greeting comes to mind—"Welcome to the greatest marketing organization on Earth" and I wonder if he can tell me how he made it that way. Instead the sentence unfolds, "Mr. Woodruff, sir, Bill Duncan says you're the greatest art director that ever lived. What's your secret?"

Bill actually called Woodruff a salesman and marketer, but I don't think he would have minded the attribution. Woodruff's gaze deepens, and his posture relaxes ever so slightly. His words are a bit halting, but the man is still all there.

"Bill worked for me for so long, after a while he knew what I was going to say, before I did!" His eyes drift out the window, as though to see if the headquarters building is in view, and he recalls, "Bill, all of our top people, almost always had good ideas—great ideas—sometimes so many ideas it was hard to choose. But, you know, the message is really simple. Heck, Coca-Cola—it's just something you enjoy drinking! But it's so easy to get too many good ideas competing for attention. All I did was remind Bill how simple the message is. You know, half our ads just said, 'Enjoy Coca-Cola.' I just reminded him to take out everything but the enjoyment." His eyes come back to me. "Just like your book—nothing gets in the way of Nell's..." He is back in the book, for a moment. Woodruff looks me in the eye for the first time, as if to complete his sentence. "Yes, it's her."

I think that of all the client compliments I have received, this one is perhaps the most soul satisfying. To design a biography devoted to an extraordinary woman, and then have the book recall that woman to the love of her life, that is about as good as one can hope to be. Jones is a little surprised—he probably didn't expect me to speak up. He does seem pleased that I have brought Woodruff some pleasant memories with the book and with my question.

> **For Woodruff, talking was for entertaining and making friends. Mentorship is leading by example, and leadership is about doing.**

As we return to headquarters, Jones asks, "So, what did you think of Mr. Cigar? That's what his executives used to call him."

"Even at ninety-two, he's a commanding personality. There were many things I would like to have asked him, you know, about how he inspired so much loyalty."

Jones smiles. "Oh, you wouldn't get much out of him; he mentored his people by example, and by making assignments and monitoring the results—not by talking. Talking, for Mr. Cigar, was for entertaining and making friends. Leadership was about doing. He would never let a compliment stick to him—he always conferred it on his team. I can't count how many times I heard him say, 'There is no limit to what can be accomplished if it doesn't matter who gets the credit.' By the way, he's not one to give out compliments often. You found a way with your rosebuds to make the design very personal."

From that day to this, whenever I prepare for a meeting with a client, I envision Bill Duncan spreading out a series of designs, and Mr. Cigar saying, "Take out everything but the enjoyment!" Woodruff is right: there is usually no shortage of good ideas. Great leaders know their mandate and lead by keeping the troops focused on the most fundamental message. The encounter gives me the courage to pare away inessential ideas, no matter how good they may be.

> *Advice from the greatest marketer on Earth:*
> **Take out everything but the enjoyment.**

Lawrence Gellerstedt, Jr.
LEADERSHIP IS DEVELOPING PEOPLE

 Lawrence Gellerstedt, Jr. (1924–2003) graduated from the Georgia Institute of Technology in 1945 with a degree in chemical engineering. He served in the US Navy, and joined Beers Construction in 1946. He would stay there his whole life, becoming president in 1960 and owner in 1969. Gellerstedt and his son Lawrence III built strong management teams and presided over the construction of many landmarks in the southeastern US, including buildings by world-famous architects Philip Johnson, Richard Meier, and John Portman. A prodigious fundraiser, Gellerstedt led many successful capital campaigns for schools, hospitals, arts organizations, and charities; his work enriched many communities. He received numerous service awards, and endowed a professorship in bioengineering at Georgia Tech. During his tenure as president, Beers annual sales grew nearly a hundredfold to $1.2 billion.

APRIL 1983 The Beers headquarters is a house in central Atlanta, surrounded by much larger commercial office towers. I enter and am shown to Lawrence Gellerstedt's office. It is decidedly modest. Beers builds very sleek, international-style buildings, so this very nonarchitectural office is homey by comparison.

"They got you some coffee, I see. Good," says Gellerstedt by way of a greeting. "Look, I'm expecting several calls on projects with crises, so we'll just have to work our conversation around that."

Gellerstedt is lean and decisive in his motions, as if everything is a move on a chessboard. He runs down the things he feels he wants to emphasize about his company: trustworthiness, strong leadership, good values, excellent craftsmanship, financial stability. This is what I expect, but I'm not learning the thing I most need to know: What makes this guy such a phenomenal success? How does he accomplish so much? How does he command the respect of so many Atlantans, both blue-collar and blue-blood? His phone rings in the middle of a sentence. He gets up from his desk to answer his phone, which he keeps on a credenza halfway between his desk and the door. There is no chair near the phone; he stands to talk.

He listens for a moment. "How did that pour go?" He is staring out the window, visualizing the progress of a partially finished structure. OK, you tell me how many extra men you need and you'll have them."

I need to figure out the real value proposition at Beers. Sometimes it is the hardest thing to isolate; even the customer does not always see it. "I have no problem telling the Beers story as you describe it. But what I'm hoping to get today is what sets Beers apart. Why is it growing, how do you finish such large projects on time and on budget? Why are Beers customers and employees so loyal?"

He takes another call to play hardball with a subcontractor who is holding up a project. He returns to my question as if there had been no gap. "You see that mud on my carpet? My cleaning staff knows they are not to vacuum that up. I need to know everything that happens, so I want my job captains to be able to walk in here without worrying whether they are messing up anything. Makes 'em feel they can tell me just about anything, no matter how bad.

"You see that Pontiac out there? Most of my competitors have Mercedes sedans. Some of 'em have their own aircraft. Our business is very cutthroat on price. Buildings are so expensive; I get a lot of price pressure. I drive up in that car and tell them this is the price to do the job right, they believe it. If I stand up in front of a civic group and tell them we urgently need to raise twenty million dollars for a clinic, and here's my check to get the ball rolling, I want them to say to themselves, 'He must really believe in this if he is willing to give money rather than buy himself a new car.'"

The pieces are beginning to fit together. I decide to ask about some of the other unexpected things I see.

"I notice you don't keep your phone within reach of your desk."

> **You see that mud on my carpet? My cleaning staff knows they are not to vacuum that up. I need to know everything that happens, so I want my job captains to be able to walk in here without worrying whether they are messing up anything.**

"I get more done standing for a lot of short conversations than sitting for fewer longer ones." I am reminded of Edelmann saying "You get comfortable, you get lazy." This man could not be

> **I get more done standing for a lot of short conversations than sitting for fewer longer ones.**

more different from Heinz Edelmann, yet they are both ferociously productive, so on that point, they agree. I must look at discomfort as opportunity!

"Mr. Gellerstedt, my job is to make this campaign—all your graphics—say the right thing, but also look and feel and sound right. What insights can you give me about what you want to get across?"

"Look at my office. I don't know anything about design or style or how to make things look good. Heck, that's why we hired you! We get these drawings from architects and I can't tell why they have designed their buildings certain ways, but I just follow their drawings and bam, the buildings look great.

"People will only hire you to do a big project when they trust you. It helps if they like you, but they absolutely have to have trust. Trust comes when what others say about you is better than what you say about yourself. When you make claims beyond your reputation, you are taking a big risk."

Here is a client who probably knows more about projecting a personal image of trustworthiness than ten branding experts, turning over exactly the control I need to do good work for his company; telling me, in effect, "That's your turf!" I realize this is his style of leadership, to pick good people and push the responsibility on them. It's a great motivator, to know you are empowered to act.

Gellerstedt goes on: "What else. I don't know that we really are all that much different. We treat our workers right. We want to keep the good ones for life. Let me give you an example. I had been calling on a big developer, John Wright, for four or five years, trying to get his business. They were happy with their relationship with Squire, and I couldn't budge him. The fact that he was loyal to Squire made me want him as a client all the more.

> **I don't know anything about design or style or how to make things look good. Heck, that's why we hired you!**

❝So here we had an endorsement from a key man in a competitor's organization bring us a relationship I couldn't win with five years of sales pitches. The way you treat people does a lot of your selling for you. ❞

"Then one day I get a call from him asking if we have the capacity to take on an office building for him. Usually someone starts you out with a small project, but this isn't a starter-type project. I said, 'What made you decide to call us now?' Wright says, 'Jimmy Saronsen called to tell me he was leaving my project. Jimmy says he has always wanted to work for Beers, and finally got the chance. So I figured, if I have to hire Beers to get Jimmy, then Beers must be as good as you have been telling me all this time!' So here we had an endorsement from a key man in a competitor's organization bring us a relationship I couldn't win, even with five years of sales pitches! If I can treat my employees and subs as well as I treat my best customers, then the word on the street does a lot of selling for us. So, to answer your question, I just you want to make us look on the outside the way we really are. An all-around good place to work with."

Gellerstedt makes it sound so simple, but clearly if it were simple everyone would be doing it. I am still at a loss for how to translate these values into visual form.

"David, I may have time for one more short question."

I have to get to the center of things, fast.

"When people talk about you and Larry and what Beers means to the community, they always seem to use the word 'leadership.' How do you define leadership? What makes your way of leading more effective than Squire's, for instance?"

"Now, I didn't say we were better than Squire, they're a damn good firm ..." For the first time in our interview, Gellerstedt pauses. Then he picks up momentum:

"Leadership is developing people. Every day, I have to push responsibility at people, ask them to do something that they feel is over their heads. Some succeed, some require help, some drop the ball. I have to force the project managers who report to me to do the same with their staff. Somebody doesn't show up for work, they have to plug in their next best person. I will tell them, 'I don't want you doing that job yourself. You reach down and pull up someone and give them the chance. I want to know who you pick.' I can't tell you how many times I've had that conversation, and that manager will say, 'I don't have anyone.' But as a boss, I can't let them push their leadership responsibility back on me. I'll say,

> **"Leadership is developing people. Every day, I have to push responsibility at people, ask them to do something that they feel is over their heads. "**

'You just give me a name!' That forces them to look at the people reporting to them with new eyes. See some potential that isn't being used. I've learned that a lot of times the person we promote does a much better job than the person who didn't show up."

"All right, David, sure have enjoyed talking to you. Now you get out of here and make us look good without promising something we can't deliver!"

"I think you've convinced me there is nothing you can't deliver," I tell him.

"Good lad, now go convince the rest of the world."

Caroline Warner Hightower
DESIGN AS MAGIC

Caroline Warner Hightower (1935—   )was born in Chicago. Her father, Lloyd Warner, was a prominent anthropologist. She began her career as the advertising manager and graphic designer for the University of California Press. In 1968, she became grant officer at the Carnegie Corporation. There she gained experience in fundraising that she then applied as a consultant to many cultural and philanthropic organizations.

Hightower was hired as the executive director of AIGA in 1977. For the better part of two decades she worked tirelessly to create a vital and dynamic organization that could effectively represent the needs of the design community. During her tenure the membership increased from 1,200 to 11,300 and chapters were established in 38 cities. Programming grew and flourished. In addition to initiating AIGA's highly influential national biennial design conferences, the national business conference, the AIGA library, and the AIGA Education Committee, Hightower was the architect of some significant stand-alone programs and publications. These include a national symposium titled "Why Is Graphic Design 93% White?" and the publications *United States Department of Transportation Symbol Signs, Graphic Design for NonProfit Organizations,* and *AIGA Standard Contracts for Graphic Designers.* Since leaving AIGA, Hightower has continued to work as a program-development and fundraising consultant. Among the institutions she has worked with are the American Numismatic Society, American Society of Media Photographers, New York University Arts Administration Program, United Way, and the Clio Awards. She was honored as an AIGA Medalist in 2004.

1987 Nine years have passed since my my interviews with the New York designers. Ed Gottschall's replacement as executive director of AIGA does not work out. The organization is in disarray—membership is down, finances are uncertain. AIGA's board reaches out to a new executive director, Caroline Warner Hightower. Hightower wades in and gets AIGA back on its feet and growing. As a member at large in Atlanta, I am a bit removed from all this, until ...

Hightower makes a visit to Atlanta and a dozen other cities. She has announced a bold initiative to start a chapter system and grow the membership. I am one of ten members at large in Georgia, so she calls, and we have lunch.

Hightower begins with some observations about the changes in the profession, the declining role of New York as the capital of the profession, and the need to involve everyone.

I begin a bit skeptically. "Why chapters, why now? All of us look at what we get from AIGA for our membership fee, and many years it amounts to a listing in the membership roster and some invitations to spend more money entering shows."

Hightower has startlingly good answers. "Let me tell you how this started. I got a letter from a member at large in Cleveland, Ohio, telling me that they had decided to form an AIGA chapter. On their own they just did it. They needed resources, a community network.

Having grown up in Cleveland, I can picture this perfectly. "Same town that started rock and roll, or at least we Clevelanders lay claim to having invented the term!"

Hightower says, "I hadn't thought of that, but I like the spirit of it. You were enumerating the benefits of AIGA membership, but you forgot the most important one—the network." I tell her the story of my first visit to Ed Gottschall, lost portfolio and all. "Exactly!" she says. "Now today I can't see every young designer that comes through, but the idea is the same. Designers need a network, a safe zone, a place where they can teach and learn from one another. Awards are nice, but we—any professional association worth its salt—are all about the network. It's both survival and growth. Designers change jobs, they have to! The business world is changing. Corporations add and cut design departments rather quickly relative to other job categories.

> *Designers need a safe zone, a place where they can teach and learn from one another. Awards are nice, but we—any professional association worth its salt—are all about building a lifelong network. It's both survival and growth.*

"Design matters more than it ever has before. We need to move beyond giving awards to each other that only designers understand, and start being about demonstrating why design matters to the world. And we need to help these wonderful creative people cope with the changes they face. AIGA has always been about the network, but the network needs to get bigger, fast. Design, for us, is a process. It can even be a fairly laborious process, when we get clients changing things by the hour. But for most of the world, who don't ever see the process, design is magic with a capital *M*. We have to be about sharing that magic."

This makes me think of George Nelson, talking about the benefits of design without saying anything to his prospects about process.

> *Design, for us, is a process. It can even be a fairly laborious process. But for most of the world, who don't ever see the process, design is magic. We have to be about sharing the magic.*

"Magic" is the wrong word to use with my clients, but she is right.

Hightower goes on. "Design simplifies, transforms, makes things look better and work better—and many people will pay a premium for it. AIGA needs to be about promoting the electricity that design brings to business, to our broader culture. Not everyone has the ability to visualize, or grasp problems in the way designers do. But except for the visually impaired, everyone sees how a great design enhances its subject."

I remember Victor Papanek designing for underserved populations and say, "Design can include the visually impared too."

Hightower gets a boost from this observation and kicks it up a notch: "I took the job at AIGA, even with the organization in somewhat of a mess, because I love designers. I love how they think so differently from other business people. I love how they reframe questions to make them more exciting. I love how they convert abstract problems into concrete images, yet it is somehow filtered through their own personality. You can give the same poster assignment to a hundred different designers, and get a hundred good posters that are wildly diverse." I find myself thinking that her conviction and confidence would make Bill Duncan proud.

> **❝I love designers. I love how they reframe questions to make them more exciting. We give the same briefing to 100 designers, and get 100 posters that all deliver the message, yet are wildly diverse. ❞**

I remember that Hightower worked for a short time as a designer but spent more time in other areas. I don't want to be rude, but I am concerned about whether someone who is not a designer can pull this off. I try to say this obliquely. "I'm curious, what makes you so convinced this is what designers need? Does the board agree?"

Hightower must have heard this question in many ways from other people. She confides that her being a design aficionado—but not a designer—caused some uneasiness among board members when she was interviewing for the job.

"When I applied for the job," she says, "the board asked how many years I had been in the profession. I told them I had only practiced graphic design for a few years, but that I been a singer in a bar for a few months. I'm not exactly sure why, but that put the designers in the room at ease. Singing in a bar seems to everyone much more difficult, fairly creative—and anyway, what difference does it make? as long as we like each other!"

"Here is the important thing: Designers are great at seeing the needs of others and making them visible, comprehensible, fun. Designers are much less good at seeing themselves. They get excited about details too small to be of any value. AIGA helps them be practical." She is "selling" her specific organization, but the comment applies more broadly as well. I muse on her comment about small details. I think of how Dorfsman would disagree—how he stressed that getting the subliminal details right makes the visual pop. I think of James Craig's discipline, keeping the powder dry until the right job comes along where you can chase perfection. Then, as always, I think of Fred Schneider's poster: "To be right is the most terrific personal state that nobody is interested in." I don't go into it with Hightower, but clearly, there is no universal answer, there is only the most comfortable resolution for each individual designer.

Hightower announces that AIGA will hold its first national convention in January of 1985, in Boston, and that she is asking all cities to have chapter officers elected by then and have at least three delegates there. I am ready to step up, but my inner skeptic resurfaces. "How do you know anyone will see the value in attending a national convention?"

She lets slip the mysterious smile of a singer who knows how to work the audience. "Paul Rand and Milton Glaser will be there." I book my tickets, and our Atlanta chapter gets off the ground.

SAUL BASS ENCORE:
WHEN THE STUDENT IS READY, THE TEACHER WILL APPEAR

1987 For some years after hearing Saul Bass's lecture, I keep looking for the film he described, *Notes on Change*, to appear in theaters or as part of a film festival, but it never does. Maybe the title changed? Then in 1989, at the second AIGA national convention in San Francisco, I see Bass again. We happen to be part of a group walking from one venue to another, and I am able to introduce myself.

> **❝I have come to be at peace with being a designer. I need the intensity of the relationship with a great team and a demanding director or client to bring out the best in myself. ❞**

"Mr. Bass, I was among the audience you addressed in Pittsburgh in 1970. I remember vividly how you read to us a script for *Notes on Change*, and I thought it was a world-beater. I have been hoping to see it and was just wondering if it ever got made?" Bass looks a bit startled, and says no, it is one of many pet projects from that period he had not been able to get funded.

"Now I have the money that I could make it myself, but I keep getting calls from the studios to do this title or that project, and I never tire of that thrill. I have come to be at peace with being a designer. I need the intensity of the relationship with a great team and a demanding director or client to bring out the best in myself. The personal projects—I don't know, someday maybe."

I thank him and tell him that I still hope he will find time to make *Notes on Change*. The old smile flashes: "If you remembered it this long, you have already seen it!"

In this short exchange, Bass resolves for me the crux of the design versus art definition that has eluded me for so long. The product—

> *Aha: What distinguishes design from art is the person doing the work. An artist is internally centered, bringing work out of an inner reservoir. The designer is other centered; finding a dynamic relationship with a client brings the work to its fullest potential. One can wear both hats, just not simultaneously!*

design or art—is not the locus of the distinction. Nor is the type of aesthetic experience—gallery contemplation vs. utilitarian satisfaction. Finally, the distinction has nothing to do with the remuneration, or lack thereof. What distinguishes design from art is the person doing the work. An artist is internally motivated, bringing work out of an inner reservoir. The designer is *other centered*, and finds motivation and satisfaction in a relationship with a client or user to bring forth the work. That is not to say that artists cannot be designers, or that designers cannot rise to the level of fine artists. The results can be equally profound and far-reaching. This definition works for problem cases like the Diego Rivera mural—there was a client, but the mural was torn out because the work was ultimately Rivera's own content, not a collaborative venture. It may be possible to categorically decide whether a given work is design or art; it may also be misleading.

George Nelson's 80-18-2 maxim: **"***You may have a hundred new ideas. Eighty have been done before. Eighteen are original but fall somewhere between mediocre and stupid. That leaves you with two good, original ideas! You have an obligation to use yourself up!***"**

Ultimately, if there needs to be a definition, placing a work somewhere on a continuum between art and design is rather more useful than a dichotomy. I remember Bucky Fuller saying "You can't do everything, you have to decide where to invest your career time." There are even lots of examples of people who were accomplished both as artists and designers—Le Corbusier, Leonardo, Bucky Fuller, Ray Eames, John Portman—it's a long and interesting list. I decide that the conflict arises when I want to make design into art. One person can wear both hats, just not simultaneously! It is actually beneficial to do so, as each activity can enrich the creative approach of the other.

Recognizing this fundamental difference, it then becomes crucial to apply George Nelson's 80-18-2 maxim.

Aha. I have always felt that the language and tools of graphic design have vast untapped potential beyond what makes sense for client work. As a result of this brief encounter with Bass, my career focus sharpens. I resolve to apply Nelson's Maxim to all my ideas, to be willing to wear two hats, and to always be conscious of which hat— my internally centered artist's hat or my other-centered designer's hat—is optimum for a given situation.

Sidney Topol
A GOOD PROPOSAL ON TIME

Sidney Topol (1925–   ) served in World War II, then received a BS in physics in 1947 from the University of Massachusetts Amherst. He later attended the Harvard-MIT Radar School. Topol began his career with Raytheon Co., and went on to serve as president of Scientific Atlanta from 1971 to 1983, CEO from 1975 to 1987, and chairman of the board from 1978 to 1990. During his tenure, the company grew dramatically and developed the concept of cable/satellite connection, which established satellite-delivered television for the cable industry. He also played a key role in the development of international telecommunications trade policies.

He is the president of the Topol Group, a venture capital firm, and the founder of the Massachusetts Telecommunications Council. He is in the Cable Television Hall of Fame and the Georgia Technology Hall of Fame. He established the Sid and Libby Topol Scholarship and the Topol Distinguished Lecturer Series at UMass Amherst. He holds an honorary doctor of science degree from UMass.

1985-1991 I am asked to participate in a panel discussion about annual reports for the National Investor Relations Institute (NIRI). Each panelist is asked to look at several dozen annuals and give opinions about the relative merits of each, then discuss them in front of a NIRI audience and take questions. I try to be candid, and in doing so, I hit a few nerves. One of the annuals on which my candor falls particularly hard belongs to Scientific Atlanta, and the next day I get a call from their corporate secretary, Margaret Wilson Jones. To my surprise, she invites me to visit their office to discuss it further.

Sidney Topol is a short, fit man with wavy hair and the aura

Aha: The goal of marketing, for the design professional, is to be hired for your expertise, in spite of your price, rather than the other way around!

of a superhero. His office is modest in size and furnishing, but there is a Kandinsky painting on the wall behind his desk. Introductions are brief and he notes the time on his watch.

"We are here to discuss?" he asks.

Jones starts, "This is the gentleman I told you about who..."

"Ripped up our annual report," Topol says congenially.

She rejoins, "Well, I thought he would be a good choice because he had most of the same criticisms you did."

Two of the criticisms on which we agree are a lack of continuity between the visuals and the narrative, and a lack of exciting imagery. Jones explains that there has never been a budget specifically for annual report photography, so they use what they can get from customers, which is uneven. I recommend that we take photographs of the most significant customer installations first, then build a narrative around that. Topol and Jones give me a quick list of a dozen such installations, and agree on a next meeting.

Driving back to the office, I realize that nobody at SA asked to see samples of our work, and we did not discuss budget, yet I had been hired. I flash back to my discovery of the Bertoli toggle, a decade before; I sense I have crossed another career boundary. For many years, I was selling from my portfolio and getting hired based on price, in spite of my expertise. Today, for the first time, I am hired for my expertise, without any portfolio. Pricing, though still important, comes later. The idea of the expertise-based sale comes alive.

We book an accomplished location photographer named Flip Chalfant and get him on the road. The team travels to several installations. I arrive in Topol's office a month later with photographs representing six customers—no design or written content. I have brought contact sheets of a thousand photographs of SA customer equipment, and prints of fifty.

Jones says, "Don't take the contact sheets to a CEO. He wants you to make the decisions. Just show him your best shots."

I take the photos to Topol, but I'm concerned—I tell him I would rather show them in the context

> **"I get that from my engineers all the time—'We can't present yet, it isn't finished.' Over and over, I remind them: A good proposal on time is better than the perfect proposal too late!"**

> **❝ You have a sort of love-hate relationship with business details. Leaders have to be about big vision, shining a light far down the right path. You have to delegate the details or you never get out of the weeds. At the same time, you need details reported to you. ❞**

of a design. Topol is studying the photographs intently, sorting them into groups. Without looking up, he says, "I get that type of comment from my engineers all the time—'We can't present yet, it isn't finished.' Over and over, I have to tell them: A good proposal on time is better than the perfect proposal too late!" Inside of a minute, he hands me back roughly a third of the photographs. "These ten pictures are brilliant. I want you to continue. Bring me twenty more images like these and we will make Scientific Atlanta a forty-dollar stock!"

The 1985 annual report for SA comes out, and looks great. Topol confides to me later, "When I handed this annual report out at the first analyst meeting of the year, I had them eating out of my hand!"

Almost immediately, we begin working on the next year's annual. I'm with the photographer on location, documenting some large SA earth stations owned by one of the network affiliates. It's cold, we are behind schedule, and we just need to take photographs and move on. The administrator of the installation is unhappy, and he decides to make an issue of it while we are there. He shows me several problems with his SA earth stations.

He says grimly, "I can't get any response out of my field rep, and frankly, I will buy my next earth stations from another company."

I'm about to say that this isn't my area, and I'm just a contractor, but instinct speaks: "Here's a major customer in a top-tier market, telling you the account is on the ropes. Do something!" It's as though, standing there in the snow, a crevasse is opening before me; I must either fall in or jump. I have no authority to make promises—or do I? Jones said I had been "deputized." As designers we make promises on behalf of our clients all the time. Making that relationship work in both directions feels risky, but it can be crucial to the success of the business. I look this distressed customer in the eye and promise to take his complaint to the top. A week later

I relate this story to Topol. I hand him a few snapshots of the problem installation. Topol is silent, his jaw tense.

I say, "I had no authority to promise him service, but the salesman in me wouldn't let me sidestep such an obvious distress signal."

"You did the right thing," Topol reassures me. "I'm just concerned how I can get this fixed fast. The relationship—if we can save it—is worth many times your design fee."

> **I learned during our go-go growth years that my people would work tremendously hard and gladly let their leader have all the magazine covers and industry awards—as long as that leadership also takes the heat when things go wrong.**

The next time I arrive at SA to sign in, the receptionist says, "Oh, Mr. Laufer, you are approved for an upper-level badge." She hands me paperwork and sends me off to get security clearance and a mug shot. A simple act of salesmanship elevates my status within the organization. Design is valuable when designers do valuable things. Sometimes those valuable things are creative, but are not design.

Topol makes the transition to chairman and is getting ready to leave Atlanta and return to his beloved Boston. I have one lunch date open before he goes, so I ask him if he will give me some valedictory thoughts on leadership. He talks about the technical achievements that have propelled SA during his stewardship of the company, but I am interested in the *how* of his leadership.

He grasps this line of thinking instantly. "You have a sort of love-hate relationship with business details. Leaders have to be about big vision, overall direction. Shining a light far down the right path. You have to delegate the details or you never get out of the weeds. At the same time, you need details reported to you. You must have the confidence of and rapport with your direct reports, and foster a working chain of command. Where there is fear in the ranks, there's a tendency to hide problems and failures from senior management— that can be catastrophic. I learned during our go-go growth years that my people would work tremendously hard and gladly let their leader have all the limelight—all the magazine covers and news clips and industry awards—as long as that leadership also takes the heat when things go wrong."

> **❝ If you read the business magazines, it sounds as though entrepreneurship is all about boldly taking risk. The vision does indeed have to be bold, but to achieve it, your team has to work at minimizing risk, making small mistakes until you have all your systems working. ❞**

We discuss the differences between leadership and management. Topol quotes the great management consultant and writer Peter Drucker: "Management is doing things right, leadership is doing the right things."

Topol elaborates, "A lot of people can, with training and experience, do things right if you supply them with good objectives. Doing the right things, on the other hand, can be a lonely endeavor. If you read the business magazines, it sounds like entrepreneurship is all about boldly taking risk. I think it's more about figuring out ways to minimize risk. The vision does indeed have to be bold, but to achieve it, your team has to make small, low-cost mistakes until you have your product working."

Under the leadership of Topol, and later CEOs, SA does indeed return to profitable operation. Ten years after Topol's retirement, the company is purchased by Cisco Systems for $43 a share—$3 per share more than Topol had promised himself at our first meeting!

Roberto Goizueta
CREATIVE FRIENDS

Roberto Goizueta (1931–1997) was born in Havana, Cuba. Goizueta was educated in a Jesuit college in Havana and graduated from Yale University in 1953 with a degree in chemical engineering. He responded to a want ad in Cuba seeking a bilingual chemical engineer, and in 1955 joined Coca-Cola, where he would remain for the rest of his career. He rose steadily, and emigrated to the US in 1960. Goizueta successfully managed many assignments during his career—he eventually became a protégé of Robert Woodruff—and held the offices of president, CFO, and vice chairman before becoming chairman in 1981. Goizueta's leadership was characterized by bold moves. He spearheaded the development of Diet Coke, which succeeded spectacularly, but also introduced New Coke, which did not. He embraced Olympic sponsorship and opened new markets around the world. Under Goizueta's leadership, Coca-Cola tripled in size and its stock price grew by 3,500 percent! Like his mentor, Goizueta was a generous benefactor to many causes, especially Emory University, which honored his contributions by adding his name to the Roberto C. Goizueta School of Business.

MARCH 1993 Twenty years after I first stormed into Penn Station with The Great Midwest Mounted Valise, the dialogues continue. Giving and seeking mentoring becomes a pattern of life. Wearing two hats—fine art and graphic design—results in less income, but my design work benefits tremendously from my fine art exploration, and vice versa. My fine art projects, which allow the visual language of graphic design to take new directions, begin to find an audience in exhibitions and collections, but also result in design commissions that require more adventurous creative thought.

I take a page from Rand's playbook, and use speaking and publishing as a way to stimulate the types of dialogues that result in business relations of trust and synergy. In early 1993, I put together an experimental lecture on spirituality in art. One such speaking engagement results in a call from the office of Roberto Goizueta, then the chairman of Coca-Cola. Mr. Goizueta, his assistant explains, has a special art need. Could I please come in to consult?

Goizueta's friend, Don Keough, is about to retire as COO of Coca-Cola. Goizuetta wishes to give him a retirement gift. Keough is an art collector, so Goizueta wants to commission something to add to Keough's collection to touch him personally—but, says the assistant, they need to know how to select it. The timing of my lecture and their need coincided, but just barely; the retirement party is in a few weeks! I'm traveling during much of that time, and Mr. G is available only seldom.

I suggest and get verbal approval for the idea of commissioning a painter to summarize Keough's career in a lighthearted way. I make a few rough sketches in pencil for discussion.

Creative work isn't made in a vacuum. It has to be about something. In a piece of fine art, the artist picks a subject, bringing the work forth from internally collected resources. In this case, the work is focused on a recipient, so the work is "other centered." All my struggles with definitions are finally beginning to pay off! I request all the nonproprietary background on Mr. K's career that can be had.

While that is being collected, I speak to a dozen artists' representatives, scrambling to see who is available. We have a very tight time frame—and there is always a risk with commissioned work that the artwork may be rejected. I call my longtime ally Will Sumpter, who represents many artists. We settle on Drew Rose, a highly accomplished artist who meets our criteria and will have a lot of ideas.

Sumpter takes the box of Keough's memorabilia with my idea sketches and goes off to brief Rose. Two days later, Sumpter calls to say he has sketches ready and is on his way to show them to me. Most top flight illustrators are fast, and Rose is exceptionally so, but this turnaround is very unexpected.

Sumpter explains, "Drew wants to be perfect for this, so he needs to save as much time for the finished art as possible."

> **Each step in the creative process involves a jump, like finding stepping stones across a stream. Those jumps that are familiar to us are unfamiliar to the C-suite, so a little forethought goes a long way.**

"Let me guess," I say. "Drew worked on it for forty hours straight and he's sleeping now." Sumpter smiles. This goes against Don Trousdell's 80/20 observation, but this is a rather unique situation!

The concept Rose proposes is different from my sketches. Forget your ego, Laufer—how does it look? Mine is safer, but Rose's is clearly better. Sumpter and I admire it together. It has pictures and dramatizations of scenes from Keough's career, gleaned from the box of materials.

Sumpter brings me the pencil drawing, and with it a similar pencil sketch for another project, along with an exquisitely finished illustration made from that pencil sketch. In that way, Goizueta can see the content, and see how the work will look when finished.

"Wilbur, supplying a sketch and a completed work is brilliant!"

"Well, you know, that comes with experience. Each step in the creative process involves a jump, like finding stepping stones across a stream. The jumps that are familiar to us are unfamiliar to the C-suite, so a little forethought goes a long way. And besides, we may not be there to make explanations."

Sumpter is right—Goizueta, who is out of the country, approves the sketch from a phone description.

A week goes by. Sumpter brings the finished painting for me to review. We preview it together; Rose has outdone himself. The surface of this coat of arms is fairly alive with witty interpretations of Keough's career, from Notre Dame's pugilistic leprechaun to the crescendo at Coca-Cola.

I call Coca-Cola Headquarters and get on Goizueta's schedule straightaway—there is barely enough time to get the work framed if we approve it immediately. I unwrap the artwork in a meeting room adjacent to Goizueta's office. He has arranged for an easel to be brought in. I walk the easel back a few paces to sit just below a light fixture, so the artwork is in a pool of light. It looks great.

A remarkably handsome man—with dark eyes and dark hair with a few streaks of silver—strolls into the room. He has just lit an unfiltered cigarette and looks like a film noir leading man. We have conducted the project remotely from airports and by phone until now; Goizueta's assistant introduces us with impeccable protocol and we address the painting. After a moment he opens his stance to me, and makes a slight circular motion with his cigarette hand, my cue to begin. I give him a little background about the artist, and recall for him the concept of making a a work that recaps Keough's remarkable career in business. He is the subject as well as the recipient. Goizueta nods, looking intently. My instinct, from so many meetings, is to keep quiet. When a work of visual art or design engages a viewer's full attention, time stands still momentarily, and a deep comprehension takes place—something outside the realm of words and numbers.

Goizueta remarks, "It's really extraordinary. I wanted to get Don something special to say 'thanks,' you know, because he has been

such a dynamic presence at the company. Because he collects, my initial thinking was, get him a piece of art. But this goes way beyond just something to add to his collection. By being so full of personal milestones, and also having a touch of humor, this expresses a thousand things about our relationship that ..." This realization pleases him; he is still nod-

Goizueta's "creative friend" comes closer than any other term to describing the ideal designer/client relationship. **Aha!**

ding, his eyes wandering around the painting. Then he snaps back, "... that were beyond saying."

"We could never have done this without you as creative friends of the organization, to understand our needs and visualize it for us." For an instant, Goizueta brings to bear the full force of a great leader's personal charm. "Thank you, David, very well done." This has the dual purpose of complimenting the team and signaling that the meeting is over.

Goizueta's term "creative friend" stays with me. "Creative friend" gets closer to describing the ideal designer/client relationship than any to date. He might have said "art consultant," or "graphic designer," or "creative director," or any number of other more conventional titles, but the way he thought of our team was as "creative friends." A friend is someone who has your best interest at heart, in a manner somehow more deeply felt than in a professional relationship. Being creative means being a problem solver with a different way of thinking. Business people think in terms of organizational behaviors, balance sheets, breakeven volumes. Creative friends solve problems that require an understanding of organizational and financial terms, but reach into emotional and even spiritual dimensions as well. We use nonscientific means and achieve results that can be deeply felt, if not always quantified.

Finding imaginative ways to share the excitement and wonder of the visual arts—or any engaging subject—with others can be a great pathway to the special relationships so necessary to fulfilling our sense of creative mission.

Reflections
THE ROI MODEL FOR CAREER OPTIMIZATION

THE FUNDAMENTAL GOAL OF THIS BOOK is to assist the reader in making good career choices. Richard Saul Wurman has famously observed that all design professionals face divergent paths in their careers, a choice between looking good and being good. In the Foreword to this book he reiterates the story of Mies van der Rohe's pronouncement: "Do good work." Clearly, to capitalize on this advice, the designer must form a working personal definition of "good" as it applies to his or her design and talents.

The astute reader will have noticed by now that the advice offered by the interviewees, and conclusions drawn by the author, are full of contradictions. This is actually very encouraging. While some of the quotations are universal, not all the advice offered works for every person, every career, or even for the same person at different stages of career development. Every career journey involves numerous personal choices. The decisions made by individuals of extraordinary talent—while they may be fascinating—will not work for the majority of professionals. The intent of the narrative has been to provide a set of tools and ideas from which to make the best possible individual choices.

There is, happily, much to be learned from the weighing of advice—analysis and reflection are valuable decision-making tools, whether a given aphorism is discarded or taken to heart. In reflecting on the aha moments, I took a lesson from my mentor Richard Saul Wurman and set about categorizing them. They fall into three broad categories: relationships, other-centered (communications), and individual-centered (professional development). These conveniently form the acronym ROI.

Closer examination of the ROI model suggests eleven categories of career management tools.

Relationships

CLIENT RELATIONSHIPS Considerable discussion revolves around finding and nurturing client relationships that result in good work. From the mentors I surveyed, one constant emerges: Productive relationships are as individual as the designer and the client. Ivan Chermayeff observes that each client has a unique "value matrix." James Craig suggests that designers develop their individualized "recipe" for a good design opportunity. Saul Bass suggests that saying no to certain relationships is the only real leverage the creative professional can exert. Roberto Goizueta's concept of the designer as a "creative friend" is rather open-ended, but designers ultimately supply value by balancing a broad range of visual, experiential, emotional, and informational issues.

EMPLOYER RELATIONSHIPS An employer is a special category of client to whom the designer says yes every day, but the opportunity to say "no" occurs only rarely. Employers are also a special category of mentor; working closely with an accomplished master can be transformational. Learning to think like the boss—the Bertoli toggle is an example—and to navigate office politics are often the first lessons in deep empathy experienced by rising creative professionals. Following Lou Dorfsman's lead and cultivating one's detractors as well as one's supporters requires patience, persistence, diplomacy, and maturity.

MENTORING Seeking the criteria for selecting "good"—good design, good opportunity, good advice—can be befuddling. Mentoring connects personal passion with a wider base of experience. Mentoring offers not only an external view of the decision-making process, but also the courage to make the right decisions. One is never too old to seek mentoring, nor too young to give it. Mentoring relationships are characterized by an implicit agreement to be utterly frank. Because mentoring is offered in the spirit of enthusiastic support, there's an understanding that offense is never intended or taken. It's rare to find an excellent designer who is not also valued by many mentees and deeply grateful to many teachers and mentors.

PEER & COMMUNITY The narrative makes frequent reference to AIGA, an organization that I find especially rewarding to work with. Obviously, many professional associations exist; the important point is to develop a wide and deep network through one or several such associations. Caroline Hightower's remark about designers needing a safe zone describes a special kind of community, where all resources may be shared. In general, sharing techniques and experience with others strengthens all practitioners, in part by improving individual specialization. Lawrence Gellerstedt's observation that the way you treat people is your best marketing tool applies doubly to professional peer relationships.

Other-Centered (communication)

MARKETING AND EVANGELIZING (PORTFOLIO) The central aha moment from these interviews is the realization that a straightforward dialogue with an audience is infinitely more effective than an entertaining monologue. A portfolio is a conversation starter. Find ways to cultivate serendipity and personal connection in interviews. The mark of a maturing career is transcending your portfolio and being hired for expertise rather than price. Successful marketing requires passion: "Welcome to the greatest marketing organization on Earth." And passion is required to continue to refresh and revitalize your portfolio. Your ten best pieces are all you need to show, except in a mentoring situation.

APPROVALS Relatively few customers know great design when they first see it. They gauge the quality of the work presented by the passion and intensity of the presenter. The focus on being good—carried to its logical extreme—is the best ticket to a smooth approval process. This means that the more carefully researched and articulated the background is, the more concrete the criteria for judgment and approval will be. George Nelson explains a novel method for approvals: the telephone sketch. He describes how he proposed the Chrysler world's fair booth not with drawings or models, but by describing it to his client by phone, then asking, "What do you think about this idea?"

The genius of this method is that the client begins visualizing on his or her own, early in the process, so that multiple variations can be discussed and eliminated before any budget is expended on expensive visual media. It is especially effective when budget and deadline are pressing. Remember Ray Eames' suggestion to work out ideas as cheaply as possible, and save the budget for production. Quick expression is the designer's salvation. Big ideas frequently face inertia—resistance to change.

LEADERSHIP Design is not a technicality. In its best sense, design is a special category of leadership. The word "architect" is derived from "chief worker" or "first builder."

Leadership is developing people. Leadership is a love-hate relationship with details: you need details to manage, but you need the largest possible field of vision to lead effectively. Leadership is about taking risks, but minimizing risk until your idea and your team are ready for prime time. Leadership may mean being unpopular, as visionaries like Victor Papanek and Buckminster Fuller sometimes were, or it may mean coping with adulation of the type that forced Herb Lubalin and other marquee names to limit their accessibility. Great leaders value articulate employees. Great leaders are democratic at the beginning of the project, collecting input and consensus, but know when the moment for autocracy arrives. When someone steps forward to ask for responsibility, give them a shot. You can pick up experience more easily than motivation.

Individual (professional development)

CRAFT, TECHNIQUE, & SKILL Mentoring, while it may ultimately be about career, philosophy, client relationships, and war stories, frequently begins with "how did you do that?" Massimo Vignelli's interest in my lettering, and my interest in Ed Gottschall's book in progress—to name just two examples—laid the foundation for deeper discussions. While the availability of interactive and mobile training makes technical information more readily accessible, there's still nothing quite like the intensity of hearing and seeing firsthand a grand master at work. Push for speed; this forces you to internalize and compress actions. Develop your own library of things that ignite passion—drawings, photographs, lettering, notes—the connections and purpose will appear later. Use yourself up! Don't die with a single good idea left inside. Adversity should never be an excuse for bad work. The public doesn't see the excuses, only the finished work. Don't think your way to doing it right, rather, do your way to right thinking.

PASSION The passion that defines so many designers is both our greatest strength and our Achilles heel. George Bernard Shaw famously remarked that "youth is wasted on the young." I'm sure that my first clients and employers lamented as I expended precious energy on petty projects out of sheer undisciplined enthusiasm. I found James Craig's mentoring provided a crucial aha moment in my professional development; it taught me to save my best for projects that could benefit and to develop a professional distance so I could work quickly and intelligently on many projects. Hermann Zapf's observation that "when you get serious, you push for speed" is doubly valuable. Speed allows balance in life and saves stamina for those projects that require extended concentration. Speed also improves the overall quality of the output, and makes the designer more valuable to employer and employee alike.

ART VS. DESIGN Fred Schneider, my boss and mentor, referred to Franz Kline's belief that "truth is so complex that it must be—can only be—stated as a conundrum, a dynamic balance of opposing forces." This idea extends to many aspects of design thinking. The key to a productive career is discovering where it is on the continuum between beauty and utility that your own skills and desires are in perfect balance. What distinguishes art from design is the person doing the work; internally driven versus other-centered. I doubt that Saul Bass realized his brief comments about being at peace with being a designer and needing the intensity of a relationship with a great team would be so profound for the stranger he coached on a San Francisco street corner. Design is more complex than art.

PROFESSIONALISM Craig said to me, "If you throw yourself into every project as though it were a gold medal candidate, you will dash yourself to pieces." Professionalism is the counterbalance that allows passion to become productive. Professionalism in design is a result of training, discipline, experience, and maturity. Ruedi Rüegg's remark

that only complete discipline brings complete freedom undoubtedly goes back many centuries. For Heinz Edelmann, destroying his
portfolio to goad himself to new creative heights was a professional
discipline few other practitioners would have the courage to embrace.
For Zapf, the ability to teach and entertain while performing calligraphic legerdemain at a chalkboard was one of the many standards
he set for his professional life. As a business proposition, a recognizable style is salable. As an innovator, style can become confining. The
construction, by each individual designer, of high professional and
creative standards is both an enormous challenge and the bulwark
and strength of our industry. Professional standards can apply to
both business practice and evaluation of the results.

Take-Aways

"LOOKING GOOD" IS A BYPRODUCT OF "DOING GOOD WORK"

Looking good as a goal is self-limiting. Fuller distinguishes between
method and result: "I never set out to design something beautiful,
but when I am done designing, if the result is not beautiful, I know
I have done something wrong." Doing good work is, in turn, the
outcome of a quest to make work that benefits people, that makes
their lives and life choices easier. Take, for example, Ian Ballantine's
dialogue with the book-buying public through his many experiments with genre covers, or Papanek's tin can radio, which users so
loved that they provided their own decoration. Neither designer was
striving for beauty, but both had clear criteria for the good work
they needed to do. A successful designer maintains a repertoire of
stories about the benefits of good design. George Nelson rarely
spoke to audiences about design; he made a greater impact by telling
stories and highlighting benefits.

KNOW THE GOAL, MAKE THE SACRIFICE

"Good" for designers
is actually not nebulous or illusive. When Kline says, "To be right
is the most terrific personal state that nobody is interested in," he
asserts that every individual is capable of excelling at something
that makes them happy, but the process of discovering and developing that capability takes tremendous focus and effort. Schneider
made courageous sacrifices for a dream, living a spartan life to test
his talent as a painter. Then, with Kline's help, he made the equally

courageous sacrifice of that dream to become a very fine art director. He used his considerable talents in service to the community of authors and scholars at Oxford, rather than becoming a merely good painter. That courage and those decisions made the mentorship I received from him particularly valuable. Similarly, Walter Herdeg's decision to exalt graphic design was a very other-centered choice: he sublimated his own creative impulses to a magazine, a vessel, to feature and promote outstanding work. Somewhere in that decision Herdeg may have decided that he was not capable of world-class creative work, but realized that he was uniquely qualified to create a forum for celebrating world-class work.

BALANCE THE ROI For business leaders, ROI stands for Return On Investment. For design leaders, the "investment" in a small but regular amount of career time reviewing and balancing the ROI elements described above—Relationships, Other-Centered and Individual (or Inner-Centered)—pays big returns. One constant among the Creative Legends is that they are alert to opportunities to express what they find most intensely interesting. They are always working, in Zapf's words, to "play their soul's music." The order of the ROI elements is significant: "Individual" is last. This is why Charles and Ray Eames emphasized "connections" as a theme in their work, and why Roberto Goizueta's term "creative friend" is a useful model. With those two categories of "good" defined, the possibility of Relationships opens up, cultivating audiences and constituencies who benefit from our creative work.

This elliptical definition, a paraphrase (from an Eric Gill's 1933 essay *Beauty Takes Care of Herself,*

> **❝ *The artist is not a special kind of person. Every person is a special kind of artist.* ❞**

though probably dating to antiquity) is perhaps the best capstone for these dialogues. The creative process is not the exclusive territory of artists and designers. Rather, the goal is to bring out the creativity innate in every individual, every team, and every culture. Design thinking is a way of provisioning a better life for all inhabitants of Spaceship Earth.

For Further Reading

Bass, Jennifer, and Pat Kirkham
Saul Bass: A Life in Film and Design, Laurence King Publishers, 2011

Berry, John
U&lc: Influencing Design & Typography, Mark Batty Publisher, 2005

Caplan, Ralph
Connections: The Work of Charles and Ray Eames, Frederick S. Wight Art Gallery, University of California, 1977

Chwast, Seymour, Stephen Heller, and Paula Scher
Seymour: The Obsessive Images of Seymour Chwast, Chronicle Books, 2009

Craig, James, with William Bevington and Irene Korol Scala
Designing with Type, 5th Edition: The Essential Guide to Typography Watson-Guptil, 2006

Elliot, Charles Newton
Mr. Anonymous: Robert W. Woodruff of Coca-Cola, Cherokee Publishers, 1982

Fuller, R. Buckminster
Nine Chains to the Moon, Lippincott, 1938
I Seem to Be a Verb, with Jerome Agel and Quentin Fiore, Bantam, 1970
Critical Path, Kiyoshi Kuromiya, Adjuvant, St. Martin's Press, 1981

Glaser, Milton
Milton Glaser: Graphic Design, Overlook Press, 1973

Gottschall, Edward
Typographic Communications Today, MIT Press, 1989

Greising, David
I'd Like to Buy the World a Coke: The Life and Leadership of Roberto Goizueta, Wiley, 1999

Hightower, Caroline (introduction)
Graphic Design in America: a Visual Language, Harry N. Abrams, Inc., 1989

Lois, George
George, Be Careful, John Wiley & Sons, 1971

Malsy, Victor and Lars Müller, eds.
Helvetica forever: Story of a Typeface, Lars Müller Publishers, 2009

McMullan, James
The Theater Posters of James McMullan, Penguin Studio, 1998

Müller, Lars, foreword by Paul Rand
Josef Müller-Brockmann: Pioneer of Swiss Graphic Design, Lars Müller Publishers, 2001

Nelson, George
George Nelson on Design, Whitney Library of Design, 1979

Papanek, Victor
Design for the Real World, Pantheon, 1971

Rand, Paul
A Designer's Art, Yale University Press, 1985

Rüegg, Ruedi
Basic Typography: Design with Letters, Van Nostrand Reinhold, 1989

Snyder, Gertrude and Alan Peckolick
Herb Lubalin: Art Director, Graphic Designer and Typographer, Amshow & Archive, 1985

Tress, Arthur
Shadow: A Novel in Photographs, Avon Books, 1975

Vignelli, Massimo
The Vignelli Canon, Lars Müller Publishers, 2010

Wurman, Richard Saul
Information Anxiety 2, Que, 2000

Wurman, Richard Saul
33: Understanding Change & the Change in Understanding, Greenway Communications, 2009

Zapf, Hermann
Hermann Zapf & His Design Philosophy, Society of Typographic Arts, 1987

Index

Photographic Credits

Portraits of Saul Bass, Herb Lubalin, Ivan Chermayeff, Lou Dorfsman, and Paul Rand, courtesy of Sahlan Simón Cherpitel, used by permission.

Portrait and design samples of Charles and Ray Eames, courtesy Eames Office, used by permission.

Photograph of Heinz Edelmann and his works courtesy of Estate of Heinz Edelmann, and School of Visual Arts, New York, used by permission.

Portraits and design examples of the following AIGA medalists and honorees are courtesy AIGA, the professional association for design www.aiga.org:
    Saul Bass,
    Chermayeff and Giesmar,
    Seymour Chwast,
    Lou Dorfsman,
    Herb Lubalin,
    Caroline Warner Hightower,
    Paul Rand,
    Massimo and Lella Vignelli

Portrait of James Burke, Jr. courtesy QuestFore, used by permission.

Portrait and designs of James Craig courtesy James Craig, used by permission

Portraits of Seymour Chwast, Max Miedinger, George Nelson, courtesy AIGA, the professional Association for Design www.aiga.org, used by permission.

Photographs of R. Buckminster Fuller, Ruedi Rüegg, Sidney Topol, collection of the author.

Portrait of Lawrence L. Gellerstedt Jr. by Peter Stevens Courtesy of Commerce Club Atlanta, used by permission.

Portrait of Roberto Goizueta courtesy Goizuetta Business School, Emory University, used by permission.

Portrait of Walter Herdeg and Graphis Magazine Covers courtesy Graphis Inc., used by permission.

Portrait of Peter Mayer courtesy Overlook Press, used by permission.

Photograph James McMullan Courtesy Society of Illustrators, NY, used by permission

Portrait of Victor J. Papanek, Tin can radio designed by Victor Papanek and George Seeger and tin can radio receiver decorated by user in Indonesia © Victor J. Papanek Foundation at the University of Applied Arts, Vienna, used by permission

Portrait of Herb Stern courtesy Herb Stern, used by permission.

Portrait of Robert W. Woodruff courtesy, Emory University, used by permission.

Portrait of Arthur Tress by Yuen Lui, used by permission.

Portrait of Don Trousdell courtesy Don Trousdell, used by permission.

Portrait of Richard Saul Wurman by Melissa Mahoney, used by permission.

Portrait of Hermann Zapf, and examples of Zapf's designs courtesy Society of Typographic Arts, Chicago, used by permission.

Keough artwork by Drew Rose, courtesy Will Sumpter Unlimited and Don Keough, used by permission.

Portrait of David Calvin Laufer by Jerry Burns, Studio Burns Atlanta, used by permission.

Photo on page 83 © WavebreakmediaMicro - Fotolia, used by permission.

All other visuals are from the photo collection of the author.

ABOUT THE AUTHOR
David Laufer

David Laufer (1950–   ) is a visual designer with a wide spectrum of experience. Born in Cleveland, Ohio, he earned a BA in Design at Carnegie Mellon University, where he was a Champion International Imagination Scholar. His work first came to international prominence with his rebranding of Oxford University Press to commemorate the 500th anniversary of book publishing at Oxford. This launched a consulting practice that includes product designs for the Museum of Modern Art design catalog and branding programs for venture fund startups and Fortune 500 companies. His design works have earned more than 50 awards and 5 US patents. His success at integrating design thinking with business strategy has made him one of the nation's leading exponents of expertise-based branding.

Mr. Laufer is a founding trustee of the AIGA chapter in Atlanta. He cofounded Brand Academy, a collaboration between AIGA and Emory University. As president of the National Investor Relations Institute chapter in Atlanta, Mr. Laufer chaired the first national survey of annual report budgets.

Laufer's iconoclastic sculptures utilize the language of graphic design for satire and social commentary. These "Fictitious Texts" have been displayed in more than 100 exhibitions, including solo shows in Minneapolis, Pittsburgh, and the Centennial Olympic games in Atlanta. He is active in the global Little Free Library movement. He is married to author and social media writer Geraldine Adamich Laufer; they have two sons. *Dialogues with Creative Legends* is his first book.